KT-173-734

Achieving QTS

Primary English

Knowledge and Understanding

Seventh edition

Achieving QTS

Primary English

Knowledge and Understanding

Seventh edition

Jane Medwell • George Moore •
David Wray • Vivienne Griffiths

SAGE | LearningMatters

Los Angeles | London | New Delhi
Singapore | Washington DC

Learning Matters
An imprint of SAGE Publications Ltd
1 Oliver's Yard
55 City Road
London EC1Y 1SP

SAGE Publications Inc.
2455 Teller Road
Thousand Oaks, California 91320

SAGE Publications India Pvt Ltd
B 1/I 1 Mohan Cooperative Industrial Area
Mathura Road
New Delhi 110 044

SAGE Publications Asia-Pacific Pte Ltd
3 Church Street
#10–04 Samsung Hub
Singapore 049483

Editor: Amy Thornton
Development editor: Jennifer Clark
Production controller: Chris Marke
Project management: Deer Park Productions,
Tavistock, Devon, England
Marketing Manager: Catherine Slinn
Cover design: Wendy Scott
Typeset by: C&M Digitals (P) Ltd, Chennai, India
Printed by: CPI Group (UK) Ltd, Croydon, CR0 4YY

MIX
Paper from
responsible sources
FSC
www.fsc.org   FSC® C013604

At SAGE we take sustainability seriously. We print most of our
products in the UK. These are produced using FSC papers and
boards. We undertake an annual audit on materials used to ensure
that we monitor out sustainability in what we are doing. When we
print overseas, we ensure that sustainable papers are used, as
measured by the Egmont grading system.

First published in 2001 by Learning Matters Ltd

Reprinted in 2001 (twice). Second edition
published in 2002. Reprinted in 2003 (twice), 2004
(twice), 2005 and 2006. Third edition published
in 2007. Reprinted in 2007 (twice). Fourth edition
published in 2009. Reprinted in 2009 and 2010.
Fifth edition published in 2011. Reprinted in 2011.
Sixth edition published in 2012. Seventh edition
published in 2014.

Library of Congress Control Number: 2014937400

British Library Cataloguing in Publication Data

A catalogue record for this book is available from
the British Library

ISBN: 978-1-4462-9523-6
ISBN: 978-1-4462-9524-3 (pbk)

Contents

Acknowledgements

Extract from *The Lion, the Witch and the Wardrobe* by C. S. Lewis copyright © C. S. Lewis Pte Ltd. 1950. Reprinted by permission (page 12); extract from *The Ghost of Thomas Kempe* by Penelope Lively published by Heinemann Educational and reproduced by permission of David Higham Associates (page 14); extract from *Fair's Fair* by Leon Garfield reproduced by permission of Hoddder & Stoughton Limited (page 133); by kind permission of John Agard c/o Caroline Sheldon Literary Agency *Poetry Jump-Up* from *Get Back Pimple* published by Viking Puffin 1990 (page 148); *Cargoes* by John Masefield reproduced by permission of The Society of Authors as the Literary Representative of the Estate of John Masefield (page 149); *Hippo Writes a Love Poem to His Wife from We Animals Would Like A World With You* by John Agard, published by The Bodley Head, reprinted by permission of the Random House Group Limited (page 157); *Gran, Can You Rap?* by Jack Ousbey © Jack Ousbey (page 161); *According to My Mood from Talking Turkeys* by Benjamin Zephaniah (Viking, 1994) copyright © Benjamin Zephaniah, reprinted by permission of Penguin Books Ltd (page 162); *Hoff the Cat Dealer from Playstage: Six Primary School Plays* © 1987 Andrews Davies, first published by Methuen Children's Books Limited, now Egmont Children's Books Limited and used with permission (page 180).

Every effort has been made to trace copyright holders and to obtain their permission for the use of copyright material. The Publisher and authors will gladly receive information enabling them to rectify any error or omission in subsequent editions.

1
Introduction

About this book

This book has been written to cater for the needs of primary trainees on all courses of initial teacher training in England and other parts of the UK. In order to gain qualified teacher status (QTS), teachers must demonstrate that they have the knowledge, skills and values necessary to be effective classroom teachers. Secure subject knowledge in English is required for the award of Qualified Teacher Status (QTS) or its equivalent. This book will also be useful to Newly Qualified Teachers (NQTs) and other professionals working in education who have identified aspects of their English subject knowledge that require attention.

This book has been written with the Teachers' Standards firmly at its core. *The Teachers' Standards in England* (DfE, 2013) came into force from 1 September 2012, replacing the standards for Qualified Teacher Status (QTS), the Core Professional Standards and the General Teaching Council for England's *Code of Conduct and Practice for Registered Teachers*. These standards define the minimum level of practice expected of all teachers from the point of being awarded QTS.

At the time of writing this book, as at most other times in education, changes are under-way in the structures of school governance and assessment requirements which affect the curriculum in schools. The Department for Education (DfE) has recently reviewed the primary National Curriculum and the majority of this new National Curriculum will come into force from September 2014. From September 2015, the new National Curriculum for English, mathematics and science will come into force for children in Years 2 and 6.

The revised Statutory Framework for the Early Years Foundation Stage, which details the Early Learning Goals set nationally for children from birth to 5 years old, became statutory in September 2012 (DfE, 2012). This framework is mandatory for all early years providers, including maintained schools, non-maintained schools, independent schools, and all providers on the Early Years Register.

This book includes information on the programmes of study for National Curriculum English, which maintained schools (but not academies, free schools or independent schools) must follow from September 2014, and on the Early Learning Goals for children in the Early Years. In any transitional period, you will need to understand about what curriculum requirements were in place before the new arrangements as the teachers you work with may well retain in their practice elements of the earlier ways of working. You will almost certainly hear colleagues discussing the differences between curriculum initiatives and referring to former frameworks, for example the Primary National Strategy for Teaching Literacy and Mathematics.

Each chapter of this book addresses particular areas of English knowledge that primary teachers need in order to become effective teachers of English and communication, language and literacy (CLL). Issues of pedagogy (how to teach English to primary aged children) are addressed in the companion volume, *Primary English: Teaching Theory and Practice* (Learning Matters, 2014). However, the authors of this book have attempted to make clear links between the knowledge you, as a teacher, need and how you will use it in teaching.

Features of the main chapters of this book include:

- clear links with the Teachers' Standards;
- information about the curriculum context, including the National Curriculum for English in England and the Early Years Foundation Stage;
- English knowledge and understanding;
- pedagogical links;
- reflective and practical activities for you to undertake;
- research summaries that give additional background insights;
- a summary of key learning points;
- suggestions for further reading.

The book also contains a glossary of terms and a useful appendix of irregular verbs. There are also self-assessment questions so that you can check on how well you have assimilated the knowledge and understanding.

English subject knowledge really does matter!

It is a basic training requirement that all trainee teachers (and serving teachers) in the UK can use spoken and written Standard English well. However, research into English teaching in primary schools has shown that in the past, some teachers seemed to have poor subject knowledge (Medwell *et al.,* 1998). This apparent anomaly refers to the fact that even when we use English very well ourselves, we may still be unable to discuss, analyse and reflect on our use of English. As teachers we are responsible for planning, teaching and assessing English lessons, setting learning outcomes, choosing appropriate activities and resources, identifying children's errors and misconceptions, asking and responding to questions, and so on. All these tasks require teachers to be able to analyse just how English is used effectively, and to be able to discuss it. This cannot be achieved without a sound, explicit knowledge of English and, probably, some knowledge of the terminology to discuss it.

In primary schools there has been an ongoing drive to raise standards of English achievement through raising expectations, target setting and a focus on assessment. The National Curriculum is intended to support the development of a coherent and progressive English curriculum in schools. A key part of this drive to raise pupils' standards of English is the need for teachers to have the necessary subject knowledge to teach confidently and effectively, motivating, challenging and extending their pupils' knowledge, understanding and experience.

The Teachers' Standards

This book refers mostly to the English-related subject standards underpinning the effective teaching of literacy and language you will be required to demonstrate in order to be awarded QTS. The book explicitly addresses the following Standards:

A teacher must:

3. Demonstrate good subject and curriculum knowledge

- have a secure knowledge of the relevant subject(s) and curriculum areas, foster and maintain pupils' interest in the subject, and address misunderstandings
- demonstrate a critical understanding of developments in the subject and curriculum areas, and promote the value of scholarship
- demonstrate an understanding of and take responsibility for promoting high standards of literacy, articulacy and the correct use of Standard English, whatever the teacher's specialist subject
- if teaching early reading, demonstrate a clear understanding of systematic synthetic phonics.

4. Plan and teach well structured lessons

- impart knowledge and develop understanding through effective use of lesson time
- promote a love of learning and children's intellectual curiosity
- set homework and plan other out-of-class activities to consolidate and extend the knowledge and understanding pupils have acquired
- contribute to the design and provision of an engaging curriculum within the relevant subject area(s).

8. Fulfil wider professional responsibilities

- take responsibility for improving teaching through appropriate professional development.

It is always difficult to decide where to begin when writing about English. Should we start with really good examples of English texts and analyse what makes them successful? Or should we begin with the smaller units of language and 'build up' to larger units? Both approaches are useful in teaching English.

In this book we begin by considering the nature and role of Standard English, because this is the variant of English generally referred to in English teaching. We then consider how spoken and written language are constituted and related and include chapters on word and sub-word units; sentences, grammar and punctuation; cohesion and text types; and finally examination and appreciation of literature. We devote substantial space to consideration of different text types because whole, successful texts (spoken and written) are the aim of English teaching. We want children (and you) to understand how language works so that they it can be used effectively.

Curriculum context

As we said at the start of this chapter, the curriculum is changing in 2014 and this sort of change may very well happen several times in your career as a teacher. Because of this, we have focused in this book on the core areas of English subject knowledge and understanding that you will need in order to develop the language and literacy of the children you work with. This will enable you to ensure that they develop effective speaking and listening skills, and become successful readers and writers. You can use your knowledge of English to underpin your planning for whatever curriculum is in place in your teaching setting. However, you will need to know about the context of the curriculum prior to any new initiatives so that you can understand how your children have been taught and why. Therefore, we have included contextual information about the primary National Curriculum programmes of study, and the Early Learning Goals for children in the Early Years Foundation Stage.

English in the National Curriculum

English in the National Curriculum is organised on the basis of five key stages: Foundation Key Stage (part of the Early Years Foundation Stage) for 3 to 5 year olds; Key Stage 1 for 5 to 7 year olds (Years 1 and 2); and Key Stage 2 for 7 to 11 year olds (Years 3 to 6) refer to primary and early years teaching. The components of the Foundation Key Stage are set out as Early Learning Goals (ELGs), which set targets for the end of the Foundation Stage and stepping stones, which set out how children can achieve ELGs. Key Stages 1 and 2 include Programmes of Study, which set out the English that children should be taught. These Programmes are organised over four age phases:

1. Key Stage 1 – Year 1;
2. Key Stage 1 – Year 2;
3. Lower Key Stage 2 – Years 3 and 4;
4. Upper Key Stage 2 – Years 5 and 6.

Within each age phase the material to be taught is split into five strands:

1. Reading – word reading;
2. Reading – comprehension;
3. Writing – transcription;
4. Writing – composition;
5. Writing – vocabulary, grammar and punctuation.

There are also requirements for the teaching of spoken language which span Years 1 to 6, and two statutory appendices – one about spelling and one about vocabulary, grammar and punctuation – which give an overview of the specific features that should be included in teaching the programmes of study.

The National Curriculum is intended to be a minimum statutory entitlement for children and schools have the flexibility and freedom to design a wider school curriculum to meet the needs of their pupils and to decide how to teach it most effectively. As *The National Curriculum in England* (DfE, 2013) itself puts it:

> *The national curriculum is just one element in the education of every child. There is time and space in the school day and in each week, term and year to range beyond the national curriculum specifications. The national curriculum provides an outline of core knowledge around which teachers can develop exciting and stimulating lessons to promote the development of pupils' knowledge, understanding and skills as part of the wider school curriculum.*

All schools are required to set out their school curriculum for English on a year-by-year basis and make this information available online.

Statutory assessment of English attainment will continue to occur at various points in the primary phase after the introduction of the new National Curriculum, although with some significant changes. Following a phased change, from 2015 onwards the statutory assessment of primary pupils, in English, will involve reporting of assessment at the end of Key Stage 1 and Key Stage 2. This assessment will include teacher assessment and some tests.

At Key Stage 1, schools may order and use the Key Stage 1 tests and tasks for English in 2014 and 2015, but they do not have to and many schools will make their own arrangements to assess reading, writing, speaking and listening. Schools are required to report the results in the summer. In addition, Year 1 pupils must do the nationally set, but teacher-administered, phonics screening check.

At Key Stage 2, Year 6 pupils will do Key Stage 2 tests in English, including nationally developed tests of English reading and English spelling, punctuation and grammar (SPaG), and teacher-administered assessments of writing.

In 2016 a new national assessment regime will be introduced which will dispense with the National Curriculum levels and sub-levels. The new approach to assessment will aim to assess annual progress and will be related to the content of the 2014 National Curriculum.

Early Years Foundation Stage and the Early Learning Goals

The *Early Learning Goals* (DfE, 2012) describe what most children should achieve by the end of their Reception year. This document identifies features of good practice during the Early Years Foundation Stage and set out the early learning goals in three prime areas and six specific areas of learning. One of the prime areas is that of Communication and Language (including Listening and Attention, Understanding and Speaking) and one of the specific areas is Literacy (including Reading and Writing).

There are thus five areas within the Early Learning Goals which specifically concern us in the present book. These are:

- listening and attention;
- understanding;
- speaking;
- reading;
- writing.

English also includes exploring and using media and being imaginative.

Specific reference will be made to these Early Learning Goals where relevant in the book.

At the end of the EYFS (the end of Reception), all providers of early years care and education complete the Early Years Foundation Stage profile, which summarises and describes children's attainment at the end of the EYFS. It is based on ongoing observation and assessment in the three prime and four specific areas of learning, and the three learning characteristics.

Outcomes

By using this book to support your subject knowledge development, you will be able to learn the knowledge you require to teach primary English and Communication Language and Literacy in the EYFS successfully. We hope that understanding a little about the different systems inherent in English and the way the 'parts' of English work together to create successful texts will enable you to develop an enthusiasm for the language and for your own reading and writing of English. Such enthusiasm is an invaluable asset to a teacher and can bring English alive for children. We hope this book will stimulate your curiosity and help you to investigate language and texts with children. Teachers who know about and enjoy all aspects of English can pass their positive attitudes to children, as well as the skills and knowledge those children need to do well.

So that you can check on how well you have assimilated the subject knowledge, you may wish to try the self-assessment questions related to each aspect that we address. You will find these in a separate section towards the end of the book. The answers to these questions are provided for you in a separate chapter.

For those undertaking credits for a Masters Degree, we have included suggestions for further work and extended study at the end of each chapter in a section called 'M-Level Extension'.

Statutory and exemplary documentation

To support you in understanding the curriculum context, you may find it helpful to refer to some of the following documentation:

DfE (2012) *Statutory Framework for the Early Years Foundation Stage.* Runcorn: DfE. **(www.education. gov.uk/publications/standard/AllPublications/Page1/DFE-00023-2012)**

DfE (2013) *2014 Key Stage 2 Tests*. London: DfE. **(http://education.gov.uk/schools/teaching andlearning/assessment/keystage2/b00208296/ks2-2013/ks2-2014)**

DfE (2013) *Teachers' Standards*. London: DfE. **(www.gov.uk/government/uploads/system/uploads/ attachment_data/file/208682/Teachers__Standards_2013.pdf)**

DfE (2013) *The National Curriculum in England.* London: DfE. **(www.gov.uk/dfe/nationalcurriculum)**

DfE (2013) *The 2014 National Curriculum*. London: DfE. **(www.gov.uk/government/collections/ national-curriculum)**

2
Spoken English and Standard English

Curriculum context

National Curriculum programmes of study

This knowledge is designed to underpin the teaching of the Key Stage 1 and Key Stage 2 programmes of study for English, which state, for example, that children should:

- be introduced to some of the main features of spoken Standard English and be taught to use them;
- understand how word order affects meaning.

Children should learn to speak competently and creatively for different purposes and audiences, reflecting on impact and response. They should learn to explain and comment on speakers' use of language, including vocabulary, grammar and non-verbal features.

Early Years Foundation Stage

The Early Learning Goals specify that, by the end of the Early Years Foundation Stage, children should:

- enjoy listening to and using spoken and written language, and readily turn to it in their play and learning;
- extend their vocabulary, exploring the meanings and sounds of new words;
- speak clearly and audibly with confidence and control and show awareness of the listener.

Introduction

English is one of the most widely spoken and written languages in the world. It is estimated that there are 300 million native speakers and 300 million who use English as a second language, while a further 100 million use it as a foreign language. It is the language of science, aviation, computing, diplomacy and tourism. It is listed as the official or co-official language of 45 countries. Chinese may be spoken by more people, but English is probably the language used for the widest variety of purposes.

It is not surprising, then, that English is a large and flexible language. There are probably between a million and two million words, not including the half a million abbreviations in English. An educated English speaker may have a vocabulary of 50,000 or so active words and half as many again that are understood without being regularly produced. Becoming a successful speaker of English is not simply about knowing the words and how to pronounce them. It also involves knowing the wide range of rules governing the way words and phrases are ordered into spoken discourse as well as the conventions that govern the ways varieties of English differ to include linguistic differences of region, class, gender, formality and relationship.

This chapter considers what Standard English is and the main types of language variation you will deal with as a teacher.

Standard English

There is no 'Standard' for English like the 'standard' metre or gram – something against which all English can be measured and corrected. Standard English is a particular variety of English which, although most educated adults recognise and use it, is difficult to define. Standard English is largely a matter of using certain grammar, vocabulary and, when written, spelling. It can be spoken in most English accents and does not have a correct pronunciation.

REFLECTIVE TASK

Which sentences are Standard English? How do you know?

They were just over here.　　　　　　　　*I did not do it.*
I've never been here.　　　　　　　　　*They was there a minute ago.*
I ain't never been here.　　　　　　　　*I never done it.*

As a fluent Standard English user you may find the answers to this activity easy, but also find that explaining your answers demands reflection on language, and vocabulary about language that you do not use every day.

Standard English is a form of English that carries prestige within a language group (people in Britain, in this case) and so it is the form of English usually learnt by foreigners and used by most people in formal, business and political situations. This form of English is a 'standard' in that the prestige of Standard English is recognised by the adults in the language community and so it has become an educational target. In Britain we aim for all children to be able to use Standard English in their writing and in appropriate speaking situations. Not to be able to do so would certainly be a disadvantage in modern life and people unable to do so would be liable to be considered poorly educated by their peers.

Despite the near universal recognition of Standard English as a powerful variant of English that all children should learn and the fact that Standard English is very widely understood, very few people actually speak only Standard English. For most of us a mixture of Standard English and a regional variety of English is used for much of the time. Spoken Standard English is likely to be used in situations where clarity and near universal understanding are required – reading the television news is an obvious example. Teachers need to be able to use, and model the use of, Standard English to their children. The most common occurrence of Standard English is in writing and so it is not surprising that, for many of us, newsreaders sound as though they are 'speaking in writing'.

Finally, it is important to point out that there are a number of 'Standard' varieties of English. English has become an international language in that it has an unprecedented worldwide presence. Yet it has also been adopted as the language of a number of countries. Because it has been used in different countries, each country has reached agreement over language issues so that the language reflects the identity of that country. As a result there is not one 'correct' Standard world English, but different Standard English varieties in different English-speaking countries. You have only to look at the language section of your word processor to be offered Standard British English, Indian English, Australian, New Zealand, American and Canadian English spelling and grammar checkers. All these Standard English variants have slightly different vocabularies, rules governing grammar and conventions of punctuation. In this book, and in teaching in UK schools, we are dealing with Standard British English, although many people say that there is also a Standard Scots English.

Although we aim to offer all children access to Standard English, there are important types of language variation that teachers and children need to learn about. These affect the ways we speak and write, as well as the nature of the language.

Historical variation

One way that English varies is over time. English has a long and complicated history (discussed in more detail in Chapter 5), which partly accounts for the complexity of the language. As a living language it is constantly changing to accommodate new situations. This means that Standard British English gradually invents, borrows or changes words, phrases and expressions, grammatical rules and conventions of punctuation.

In terms of grammar, there are broadly agreed grammatical rules and conventions that make Standard English understandable and relatively stable. For example:

- It is usual for the subject and verb in a sentence to agree.

  They were, NOT *they was*
  He is, NOT *he are*

- There are complicated spelling and grammatical conventions about the formation of past tense verb forms.

  I fell, NOT *I falled*
  She stopped, NOT *she stoped*
  I did, NOT *I done*
  I have done, NOT *I have did*

However, there are always some 'grey areas' where standard usage is changing.

REFLECTIVE TASK

Which of these sentences seem like appropriate usage to you? Which do not, and why?

  It was something I couldn't put up with.
  I wanted to quickly leave.
  I did not understand the relevance of it.

An example of change in grammatical usage is the use of the split infinitive. Less than 50 years ago many people felt that the infinitive form of a verb ('to go', 'to be', etc.) should not be split. Today, however, most people have accepted the use of phrases such as 'to quickly leave', while 'to boldly go' must be the most famous split infinitive in the world. This sort of change is evident in every aspect of English. The words of English change. New words are invented or borrowed and meanings change. Some words and expressions have changed in our lifetime. (This topic is discussed in more detail in Chapter 5.)

PEDAGOGICAL LINK

Children need to be able to use morphology and etymology to spell new and unfamiliar words. Dictionaries contain more than just definitions – they include information on word class, formation and origin. All primary teachers need to become familiar with a really good dictionary such as *The Concise Oxford English Dictionary,* which gives some information about word origins. *The Oxford English Dictionary* contains all the information about a word you could need and is now available online.

PRACTICAL TASK

Think of some modern equivalents of these words, phrases and expressions:

Wireless	*LP*
Parlour	*charabanc*
Spooning	*vexed*

How have these words and expressions changed meaning?

He is a <u>sad</u> little man.	*presently*
regular	*gay*

Here are some words from a 1990 *Dictionary of New Words*. Which ones remain part of Standard usage and which ones don't? Why? How long do you think they will remain?

mad cow disease   skorts
bumbag   bimboy
diffuser   fatwah
cardboard city

In order that children can use knowledge of word structure and origins to develop their understanding of word meanings, they need to study and collect new words.

It is not only spoken Standard English that changes. In recent years new conventions have entered written English. Fifteen years ago few people used bullet points to punctuate lists of sentences, phrases or words but bullet points are now a Standard written convention. The dash to signal parenthesis or an afterthought in writing has become a very common usage and is accepted in Standard English. These changes raise the question of who decides what is correct usage in Standard English? The answer is not simple. At root, usage that is generally accepted as appropriate by the language group is correct – in this case, the British public. It can be difficult to decide whether something is accepted appropriate usage, especially when the English language is changing so quickly. It is important for teachers to maintain awareness of language usage in society, on television and radio, in newspapers, books and online and to keep in mind the goal of clarity of expression. However, this underlines that there can never be an absolute statement of correct Standard English – the aim is appropriate use of English.

Regional variation

Standard English has the features of a dialect in that it uses particular words and grammatical forms. However, unlike most dialects it does not tell us where the speaker comes from. Many regional varieties of English tell us about the speaker's origins in terms of geography or class. There are two main elements of regional variation: accent and dialect.

A **dialect** is a variety of English that includes particular words and grammatical rules that indicate the origins of the speaker. In UK schools one of the most obvious examples of word variation is the word for shoes worn for PE. Do you call them daps (south west and Wales), plimsolls (south east), pumps (midlands), sandshoes (north east) or even rubbashoes (Gibraltar)? There are many other dialect words you might use and linguists have researched and recorded the distribution and change of dialect words. As a teacher, it is important to know local dialect terms that children might use appropriately in speech, if not in all types of writing.

Each dialect may also have a consistent, but often non-Standard, grammar. For instance, although Standard English uses the third person plural of the verb to be ('were') and demands that it agree with the third person pronoun ('we were'), in some dialects 'we was' is consistently used. The sentence 'I ain't never been there' is identifiably not Standard English because of the formation of 'have not' and the double negative. In Standard English the sentence would be 'I have never been there'. However, in parts of north London, this is a popular dialect usage.

The dialect (or language) primarily used at home by young children is very important for a number of reasons. It is the language variety through which they have learnt about the world and their place in it. It is also the language variety that marks them out as part of the social group of their home community. For these reasons it is important to recognise that non-Standard dialects have an important role in children's lives and are not simply 'wrong' use of words and grammar. At the same time it is also vital to teach children both how to use Standard English and when it is appropriate to use it. Very young children will begin to use Standard English in school discussions and structured play. As schooling progresses children will be taught to consider critically what they speak and write and to correct Standard English in writing and, when appropriate, in speech.

Study of direct speech in children's literature is one way in which children can study the differences between dialect and Standard English.

PEDAGOGICAL LINK PEDAGOGICAL LINK PEDAGOGICAL LINK PEDAGOGICAL LINK

Children need to be able to identify how talk varies with age, familiarity, gender and purpose and how it varies between formal and informal occasions. This involves both listening to speakers and study of children's books and plays that include direct speech.

PRACTICAL TASK PRACTICAL TASK PRACTICAL TASK PRACTICAL TASK PRACTICAL TASK

Here is an extract from *The Secret Garden* by Frances Hodgson Burnett. It is the story of Mary, an orphan who is brought up in her Grandfather's house in Yorkshire.

For two or three minutes he stood looking around him, while Mary watched him, and then he began to walk about softly, even more lightly than Mary had walked the first time she had found herself inside the four walls. His eyes seemed to be taking in everything – the grey trees with the grey creepers climbing over them and hanging from their branches, the tangle on the wall and among the grass, the evergreen alcoves with the stone seats and tall flower urns standing in them.

'I never thought I'd see this place,' he said at last in a whisper.

'Did you know about it?' asked Mary.

She had spoken aloud and he made a sign to her.

'We must talk low,' he said, 'or someone'll hear us an' wonder what's to do in here.'

'Oh! I forgot!' said Mary, feeling frightened and putting her hand quickly against her mouth. 'Did you know about the garden?' she asked again when she had recovered herself.

Dickon nodded.

'Martha told me there was one as no one ever went inside,' he answered. 'Us used to wonder what it was like.'

He stopped and looked around at the lovely grey tangle about him and his round eyes looked queerly happy.

> *'Eh! The nests as'll be here come springtime,' he said. 'It'd be th' safest nestin' place in England. No one ever comin' near an' tangles o' trees an' roses to build in. I wonder all th' birds on th' moor don't build here.'*
>
> Note down the grammatical and lexical features which indicate Dickon is speaking in a regional dialect, using Standard English as a reference point. What is the effect of using this dialect in the passage?

Another feature of geographical and social variation in spoken English is **accent**. This is represented in the passage above through spelling and punctuation. Standard English can be spoken in the whole range of regional accents and there is no Standard accent. A particular type of accent, which has been called 'BBC' or 'The Queen's English', is widely recognised by foreign learners of English. This accent is known by linguists as RP, or 'received pronunciation'. In the late eighteenth and nineteenth centuries this accent developed as the accent spoken by those who 'were received in society'. However, in recent years the incidence of RP has declined and now few people speak in an RP accent, with even most RP speakers including a number of regionally identifiable sounds. It is important to recognise that, although most regional dialects are spoken in a regional accent, Standard English can be spoken perfectly clearly in a regional accent.

PRACTICAL TASK PRACTICAL TASK PRACTICAL TASK PRACTICAL TASK PRACTICAL TASK

This is a transcript of a conversation with two twelve-year-old African-Caribbean girls and illustrates the West Yorkshire dialect. The girls were born and live in Yorkshire but follow certain aspects of Rastafarian culture, like beaded hair, which come into conflict with school rules.

Marilyn	*They (teachers) used to say we couldn't wear (beads in our hair) before.*
Charleen	*Yeah, 'cos last – when my sister were in this school, right, 'er friend wore beads in 'er hair, and one of t'teachers told 'er to tek 'em out, and she said no, she 'adn't to tek 'em out, so she (teacher) just got 'er hair and just took 'em out, and she (girl) just put 'em back in.*
VG	*But now they let you wear them do they?*
Marilyn	*They don't say owt to me.*

(from *Adolescent Girls and Their Friends*, Vivienne Griffiths, 1995, p45)

This passage contains some dialect words (e.g. 'owt' – anything) as well as some characteristic grammatical structures (e.g. 'my sister were') and abbreviations. Now try to find some other examples.

The very prejudice with which people treat accents in Britain suggests it is an important issue. In market research surveys, accents are frequently rated in terms of popularity, with Scots accents and Newcastle accents often rated as 'warm and trustworthy' and RP rated as 'intelligent and cold'. This is pure prejudice – accents may indicate a person's social or geographical origins but do not indicate anything about their intellectual ability or personality. Accent, like dialect, can be an important part of a person's social identity. It is important for teachers to teach children to speak clearly and use Standard English. It is not appropriate or necessary to change a child's home accent.

'We've fallen on our feet and no mistake,' said Peter. 'This is going to be perfectly splendid. That old chap will let us do anything we like.'

'I think he's an old dear,' said Susan.

'Oh come off it!' said Edmund, who was tired and pretending not to be tired, which always made him bad-tempered, 'Don't go on talking like that.'

'Like what?' said Susan; 'and anyway, it's time you were in bed.'

'Trying to talk like Mother,' said Edmund. 'And who are you to say when I should go to bed? Go to bed yourself.'

(from *The Lion, the Witch and the Wardrobe*, C.S. Lewis, 1950, p10)

Although the passage is written in Standard English, there are indications of the period when it was written and the class background of the children. What are these? Find some other examples in the text that help to date this extract.

Children should be able to listen for language variation and identify ***how*** it varies, including accents. This involves study of children's books and plays that include direct speech. Accents may also be a feature of drama work in speaking and listening and children may find audio clips useful.

Individual variation – register

The way we speak English depends not only on which accents and dialects we have access to, but also on the social situation in which we are speaking. Dialects and accents are variety of languages which are linked to groups of people, but language can also vary depending on its use. The term language register has been used to describe the way speakers (or writers) use different words and grammatical formations depending on the situation.

This diagram was originally used by James Murray to introduce the first volume of the *Oxford English Dictionary* (1888). It describes the way word choice varies in a number of situations. Some linguists dispute the differences between common and colloquial vocabulary, since many colloquial words become common.

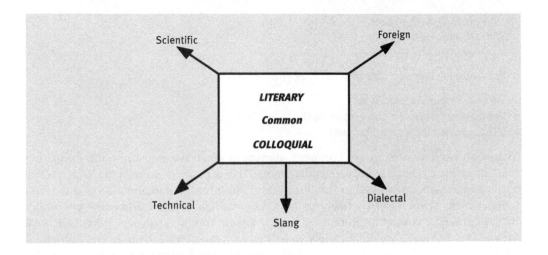

When we speak (or write) in any situation the language we use reflects a number of things: the degree of familiarity between the speaker and listener, the social situation of school, work, home, etc. and the formality of the situation.

We use certain words and expressions for formal situations and completely different ones for informal situations. The classroom is a relatively formal situation. A teacher might say 'Please, be quiet!' to a child, but that child might simply say to a friend 'Shuddup, you!' without any intention of rudeness or malice. The difference between the utterances is the relationship between the speaker and listener. Children learn the unwritten rules of vocabulary selection for the classroom easily, but may need to consider and discuss their choice of words in less familiar contexts.

PRACTICAL TASK PRACTICAL TASK PRACTICAL TASK PRACTICAL TASK PRACTICAL TASK

There are many ways to say that someone has died, or is dead. How many can you list? Choose words or phrases to suit these situations:

1. A lawyer discussing a client who has died, leaving a will to be administered.

2. An undertaker talking to bereaved relatives.

3. A newsreader reporting a major flood disaster in a distant country.

4. A man telling a friend about the death of a local person some 20 years ago.

5. A comedian making a joke.

It is not only word choice that varies according to the situation. We also use grammatical structures differently.

This is a discussion between two seven-year-old boys finishing their work in school:

You done it?
No. Hang on.
You what? She'll do you.
Nearly done it. Not long.

Get on with it! Come on!
OK, OK keep your hair on, bro.
I got to go. Can't wait, sorry.

What evidence can you identify that tells you:

- that this is informal conversation?
- that the discussion was spoken, not written?
- that the children knew each other well?

In speech we tend only to use complete sentences when we speak in quite formal settings or where a person is not well known to us. This is partly to do with the level of clear, explicit information we need to put into speech. In informal conversation about a very familiar topic, speakers can actually leave out a great deal of detail and some expression that is conveyed through gesture or is already known to both speakers. When we speak (or write) to someone we do not know well or when a speaker needs to be very precise in a formal situation, full sentences with explicit detail become useful. Informal conversation tends to consist of linked clauses or phrases, often with sentence elements implied or left out. This is why it can be difficult to transcribe speech.

PRACTICAL TASK PRACTICAL TASK PRACTICAL TASK PRACTICAL TASK PRACTICAL TASK

Below is an extract from *The Ghost of Thomas Kempe*, by Penelope Lively (1975). Two boys are talking about a notice they have seen, purporting to be from 'Thos. Kempe Esq. Sorcerer':

'There!' said James, with a mixture of triumph and despair. 'There! Now do you believe me?'

Simon took his glasses off, scrubbed round them with his fingers and read the notice for a second time.

'Well,' he said cautiously.

'Well what?'

'Somebody could have put it there.'

'Such as who?'

'I don't know.'

'Such as me, perhaps?' said James in a freezing voice.

'No. Not you. You've been with me all morning . . .'

'He just wants things done like they were in his time,' said James. 'With him doing them. And me helping.'

'Oh,' said Simon. 'I see.' He sounded polite. Too polite.

James said, 'You don't believe he's a ghost, do you?'

'I didn't say I didn't.'

'But you don't.'

'I kind of half do and half don't,' said Simon with great honesty. 'I do when I'm with you but I think if I was by myself I wouldn't.'

What has the author used to replace the facial expression and actions between the two characters?

What does the passage tell you about the relationship between the two characters?

PEDAGOGICAL LINK PEDAGOGICAL LINK PEDAGOGICAL LINK PEDAGOGICAL LINK

Children need opportunities to talk in a range of situations, including in groups, to the whole class and in drama. Some group discussion activities (such as circle time or debates) are used to teach children about the conventions of turn-taking. Others such as a child instructing a partner how to build a model that cannot be seen are designed to teach children to be precise and explicit in speech. In these ways and by discussing how to talk effectively, children can learn to use talk flexibly.

It is not only the words and grammar of speech that change depending on the situation. The very volume and pace we use for speech and the degree to which we prepare what we say depends on the purpose and audience for that speech. However, this is not to suggest there are no rules. When speaking in a formal situation a speaker would try to use clear, well-thought-out language at a volume everyone could hear. In discussion with a few friends a speaker might produce a tentative idea, rephrase it several times and use pauses and 'ums'.

In conversation there is a clear turn-taking structure that speakers must follow if their contributions are to be acceptable and there are appropriate levels of acceptable inter-ruption. In class we teach children that if they are chosen to speak to the whole class their contribution will generally be listened to in full, but in a tentative discussion about a group task children are likely to interrupt one another repeatedly, finish one another's utterances and talk at the same time.

PRACTICAL TASK PRACTICAL TASK PRACTICAL TASK PRACTICAL TASK PRACTICAL TASK

With a partner, choose one formal and one informal conversation to role play, as though you are on the telephone:

Informal

- **asking a friend to a party (pub or club)**
- **talking to someone in your family**

Formal

- **making a doctor's appointment**
- **making a complaint about a faulty washing machine (car, television)**

Compare the way you speak in the two situations in terms of:

- **vocabulary**
- **length of utterance**
- **grammatical structures**
- **acceptable interruptions**

How would these utterances change if you were not on the telephone, and why?

PRACTICAL TASK PRACTICAL TASK PRACTICAL TASK PRACTICAL TASK PRACTICAL TASK

Here are some language autobiographies. You may find it useful to read them and think about language variation in these cases.

Maggie took A-levels and then went on to a B.Ed. course, specialising in maths.

I was born in Jersey and spent the first few years of my life there. My grandma spoke Jersey French (a French patois) which my Mum and Dad understood but didn't really speak. Once my Nan wrote some down for me and I took it proudly to school. The teacher took one look and said, 'That's not proper French.'

I took quite a long time to learn to speak, which, looking back, may have been something to do with being hearing impaired. But this wasn't diagnosed until I was at college. My Mum and Dad knew something wasn't right, but they didn't want to acknowledge it. Now they say things like, 'When you were little, if you went on ahead and we called you, you didn't turn round.' But at the time they didn't do anything about it.

When I was seven we moved to Cornwall. I had a bit of a Jersey accent which I wasn't really aware of at the time. I always remember the first day I was in the playground, a girl came up to me and said, 'Don't worry. We'll soon teach you how to talk properly.' I used to call my Granddad 'Papa' which was the Jersey way – and obviously came from the French – but the other children thought that was odd so I soon learnt to say 'Granddad' instead when I was at school. Also I remember one of my favourite things to eat as a child was Jersey pudding – made from flour, milk and suet basically – you eat it with gravy. People used to say, 'There's no such thing as Jersey pudding! Don't you mean Yorkshire pudding?'

Later when I went to grammar school we moved from rural Cornwall to Essex and I went to Nellswood School for Girls [*said in a 'posh' voice*]. This was quite a big change too and I felt very aware of being different. Maybe it was because of this – and my hearing impairment – but I found it difficult to put words together and I never had the confidence to speak in groups, something which I still find hard today.

1. What impact do you think the teacher's reaction to the Jersey French had on Maggie?
2. How did Maggie's hearing impairment affect her language development and her confidence as a speaker? Discuss the possible effects of the late diagnosis.
3. Look at the points when Maggie moved, first to Cornwall and then to Essex. How did these moves affect her language identity and self-esteem?

Jon took a degree in biology, then a PGCE, specialising in science.

I grew up in Eastwood, Nottinghamshire. Eastwood's a peculiar place. It's on the Nottinghamshire/ Derbyshire border so it has a dialect that's neither one nor the other but a meld of the two. It's where D.H. Lawrence grew up, and the English side of my family is connected: my grandfather ran a pub that's in one of Lawrence's books. My mother's family is firmly rooted in the area. My father, who's Polish, was stationed in Hucknall nearby during the war. He was originally going to Canada, but he met my mother at a dance, married and stayed, so the family's firmly embedded.

Some elements of my family were racist. I remember arguments over family tea about my father, how he couldn't speak English properly. We were subject to racist attacks – windows broken – and I was assaulted several times on the way home from school. Nottingham had a large Polish community, which tended to cluster round certain places, so my father had some Polish friends.

There was a Polish school on Saturday mornings. I wanted to go to it, but my grandmother, who was the matriarch of the family, said it would be more useful for me to go to music school than Polish school. So I grew up with very little knowledge of Polish, no conversational Polish except a few words: 'Jen dobre' (hello), 'badso' (my friend), 'dai bugie' (give us a kiss), and 'Jadek' (grandfather) and 'Babja' (grandma) which my children call my parents to distinguish them from their other grandparents.

I had a very strong sense of belonging to a time-warped community. There was a joke about Eastwood: everywhere else had mods and rockers in the '60s, but they didn't take hold in Eastwood till 1975. It was a small, insulated mining community, with just the pit (mine). I grew up in an odd atmosphere, but adopted the Eastwood dialect. It's a very broad dialect, with lots of important words. I spoke it all the time. For example, you'd say, 'Eh oop sorry, 'owta gooin' on?' The response is, 'Middlin, middlin'. 'Sorry' means 'my dear', or we'd sometimes say, 'me duck' (pronounced 'dook'). I had very little exposure to 'outside', mainly through visits to a Polish family. They'd either speak Polish, which was a closed book, or converse in more Standardised English than I was used to. When I left college and came to Sussex, after two to three years people would say to me, 'You come from Birmingham'. After three or four years away I had a London accent. I couldn't maintain the Eastwood dialect as people wouldn't understand me. But given two weeks' immersion I'd be in it again.

Lawrence's dialect is his Standardised version, but watered down to a degree so it's accessible. The only time I've seen it written down as I remember it is a poem which was in the *Eastwood & Kimberley Advertiser*. It encapsulated my roots in terms of language.

1. How does Jon convey the sense that Eastwood was a closed community?

2. How do you think this affected his language development?

3. What attitudes did his mother's family and the community have to Jon's father being Polish and how were these expressed?

4. Look at the dialect in one of D.H. Lawrence's novels (e.g. Mr Morel in **Sons and Lovers**, or Mellors the gamekeeper in **Lady Chatterley's Lover**) and try to identify some of its main characteristics, bearing in mind what Jon says about it being 'watered down'.

A SUMMARY OF **KEY POINTS**

➢ Standard English is a powerful, flexible and useful variety of English, which all speakers and writers should be able to use. This does not mean that other language varieties will cease to be used or should be penalised.

➢ Spoken English is affected by historical, regional and personal variation. This is why it is so flexible.

➢ Accent is the way words are pronounced. Dialect is the grammar and vocabulary of the language.

➢ It is important to teach children not only how to speak and write Standard English but also when Standard English usage is appropriate.

➢ Speaking and listening about texts as part of English teaching, discussion in group and class activities and drama all have a part to play in learning to use Standard English and other dialects. However, such learning also involves explicit discussion of the rules covering Standard English, as well as of dialects and accents.

➢ In practice, issues such as dialect and formality can only really be discussed when children have knowledge of Standard English as a reference point and are able to discuss and reflect on their own language.

M-LEVEL EXTENSION > > M-LEVEL EXTENSION > > M-LEVEL EXTENSION

You might like to think about your own language biography. Do you speak Standard English or are there any regional variations in the way you speak? (You would be very unusual if your natural way of speaking was entirely Standard!)

If there are non-Standard features in your speech, what do you think you should do about this? There are some possibilities you might think about, which can be illustrated by some examples.

1. One teacher found that her class did not at first understand the word 'pumps' that she used to refer to the shoes the children wore for PE. Rather than change her word, she taught the children that this was an interesting feature of her speech. They quickly got to understand the word and saw their teacher as a more interesting person because of this slight language difference.
2. Another teacher found that her class naturally used the construction 'we was going'. In her dialect (which she had deliberately suppressed in favour of the Standard English variant), she would have said 'we were going' but also 'I were going'. By contrasting these usages she was able to raise her children's awareness of Standard and local English.

The British Museum has a great website called 'Sounds Familiar' **www.bl.uk/learning/langlit/sounds/changing-voices/**

Use of this site will help you to explore variation in speech more thoroughly. The activities available will enable you to recognise how accent is largely expressed through vowel sounds in English. You can also explore accent in your area. This is important background for your phonics teaching as well as a topic of study for your class.

FURTHER READING   FURTHER READING   **FURTHER READING**   FURTHER READING

DfE (2013) *Teachers' Standards*. London: DfE. **(www.gov.uk/government/uploads/system/uploads/attachment_data/file/208682/Teachers__Standards_2013.pdf)**

DfE (2013) The 2014 National Curriculum **(www.gov.uk/government/collections/national-curriculum)**

Holderness, J. and Lalljee, B. (eds) (1998) *An Introduction to Oracy: Frameworks for Talk*. London: Cassell.

Hughes, A., Trudgill, P. and Watt, D. (5th edn) (2012) *English Accents and Dialects: An Introduction to Social and Regional Varieties of English in the British Isles*. London: Routledge.

Hughes, M. (1994) 'The oral language of young children', in Wray, D. and Medwell, J. (eds) *Teaching Primary English: the State of the Art*. London: Routledge.

Maybin, J. (1994) 'Children's voices: talk, knowledge and identity', in Graddol, D., Maybin, J. and Stierer, B. (eds) *Researching Language and Literacy in Social Context*. Clevedon: Multilingual Matters.

Trudgill, P. (2nd edn) (1999) *The Dialects of England*. Oxford: Blackwell.

Trudgill, P. and Hannah, J. (5th edn) (2008) *International English: A guide to the varieties of standard English*. London: Routledge.

3
The acquisition of language

Curriculum context

National Curriculum programmes of study

This knowledge underpins your teaching of the Key Stage 1 programme of study for English, which states, for example, that to speak clearly, fluently and confidently to different people, pupils should be taught to:

- speak with clear diction and appropriate intonation;
- choose words with precision;

- organise what they say;
- focus on the main point(s);
- include relevant detail;
- take into account the needs of their listeners.

In working towards these objectives, enjoy listening to and using spoken and written language and readily turn to it in play and learning; use talk to organise, sequence and clarify thinking, ideas, feelings and events; use language to imagine and recreate roles and experiences; speak clearly and audibly with confidence and control and show awareness of the listener; extend their vocabulary, exploring the meanings and sounds of new words.

Early Years Foundation Stage

The Early Learning Goals specify that, by the end of the Early Years Foundation Stage, children should:

- enjoy listening to and using spoken and written language, and readily turn to it in their play and learning;
- extend their vocabulary, exploring the meanings and sounds of new words;
- use talk to organise, sequence and clarify thinking, ideas, feelings and events.

Introduction

Language acquisition is one of the key topics in the study of learning. Every theory of learning has tried to explain it and probably no other topic has aroused such controversy. Being able to use and understand a language is the quintessentially human characteristic: all normal humans speak, no non-human animal does. Language is the main vehicle by which we express what we are thinking, which suggests that language and thought must be closely related.

When we speak we do not only produce strings of words that relate in some way to the world around us or our reactions to it: we combine those words into groups according to some very complex rules – what we call grammar, or syntax. And we should not underestimate the complexity of these rules. As an example of this, look at the following pair of sentences.

(a) Bill saw Jane with her best friend's husband.
(b) Who did Bill see Jane with?

You will agree that sentence (b) is a perfectly logical question form derived from sentence (a). Now look at sentence (c).

(c) Bill saw Jane and her best friend's husband.

Following the 'rules' used in (a) and (b), it would be logical to accept the question form in (d).

(d) Who did Bill see Jane and?

You know, however, that that does not work. But can you explain why the question-forming rule works in one case and not in the other?

The same difficulty appears in the following four sentences. Why is sentence (d) not acceptable?

(a) David drove the car into the garage.

(b) David drove the car.

(c) David put the car into the garage.

(d) David put the car.

Explaining these things is quite difficult, and most people will respond by saying that the (d) sentences 'don't sound right'. Nevertheless, learning a language, and learning, implicitly, complex rules like these is something every child does successfully, in a matter of a few years and without the need for formal lessons. It is not surprising that children's acquisition of language has received so much attention. How on earth do they do it?

Theories about language acquisition

How do children acquire language? There have essentially been three competing theoretical explanations for this phenomenal process.

1. The behaviourist account

Behaviourist views of learning are characterised by the use of the stimulus–response–reward loop. Broadly speaking, stimulus–response learning works like this. An event in the environment (the stimulus) produces a response from an organism capable of learning. That response is then followed by another event, which rewards the organism. That is, the organism's response is positively reinforced. If the stimulus–response–reward sequence happens a sufficient number of times, the organism will learn to associate its response to the stimulus with the reward it gets. This will consequently cause the organism to give the same response whenever it meets the same stimulus. In this way, the response becomes a conditioned response. Behaviourist learning theorists are renowned for their work with non-human subjects (e.g. teaching pigeons to peck at buttons of certain colours to get food) but their theories have also been applied to human learning. Many of you will be familiar with approaches to child behaviour management that stress finding good behaviour and rewarding it, with the aim that this rewarded behaviour will continue and non-rewarded (less desirable) behaviour will disappear.

A behaviourist view of language acquisition simply claims that language development is the result of a set of habits. In 1957, the psychologist B.F. Skinner produced a behaviourist account of language acquisition in which linguistic utterances served as stimuli and responses. His theory claimed that language learners receive linguistic input from speakers around them, and are rewarded for their correct repetitions and imitations. As mentioned above, when language learners' responses are reinforced positively, they tend to repeat those responses. Through ongoing experience of imitation, reward and repetition, learners' language becomes progressively closer to adult language.

2. The generative/innatist approach

The claims of the behaviourists about the process of language acquisition were strongly criticised in Noam Chomsky's 1959 review of Skinner's book *Verbal Behavior*. Chomsky fundamentally questioned the relevance of the stimulus–response–reward sequence to the learning of language. His attack was centred on the identification of a basic problem with the behaviourist account – that is, how could the behaviourists explain the fact that young children commonly produce language utterances they can never have heard before? If language learners were learning largely through imitation, where did novel utterances come from? And it is clearly the case that children say things they have never heard. Here are just a few of the things that Alexander said sometime between his second and third birthdays:

'I goed there last week.'
'I see your foots.'
'Don't kick it where I'm not are.'

None of these was an expression he had ever heard his parents make. Alexander cannot therefore have produced them simply through imitation. Some other learning process had clearly been operating.

PRACTICAL TASK PRACTICAL TASK PRACTICAL TASK PRACTICAL TASK PRACTICAL TASK

Collect some other examples like this from young children you have access to. In each case, try to suggest an explanation for why the child has produced this expression. Is it simply a mistake, or is there something else going on?

Following the ideas of Chomsky, two main points became established in theories about language acquisition. First, it seemed to be the case that young children, instead of simply imitating what they heard, used this input data to develop their own rules about how language was produced. So Alexander, having heard lots of examples where the past tense of a verb had been formed by the addition of 'ed', applied this 'rule' to the verb 'go'. Similarly, having realised that nouns were commonly made plural by the addition of 's', he applied this to the noun 'foot'. He was generating new language forms from the rules he was developing. Notice that both the 'rules' applied in these examples actually produced incorrect language forms. Later Alexander went on to realise that there are plenty of exceptions in the English language to the rules he had devised, and adjusted his speech accordingly.

Chomsky's second point was that the process of deriving, testing and adjusting rules of language was so complex that what was really amazing about language acquisition was that young children did it so quickly. Most children by the age of three have learned more about the workings of their language than expert linguists can describe. How could this happen so fast? Chomsky's answer was that children must be born with a pre-existing mental capacity that allowed them to learn language quickly. Thus there was a dimension to language acquisition that was innate. This became known as the Language Acquisition Device, or LAD.

3. The social/interactive approach

The Chomskyan approach to language acquisition clearly seemed much more attuned to the observable evidence about young children's language development. Yet, as time has passed and new research evidence has emerged, some problems have become apparent. First, research has suggested that the language that carers direct at young children is not actually their normal language. If Chomsky was correct in his theory that children derived their own rules from the language that surrounded them, rules that gradually approached those of adult language users, then it might be thought that children were constantly exposed to models of correct adult language from which such rules could be derived. In fact, parents and other adults tend to speak to children in non-standard ways, in what has become known as 'motherese' (Durkin *et al.*, 1982). A new approach to language acquisition has developed from (rather than replaced) the Chomskyan position and stressed the importance of the adult's input to children's development.

This new, social/interactive model stresses that language is actually a by-product of communication, which is essentially what human beings are programmed to do. Children 'communicate' with their carers almost from birth, and there is research evidence that babies as young as a few days can copy their mothers' facial expressions and, to a degree, the sounds they utter. Language is acquired and used because it dovetails with this need for communication. Children learn language through using it in interaction with others to achieve particular ends.

The new model lays stress, not so much on the LAD, the innate propensity that young children probably must have for learning language, as on the LASS, the Language Acquisition Support System, which parents and other carers seem to instinctively operate when faced with the young of the species. Adults seem to know when to use which language forms with youngsters, when to use 'baby-talk', when to repeat their messages, and when to elaborate ideas in more complex language. So it is through this constant interaction with adults that young children come closer and closer to adult language usage.

PRACTICAL TASK PRACTICAL TASK PRACTICAL TASK PRACTICAL TASK PRACTICAL TASK

Try to eavesdrop on some adults as they talk with young children. As they talk, try to find any examples of the following.

- Adults talking in simpler forms than they would use in normal conversation.
- Adults expanding what a child says (e.g. Child: Mummy go. Adult: Yes, Mummy is going to the shop.).
- Adults correcting the talk of the child.
- Adults responding to what a child means, even if it is expressed incorrectly.

What can you learn about adult methods of supporting children's emerging talk from these conversations?

How children learn language

If we accept a social-interactive position on the ways in which children become users of language, we can examine more closely some of the processes by which this happens.

All normal children, from the moment they are born, are surrounded by spoken language. One of the most noticeable facts about babies is that people talk to them, and this begins long before anyone could expect these babies to understand what was being said. And the remarkable thing about the way people talk to babies is that they generally do it meaningfully. Of course, there is a certain amount of 'goo-gooing', but, more often, the talk will be similar to, 'Who's going to see his Nana? Yes, he is. Oh, there's a clever boy'. Many babies spend almost the whole of their waking life being played with; play which almost inevitably is accompanied by talk. This talk is invariably meaningful, even if not precisely expressed in adult forms. In addition to this, young children are also surrounded by talk which is not directly addressed to them. Again such talk is invariably meaningful and much of its sense is obvious from its context. Children then begin life bathed in meaningful talk.

Because the talk that surrounds them is meaningful, young children are receiving continual demonstrations of the functions of spoken language. If an adult says to a child, 'Who's dropped his ball then? There we are. Back again', and returns the ball, the adult is demonstrating the connection between talk and the action it refers to. When the child says, 'Daddy blow', and the adult responds with, 'Yes, Daddy will blow the whistle now', the demonstration is not only of the connection between language and action, but also of an appropriate form of speech. Children receive millions of demonstrations of meaningful talk, not only directed at them, but also taking place around them. From these demonstrations they have to work out how the system of language works, so that they can begin to take part in it.

The simple fact of witnessing demonstrations of language would not be sufficient to turn children into language users unless some other factors were also present. First among these is engagement, that is the desire on the part of children to take part in the language behaviour they see around them. This desire arises because children witness the power of language in the world, and want to share in it. They see, for example, that if you can ask for a biscuit rather than just scream loudly, you are more likely to get what you want. They also see that using language to achieve what they want is not so difficult that they are unlikely to master it. On the contrary, language is presented to them from the very first as something they can do. This produces a crucial expectation of success, which we know to be vitally important in actual achievement. There is plenty of evidence that children, both in and out of school, achieve very much what they are expected to achieve by other people. It is likely that this works because children internalise others' expectations about them, and come to hold these expectations of themselves. The most familiar example of this concerns children whom adults label as 'not very clever', and who come to believe this of themselves. Because they do not believe they can 'be clever', they stop trying to be.

In the case of spoken language, however, every child is expected to be able to master it (unless some medical condition makes this impossible). Asking any parent the question, 'Do you expect your child to learn to talk?' is likely to produce only a very puzzled response. The question seems ludicrous because the answer is so obvious. Because the adults around them believe so firmly that they will become talkers, the children themselves come to believe they will do it, and they do, generally effortlessly. There is an 'absence of the expectation that learning will not take place'.

When children are learning to talk, it is highly unlikely that the adult expert talkers who surround them will decide to administer a structured programme of speech training. Adults who have tried to be even a little systematic in helping children to develop language have found that it simply does not work. The following much quoted exchange between child and carer is an example of what can happen.

Child: Nobody don't like me.
Mother: No, say 'Nobody likes me'.
Child: Nobody don't like me. (Eight repetitions of this dialogue)
Mother: No, now listen carefully: say 'Nobody likes me'.
Child: Oh! Nobody don't likes me.

Instead of this situation, in which the adult has tried to take responsibility for what the child should learn, it is much more usual for the child to take the responsibility. Learning to talk is the child's task, which can be supported by adults but is not sequenced, structured or taught by them. This is implicitly accepted by the majority of adults who rarely try to force the pace when children are learning to talk, but instead take their lead from the child's performance.

During this learning, nobody expects children to perform perfectly from the very beginning. If children had to wait until they had perfect control of all facets of spoken language before speaking, they would not produce any speech until at least nine or ten years of age. What happens is that children produce spoken language forms that are approximations to adult forms, and these approximations gradually become closer and closer to the desired end product. 'Baby talk' is not only accepted by carers but is actually encouraged by being received with amusement and pride. It is also usually responded to as a meaningful utterance, and elaborated by the adult into a more fully developed form. When a child says, for example, 'Daddy you naughty', the adult is much more likely to respond with something like, 'Oh, fancy saying Daddy is naughty. He's a good Daddy', rather than, 'No. Say "Daddy, you are naughty"'. The adult responds to the child's attempts at fully fledged speech forms by interpreting and adding meaning, rather than by correcting them. Approximations are accepted and responded to by adults, and gradually children realise for themselves that they are approximate and how to make them more 'adult'.

Any learning, to be effective, requires a great deal of practice on the part of the learner, and learning to talk is no exception. For the vast majority of children this is no problem at all. They are constantly surrounded by talk and are expected, and given chances, to join in with it. Even when by themselves they carry on practising, from early babbling in which language sounds are practised to later oral accompaniments to actions such as play. Significantly this practice occurs for completely different purposes than to help children learn to talk. For example, adults rarely hold conversations with babies and young children because they know this is good for their language development. Nor do children talk to themselves when playing because they think this will make them better talkers. Both activities occur for more fundamental, human reasons. Conversations take place because there is something to converse about and children are included in the conversation that accompanies everyday action from very early in their lives. Children talk to themselves because this is how they represent their actions to themselves and how they reflect on these actions. This kind of talk becomes more and more elliptical and eventually fades altogether, occurring inside the head as 'inner speech'. It is the beginning of thought.

For all the importance of the above processes in children's growing capacity to produce meaningful speech, none of them would work were it not for the fact they all operate in a two-sided situation. Children are immersed in language, receive a myriad of demonstrations of it, are expected to try to emulate these and given freedom and opportunities to do it at their own pace and level of approximation, but the crucial factor is that all this happens in the context of real dialogue with other people. Adults talk, not just across children, but to them; they expect children to talk back to them, and when they do, adults respond. This constant interaction is at the heart of growing language use. And it is the need for interaction which comes first. Relationships need to be developed and things need to be achieved together. Language comes into being as a means of helping these things happen. It is therefore learned as a means of coping with the demands of being human.

Because of the interactive nature of language learning the process inevitably involves response. Children respond to adult language, and adults respond to children's attempts at language. Such response not only reaffirms the relationship that forms the context of the talk, but also gives children feedback about their language, and, perhaps, a more elaborated model on which to base future language.

A SUMMARY OF **KEY POINTS**

➢ **Because they are human, children are born with the need to communicate.**

➢ **Adults talk to children, thereby giving them plenty of demonstrations of purposeful language.**

➢ **Children work out the 'rules' of language from the interactions they have with other language users.**

➢ **Many of their initial attempts at these 'rules' will be incorrect but they are steps along the path to correct adult usage.**

➢ **The freedom to experiment and the freedom to be wrong are crucial elements in the learning of language.**

➢ **Interaction between adults and children is vital in language learning and this interaction, and shared attention, is not the same as listening to a TV or computer.**

M-LEVEL EXTENSION > > M-LEVEL EXTENSION > > M-LEVEL EXTENSION

Recent research in the US has been exploring the importance of children being talked to by adults in their early years. The project is known as the Thirty Million Words project (**http://tmw.org/tmw-initiative/**) because of the finding that some children, by their fourth birthdays, have been exposed to thirty million words more than other children, and the claim that this is linked to later school performance. It would be worthwhile exploring the papers and discussion on this website to find out more about this.

If the above features are characteristic of young children's learning of language, it might be thought that they would have strong implications for language use in early childhood settings and in schools. Do settings and schools provide the conditions in which language development will flourish? Or do they tend to emphasise a more limited conception of how language is learnt?

Make notes about the environment for language development that seems to be provided in any classrooms you are able to work in/visit. Focus particularly on the extent to which children in these classrooms are given the freedom to experiment and the freedom to be wrong in their language learning.

FURTHER READING   FURTHER READING   FURTHER READING   FURTHER READING

Clark, E.V. (2002) *First Language Acquisition*. Cambridge: Cambridge University Press.

DfE (2013) *Teachers' Standards*. London: DfE. (**www.gov.uk/government/uploads/system/uploads/attachment_data/file/208682/Teachers__Standards_2013.pdf**)

Leffel, K. and Suskind, D. (2013) 'Parent-directed Approaches to Enrich the Early Language Environments of Children Living in Poverty'. *Seminars in Speech and Language*. 34 (4): 267–77 **(http://tmw.org/wp/wp-content/uploads/2013/09/SSL-00517.pdf)**

Lust, B.C. and Foley, C. (2004) (eds) *First Language Acquisition: The Essential Readings*. Oxford: Blackwell.

Trott, K., Dobbinson, S. and Griffiths, P. (2004) (eds) *The Child Language Reader*. London: Routledge.

4
Representing sound in writing

Curriculum context

National Curriculum programmes of study

This knowledge is designed to underpin the teaching of the Key Stage 1 and Key Stage 2 programmes of study for English, which require that pupils should be taught to:

- apply phonic knowledge and skills as the route to decode words Y1
- continue to apply phonic knowledge and skills as the route to decode words until automatic decoding has become embedded and reading is fluent Y2
- respond speedily with the correct sound to graphemes (letters or groups of letters) for all 40+ phonemes, including, where applicable, alternative sounds for graphemes Y1
- read accurately by blending sounds in unfamiliar words containing GPCs that have been taught Y1
- read accurately by blending the sounds in words that contain the graphemes taught so far, especially recognising alternative sounds for graphemes Y2
- read accurately words of two or more syllables that contain the same graphemes as above Y2
- read words containing common suffixes Y2
- read common exception words, noting unusual correspondences between spelling and sound and where these occur in the word Y1/2/3/4

- read words containing taught GPCs and –s, –es, –ing, –ed, –er and –est endings Y1
- read other words of more than one syllable that contain taught GPCs Y1
- read words with contractions [for example, I'm, I'll, we'll], and understand that the apostrophe represents the omitted letter(s) Y1
- read most words quickly and accurately, without overt sounding and blending, when they have been frequently encountered Y2
- read aloud accurately books that are consistent with their developing phonic knowledge and that do not require them to use other strategies to work out words Y1
- read aloud books closely matched to their improving phonic knowledge, sounding out unfamiliar words accurately, automatically and without undue hesitation Y2
- re-read these books to build up their fluency and confidence in word reading Y1/2
- apply their growing knowledge of root words, prefixes and suffixes (etymology and morphology) as listed in English Appendix 1, both to read aloud and to understand the meaning of new words they meet Y3/4/5/6.

Pupils should be taught to:

- spell:

  o words containing each of the 40+ phonemes already taught Y1
  o common exception words Y1
  o the days of the week Y1

- name the letters of the alphabet:

  o naming the letters of the alphabet in order Y1
  o using letter names to distinguish between alternative spellings of the same sound Y1

- add prefixes and suffixes:

  o using the spelling rule for adding –s or –es as the plural marker for nouns and the third person singular marker for verbs Y1
  o using the prefix un– Y1
  o using –ing, –ed, –er and –est where no change is needed in the spelling of root words [for example, helping, helped, helper, eating, quicker, quickest] Y1
  o use further prefixes and suffixes and understand how to add them (English Appendix 1) Y3/4/5/6

- spell by:

  o segmenting spoken words into phonemes and representing these by graphemes, spelling many correctly Y2
  o learning new ways of spelling phonemes for which one or more spellings are already known, and learn some words with each spelling, including a few common homophones Y2
  o learning to spell common exception words Y2
  o learning to spell more words with contracted forms Y2
  o learning the possessive apostrophe (singular) [for example, the girl's book] Y2
  o distinguishing between homophones and near-homophones Y2

- spell further homophones Y3/4
- spell words that are often misspelt (English Appendix 1) Y3/4
- place the possessive apostrophe accurately in words with regular plurals [for example, girls', boys'] and in words with irregular plurals [for example, children's] Y3/4
- spell some words with 'silent' letters [for example, knight, psalm, solemn] Y5/6

- use knowledge of morphology and etymology in spelling and understand that the spelling of some words needs to be learnt specifically, as listed in English Appendix 1 Y5/6
- continue to distinguish between homophones and other words which are often confused Y5/6
- use dictionaries to check the spelling and meaning of words Y5/6
- use the first two or three letters of a word to check its spelling in a dictionary Y3/4
- use the first three or four letters of a word to check spelling, meaning or both of these in a dictionary Y5/6
- use a thesaurus Y5/6
- apply simple spelling rules and guidance, as listed in English Appendix 1 Y1/2
- write from memory simple sentences dictated by the teacher that include words and punctuation taught so far Y1/2/3/4.

Early Years Foundation Stage

The Early Learning Goals specify that, by the end of the Early Years Foundation Stage, children should:

Reading
- read and understand simple sentences;
- use phonic knowledge to decode regular words and read them aloud accurately;
- also read some common irregular words;
- demonstrate understanding when talking with others about what they have read.

Writing
- use their phonic knowledge to write words in ways which match their spoken sounds;
- write some irregular common words;
- write simple sentences which can be read by themselves and others;
- spell some words correctly and others in phonetically plausible ways.

Introduction

Most children learn to understand and speak English before they learn to read and write the language. So the spoken language develops first and is written down. However, English is a language with a long and complex history and written English is not a simple coding of spoken English. Effective readers and writers use several different types of patterns in English to read and spell. This chapter deals with some of the relationships between written and spoken English because it is important that teachers know about the patterns found in spoken and written English if they are to teach them to children in the most effective ways.

The sounds of English

We learn to speak so naturally that it is easy to take for granted not only what we learn to do, but also what we learn about speech itself. For instance, when we speak there is no temporal break between words – just try pausing between each word as you speak and see how unnatural it sounds. We know where words begin and end because we have used those words again and again in different combinations, because of intonation and because we can also recognise units greater and smaller than words. Children need to develop explicit awareness of units of sound – **phonological awareness**. Once children know about how sound works in speech they can manipulate it and use it in their literacy learning. Children naturally play with sound as part of the development of speech and become aware of different units of sound as they develop.

One of the earliest units of sound children learn to pick out (although not to discuss explicitly) is the **syllable**. The syllable is a group of sounds, usually a combination of consonants and vowels, which act as a unit of rhythm in speech. Some words have only one syllable but others are polysyllabic.

Examples:

    cat   (one syllable)

  zigzag   (two syllables)

undoing   (three syllables)

   cow   (one syllable).

It is important to remember that the syllable is a unit of sound and it can be difficult to decide where syllable boundaries occur when the word is written down. In the teaching of phonological awareness and use of syllables in poetry it is the number of syllables that is important, not where the syllable boundaries occur. However, the number of syllables can vary with pronunciation, another reason why it is important to remember that the syllable is a unit of sound, not writing. The key point is that each syllable has one vowel or vowel-like sound.

PEDAGOGICAL LINK PEDAGOGICAL LINK PEDAGOGICAL LINK PEDAGOGICAL LINK

It is important to understand how phonologically aware young children are as a basis for teaching phonological awareness and phonics in reading. One way to find out whether young children can discriminate syllables, which are usually the first unit discriminated, is to get the children to 'clap' their names or a short message to one another in circle or sharing time. You can also use shakers and other percussion instruments for the same purpose. These games help children to develop this awareness and a sense of rhythm in speech and allow you to assess their phonological awareness.

PRACTICAL TASK PRACTICAL TASK PRACTICAL TASK PRACTICAL TASK PRACTICAL TASK

How many syllables are there in each of these words? It will help to clap out the beats (or even to shut your eyes, if the spelling distracts you).

being	*extraordinary*
syllable	*despite*
dog	

When children are aware of syllables in speech they then become aware of smaller units of sound within these syllables. Most English **syllables** have a vowel (V) as their **nucleus** (or in a few cases a consonant (C) known as a syllabic consonant such as the sound for l, r and n) and may have consonants before the nucleus or after it. The nucleus of the syllable is very important as it carries the stress, loudness and pitch information for that syllable. This is why the syllable is such an important rhythmic and expressive unit, and why poetry often uses regularly patterned syllables.

Examples:

go (CV)	*at* (VC)
cat (CVC)	*stun* (CCVC)
*thi*s (CCVC)	*zigzag* (CVC CVC)

The consonant(s) at the beginning of the syllable is called an **onset**. The rest of the syllable is known as the **rime** and will include the syllable nucleus (a vowel or vowel-like sound) and, possibly, a consonant or consonants. When children are aware of syllables they will usually then be able to pick out the onset and rime within each syllable. For instance, c-at in cat, th-is in this. This is an important ability, as children can then use analogy to combine different onsets and rimes to make a vast range of syllables. So a child may be able to segment c-at and then make b-at, r-at, s-at, p-at, etc. This use of analogy may be a key skill in later spelling. For early years teachers, children's ability to identify onsets and rimes and to use analogy is a key step in developing phonological awareness. However, it is important to use single-syllable consonant–vowel–consonant (CVC) words such as dog, cat, bin, etc. when doing this early work, as onsets and rimes occur within syllables and a polysyllabic word like zigzag has two onsets and two rimes. It is also important to know that young children do not need to know or use the terms 'onset' or 'rime'. These units are useful for teachers to recognise but children do not need to discuss or reflect on them.

PEDAGOGICAL LINK PEDAGOGICAL LINK PEDAGOGICAL LINK PEDAGOGICAL LINK

Young children need to be able to rhyme and use analogy to generate new words. They will enjoy taking part in word games and singing rhyming songs to practise these skills.

RESEARCH SUMMARY RESEARCH SUMMARY RESEARCH SUMMARY RESEARCH SUMMARY

Goswami and Bryant (1990) review research into the development of phonological knowledge and suggest a particular model for the development of reading in young children and the role of phonological awareness within it. The model proposes that children given experience of rhyme and alliteration develop an awareness of these before they begin to learn to read. They actually begin reading using only a visual approach to recognising words but very quickly their awareness of onset and rime allows them to apply analogies in order to recognise new words. Through experience of reading they begin to become aware of the phonemic basis of alphabetic script and to develop skill in using this new-found awareness. Phonological awareness, in its various forms, is therefore both a precursor to and a product of reading.

The smallest unit of sound in a word is a **phoneme,** and different languages use a different range of phonemes. Around 44 phonemes are used extensively in English (the number varies depending on how they are classified). It is the millions of combinations of these phonemes that make up the rich and varied vocabulary of English. It is important for teachers to understand the nature and role of phonemes in speech because **phonemic awareness**, that is awareness of the individual sounds in words, is essential to reading and spelling.

Linguists use the International Phonetic Alphabet (IPA) to write these sounds precisely and you will see the IPA symbols in the National Curriculum English Appendix 1 (Spelling) and some dictionaries. There is a list of the IPA sounds in the appendix to the 2014 National Curriculum if you prefer to use these symbols. For the purposes of this book we have tried to avoid using the IPA, but this makes it difficult to be specific about which sound is being discussed. When a phoneme is being discussed we have used // around it and tried to give a common word in which it is usually pronounced. It is important to recognise that all the pronunciations given are those of the received pronunciation accent and the pronunciation of some phonemes, especially vowels, may be different in different accents, without being wrong.

The easiest way to group the phonemes of English is into vowels and consonants, because these sounds have different methods of production (a **phonetic** point of view) and different functions in spoken English (a **phonological** point of view). English speech sounds are produced by converting a stream of air that is forced out of the lungs through the nasal or oral cavities (or both) into soundwaves. Consonants (unlike vowels) are produced by a closing movement somewhere in the vocal tract, involving either the lips, tongue or throat. The 24 consonant sounds in most English accents are relatively easy to write down using the 21 letters of the English alphabet reserved for consonants but you will notice that some consonants require two letters to spell them, even approximately, and others, such as /th/ (they) and /th/ (thigh) use the same letters although they sound different. This is discussed further below.

Consonant	Word in which it appears
/p/	pie
/b/	by
/t/	tie
/d/	odd
/k/	ache
/g	go
/ch/	each
/j/	jaw
/f/	fee
/v/	view
/th/	thigh
/th/	they
/s/	so
/z/	zoo
/sh/	shoe
/g/	genre
/h/	he
/m/	me
/n/	in
/ng/	hang
/l/	lie
/r/	row
/w/	way
/y/	you

When teaching children to discriminate between and learn the phonemes commonly found in English words, most teachers begin with the consonant phonemes and the short vowels /a/ /e/ /i/ /o/ /u/ so that children can blend and segment consonant–vowel–consonant words (CVC words) from the start.

Consonants usually occur at the edges of syllables (/b//o//b/) and can appear in clusters or strings with up to three consonants at the beginning of an English word and four at the end. However, not all consonants are easy to hear or to discriminate from one another or from vowels. Some pairs of consonants sound very similar – /b/ and /p/, /t/ and /d/, /k/ and /g/, /f/ and /v/ or /s/ and /z/. This is because some consonants (/b/, /d/, /g/, etc.) involve the vibration of the vocal cord and are called voiced consonants whereas others do not involve the vocal cords at all and are called unvoiced (/p/,/t/, etc.). Not surprisingly, teachers aim to pronounce these sounds as clearly as possible to help children learn to recognise and spell them. This often results in teachers adding a vowel to make the consonant sound clearer. Try saying /p/ or /b/ clearly and loudly as you would to a class of children – you may find you say 'puh' or 'buh'. This should be avoided, as it makes it very hard for children to blend phonemes if they include extra vowels.

PRACTICAL TASK PRACTICAL TASK PRACTICAL TASK PRACTICAL TASK PRACTICAL TASK

Say the following words to yourself, one at a time. How many consonants are there in each word? Remember that you are listening to the sounds, not the spelling, and that a sound can be written down with more than one letter.

rouge	*slip*
thyroid	*yellow*
gnome	*machine*

The vowels are another major category of phonemes in English speech. Vowels are the most sonorant and audible sounds in spoken English and the consonants around them sometimes depend on the vowel for their audibility. The vowels are produced in a rather different way from the consonants, using an open vocal tract and depending on the vibration of the upper vocal tract. There are 20 or so vowels in English speech and their sound quality varies from accent to accent. Although the consonants of English are relatively easy to classify and write down, the vowels are much more complicated. The IPA uses several special symbols to represent vowel sounds but we will attempt to list them without the symbols. In doing this, the most common vowels from all the systems of classification are listed.

Vowel sound	*Words including that sound (note different spellings)*
/a/	sat, hand
/e/	get, head
/i/	pig, him, women

/o/	dog, swan, cough
/u/	son, sun, does
/ae/	pain, ape, waist
/ee/	sea, feet, me
/ie/	cry, shine, die, high
/oe/	so, road, bone, cold
/ue/	moon, do, blue
/oo/	put, would, look, wolf
/ar/	calm, are, father
/ur/	bird, her, heard, learn
/or/	poor, sure, tour, door
/au/	all, saw, more
/er/	about, wooden, circus, sister, sofa
/ow/	down, house, how, found
/oi/	coin, toy, noise, voice
/air/	stair, stare, bear, hare
/ear/	beer, here, fierce, near

PEDAGOGICAL LINK PEDAGOGICAL LINK PEDAGOGICAL LINK PEDAGOGICAL LINK

Given that the vowels are most likely to appear in the nucleus of a syllable and that they vary widely, it is not surprising that English speaking children are usually able to discriminate the consonants in speech before the vowel sound. Look at this piece of a young child's writing and decide which sounds the child has been able to discriminate.

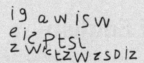

David, nearly five years old, has written about his attic conversion. He uses initial consonants but does not 'hear' most of the vowels. A notable exception is the letter name A. The piece reads: 'I got a room in the roof. It is painted white and the radiator is on. The stairs are there.'

Daniel and Ben (both aged five) have written advice for new children about writing on the class word processor. Their writing shows that they can hear vowels, but that it is very difficult to spell them – look at how they both spell **sounds**!

Ben's advice

Writing

We trid at home at my desk
you need to pradis and, you
yos the sawnds
The author's cer is for
authors
You need to Mack spasis and
it has to be intresding .

c

Writing

Went I went to skool
I cont do no writing
but I can naw
becoots I trid I
dodth it at home. I
yostt the sans and I
nedid sum hep.

When teaching children phonemes, teachers start with consonants and short vowels.

REFLECTIVE TASK

Think about the ways in which these young children write. What does it tell you about:

- their awareness of sounds?
- their understanding of the way in which English spelling works?

As a fluent writer yourself, what understandings do you think you have that these children do not yet have?

The symbols of English

Written English is never simply a case of 'speech written down' and it never really has been. Speech and writing change at different rates and so written language is always 'behind' the changes in speech. Also, if writing were simply a transliteration of speech, whose speech would we transcribe? Would we choose a particular accent to transcribe? Standard English spelling gives us a shared ways of recognising words, but it also means that written English is not a close representation of speech.

RESEARCH SUMMARY   RESEARCH SUMMARY   RESEARCH SUMMARY   RESEARCH SUMMARY

Most researchers into reading would now agree that it actually involves both decoding printed symbols into recognisable language and constructing meaning through interactions with these symbols. Both are necessary parts of the reading process and neither is sufficient by itself (Adams, 1994). This is why reading teaching focuses on both the decoding of language and comprehension.

There are a number of patterns in written English that are used to spell our words. Some are patterns of sound written down, some are visual patterns of letters we recognise easily and some are patterns that have developed because of meanings (these are discussed in later chapters). None of these patterns is complete, in that there is not one single system governing the spelling of all English words. However, if we know these patterns we can use them to read, write and spell.

The most obvious pattern is the representation of the sounds of English by letters and combinations of letters. If you have read the section above you can see that it is difficult to express the sounds of English in writing, with the limited 26 letters of the English alphabet. As it is so basic to our system of writing, sound–symbol correspondences (also called Grapheme–Phoneme correspondences or GPCs) are a very good system for children to learn about early in their reading and writing careers. As soon as children know that written words 'say' something, they will begin to want to know how to work out what. Teaching them about sounds can help them to 'crack' the code of writing, especially if the text they want to read is relevant, compelling, short or predictable.

Phonics teaching involves teaching children to match sounds (phonemes) with letters and combinations of letters (graphemes) and to blend and segment the sounds to create or decode words. The knowledge to be learnt includes the range of grapheme–phoneme correspondences (GPCs) and the skills used include blending and segmenting. These are key skills and all children need to learn them early on to make progress at early reading. However, successful phonics teaching begins when children are familiar with lots of stories and environmental print. Children do not learn to read using phonics alone and they need to know certain things to use phonics. These include knowing that text is readable, why you might want to read texts, which bits of a text you read, how text proceeds from left to right and that reading is a relevant, enjoyable activity. Most children learn these lessons very early when reading with their parents or at nursery. These ideas are also a key part of literacy teaching and reading in the Early Years Foundation Stage.

The simplest representations of sound in writing are the consonants and short vowels represented above, which can be blended together to produce consonant vowel consonant (CVC) words. Most teachers will teach these sound–symbol correspondences by using items and words containing these consonants and short vowels and repeatedly writing the words and using the letters.

PEDAGOGICAL LINK PEDAGOGICAL LINK **PEDAGOGICAL LINK** PEDAGOGICAL LINK

The very early stages of modern phonics schemes, designed for use in the EYFS, start with teaching consonants and short vowels and give one spelling of each. This means that children are quickly enabled to spell most things, although not correctly. Later they will learn other spellings.

Even at this simple level of representing speech in writing there are teaching decisions to be made. Most teachers teach the little (lower case) script before the capital (upper case) script. Most teachers also make the important distinction between the letter name and the sound the letter represents and teach this explicitly to children. To literate adults the idea that /c/ represents the sound at the beginning of 'cat' may seem simple, but for young learners it is very complicated. They must have the phonological awareness to discriminate the sound /c/ aurally in a word, they must recognise this as /c/ pronounced out of context by their teacher (who will sometimes pronounce it 'cuh', which is rather different from the sound in 'cat'). Then the young learners must associate this range of sounds with the shape

C (which they will also learn to write) and they must know that the shape is called 'see'. Finally, they must accept that this doesn't always work, as in words like cherry, chip and cheese. It really is amazing just how quickly and easily most children learn sound–symbol correspondences and the National Curriculum Programmes of study expect all children to have learnt a GPC for each of the 44 phonemes by the time they begin Year 1.

Many consonant sounds can be represented by one letter but this is not true of all. Some of the most commonly used are represented by more than one letter:

/ch/	– in **ch**eese, **ch**eek, **ch**erry and wat**ch**
/th/	– in **th**igh
/th/	– in **th**ey
/sh/	– in **sh**oe
/ng/	– in ri**ng**
/j/	– in nu**dge**

Sounds that need more than one letter to represent them in the written forms are called **consonant digraphs** (or, less commonly, **consonant trigraphs** – /j/ ju**dge** – if there are three letters). Teachers usually teach the very common consonant digraphs ch, th and sh at the same time as children learn the one-letter consonants because they aim to teach one spelling of each of the consonants and short vowels quickly.

The consonants are represented in writing in a reasonably regular way. Unfortunately, vowels are not quite as simple. The 20 vowels listed earlier can be spelt in many different ways (see the table, above). Some vowels are spelt simply by a single letter (a, e, i, o, u) but many are written using not only the five letters we traditionally call vowels (a, e, i, o, u) but also some letters we call consonants, usually r, y and w (/oi/ in b**oy**, /ou/ in c**ow**, sh**ou**t, /er/ in ci**r**cus, wood**e**n, sist**er**). Vowels represented by more than one letter are called **vowel digraphs** (r**oa**d, m**oo**n, bl**ue**, d**ow**n) or, less commonly, vowel **trigraphs** (st**air**, b**ear**, l**eer**, h**ere**).

The complexity of spelling vowels is not surprising since accents in English often use different vowels, so there are many words that are pronounced differently in different accents. One person may say b/ar/th or f/ar/st and another b/a/th or f/a/st, but they are both spelt bath and fast. As a teacher you need to know the accents of your children before selecting examples of words with particular vowel sounds.

PEDAGOGICAL LINK PEDAGOGICAL LINK PEDAGOGICAL LINK PEDAGOGICAL LINK

In Year 1 and 2 of the National Curriculum Programme of Study (English), in Appendix 1 there is a list of statutory sound symbol (grapheme–phoneme) correspondences which must be taught, although the order they are taught in is not statutory.

Visual patterns in English

There is considerable evidence that adult spellers also use visual patterns to spell. Visual strategies include remembering almost automatically how some words look. The common, short and often phonically irregular words such as and, because, but, where, a, on, in are often learnt by sight, so that they do not need to be 'sounded out' each time they are used. Learning these words can be very helpful in becoming a fluent reader or writer.

For this reason word lists of common words are often compiled for suggested words that children should know early in their school experience and these are often referred to as sight or tricky words. However, these common words are difficult to remember because, on their own, they are not particularly meaningful. Most teachers have encountered children who can spell 'tyrannosaurus' before they can spell 'because'!

PEDAGOGICAL LINK PEDAGOGICAL LINK PEDAGOGICAL LINK PEDAGOGICAL LINK

The phonics scheme in use in any EYFS (Reception) class or KS1 class will include an order in which the sight words are taught. It is important to know this, because it tells you which sight words the children have already been taught when you plan lessons and resources.

Teachers use flashcards (paper and electronic), whiteboards, spelling tests, repeated demonstrations of such words, word banks and word books to help children learn more complicated but important words and the National Curriculum has lists for Years 3–6. These words are worth examining to look at unusual spelling patterns and origins. However, a powerful strategy for learning words is one suggested by Peters (see below) called Look, cover, write, check. This involves children using a fan of paper or book to look carefully at the word, analysing its shape and sometimes tracing over it with a finger or pen then covering up the word. The learner might 'close their eyes and visualise the word on their eyelids' as they do this. The word is written down from memory and checked. If it is correct, the learner moves on; if not, the process is repeated. This common strategy aims to get children to develop a mental picture of the word.

RESEARCH SUMMARY RESEARCH SUMMARY RESEARCH SUMMARY RESEARCH SUMMARY

Margaret Peters (1985) researched the strategies used by mature spellers and whether spelling was 'caught or taught'. She concluded that a lucky few do seem to 'catch' spelling by becoming aware of patterns early and using strategies to remember them. However, most children need to have the patterns in English spelling made explicit to them and need to use a range of strategies to remember. Peters was keen to emphasise that spelling teaching should be based on the patterns inherent in English words, to give children the greatest chance of getting the words right. She emphasised the visual basis of much of adults' spelling and the possible link with fluent handwriting, and stressed that children need very fluent and swift handwriting from an early age.

One aspect of Peters' work that has been very popular in schools is her emphasis on the visual patterns of words. Although the common words mentioned above may not share a pattern and so may be hard to learn, some collections of words share a visual (not sound) pattern that can make them easier to learn, for instance, weir, their, weight and eight do not share a sound pattern but they all contain the very common visual pattern **ei**. It may be that learning words that have a shared visual pattern can help to fix them in mind. Cripps and Peters (1990) have also linked this to handwriting by emphasising the kinaesthetic learning of shape patterns. They suggest that the early learning of fluent handwriting and joined script can help children to learn common letter combinations 'by hand'. In many schools this has resulted in the teaching of handwriting being linked with the teaching of spelling and spelling tests.

Finally, in terms of visual strategies for spelling, the ability to use dictionaries, spellcheckers and word banks are all valuable skills that even mature writers need. Children must be taught these skills. Good spelling involves knowing:

- the sound and visual patterns in language, and how to use them;
- how to check spellings;
- when to make the effort!

Morphemic and etymological patterns in English

In addition to sound-symbol patterns, and sight words, there are other important patterns for children to know about if they are to be able to read fluently and write conventionally. Many of the patterns in words relate to the origins of words – their **etymology**. For instance, biscuit is a word whose origins are from the Norman French. The word refers to something which was twice (bi-) cooked (-cuit). You might see the prefix bi- in other words like bicycle. Other patterns are related to the meaning and grammatical function of words – **morphological** patterns, such as the use of –s or –es as a plural suffix. The knowledge of these patterns needed for teaching primary English is discussed in Chapter 5 of this book. However, it is important to recognise that all these patterns are important as ways of spelling and are a great basis for curiosity about words.

PEDAGOGICAL LINK PEDAGOGICAL LINK PEDAGOGICAL LINK PEDAGOGICAL LINK

The National Curriculum Programme of Study (English) includes statutory word patterns that must be taught in Years 1/2, 3/4 and 5/6.

Handwriting in English

Handwriting is a very visible part of writing, by which individuals are often judged. However, handwriting is a skill which some people develop more easily than others and which most people become competent at with practice. An individual's handwriting does not tell you about their intelligence or personality, although it might give you clues about the amount of effort they have put in!

RESEARCH SUMMARY RESEARCH SUMMARY RESEARCH SUMMARY RESEARCH SUMMARY

Although handwriting is often considered a matter of presentation, a substantial body of international research suggests that the role of handwriting in children's composing has been neglected. Automaticity in handwriting is now seen as of key importance in composing but UK policy and practice tends to have assumed that, by Year 6, handwriting is a matter of presentation, unrelated to composition processes. Recent research has been undertaken into the handwriting speed and orthographic motor integration of Year 6 pupils in relation to their composition (Medwell *et al.*, 2009) and into similar aspects of the writing of Year 2 children (Medwell *et al.*, 2007). These studies both suggest that handwriting is an important factor in composition, and that a proportion of children suffer from low levels of handwriting automaticity, which may be interfering with their composition. The teaching of handwriting is, it seems, not just important in improving children's presentation skills, but their composition skills too.

As handwriting has developed through the centuries it has become much more widespread, more fluent in use and more adapted to a great range of purposes. This means that most people need to be able to write a 'fair' hand for public use, although this is becoming rarer today as word processing assumes this role. People also need to be able to write fast, legible notes for their own consumption and a 'middling' or 'rough' hand for other occasions. Learning handwriting involves learning how to do it and when to do it. Typing is not the same as handwriting and there is some evidence that handwriting helps children to fix their knowledge of phonemes so typing is unlikely to totally replace writing by hand. There is also evidence that slow writers tend to type slowly, too.

Young children generally develop a hand preference at around 3–4 years. Some children in the EYFS will still be developing a hand preference and may swap hands. Teachers in this age phase aim to get children to develop a pen grip, scribble, paint and make marks across the page and become increasingly precise in their drawings. When children start to write they usually start with their names – these are very significant words – and may also start 'scribble writing' long messages. It is very obvious when you work with young children that they begin to write letters using capital letters. At first this is surprising to new teachers (some suggest the parents are teaching children wrongly) but it is quite logical when you consider how difficult the round movements of a small letter 'a' are, compared to the bold, easy strokes of a capital letter.

In some countries there is almost a national 'style' of 'script' and all children are taught the same letter formation – French handwriting appears distinctive to British people for this reason. In the UK the script (letter formation and joins) taught to children is decided by the school. However, it is a decision that causes much discussion because we are all attached to our particular formation of b, k, f, etc. The key requirements for script are made clear by Sassoon (1990). All scripts are basically formed from ovals and vertical strokes. Any script must join easily and fluently and must be used consistently in the school. Most schools now use letter formations that include exit strokes (kicks, or flicks) but not entry strokes. These are easy to form, clear and join logically. The formation of letters can be taught in order of the shapes or letter 'families', and joins can be taught in a number of orders. Some schools do the 'natural' vertical joins first, then the horizontal joins; others the reverse. In either case it is good practice for the teacher to use the same script when modelling handwriting, especially in the EYFS.

PRACTICAL TASK PRACTICAL TASK PRACTICAL TASK PRACTICAL TASK PRACTICAL TASK

Copy the preceding paragraph as quickly (and neatly) as possible. You will notice that writing neatly slows you down!

Examine your writing. Do you see any letters that should be joined but are not? Most writers tend to abandon the 'unnatural' joins when they write fast but be careful when you write as a model for children in class.

The most important point in teaching early handwriting is that fluent letter formation movements must be learnt early – they are very hard to change and poor letter formation inhibits joining letters. If writers cannot easily join letters, their handwriting will be less fluent in later life. It is also important for letter formation to be automatic.

Finally, there is a need for children to have the skill of accurate and fast use of the keyboard. Although not all schools teach touch typing, it is likely to be on the curriculum of many schools in the near future.

A SUMMARY OF **KEY POINTS**

➢ **Young children become aware of syllable and word boundaries before they can hear sounds (phonemes) in words.**

➢ **Individual phonemes can be difficult to discriminate, especially if you already know the spelling.**

➢ **Most sounds (especially vowels) can be represented in more than one way.**

➢ **The same spelling can produce more than one sound (e.g. in field and tried).**

➢ **Phonics is a method of teaching sound–symbol correspondences and the skills of blending and segmenting.**

➢ **All children need to learn to use sound–symbol correspondences to read and spell.**

➢ **Correct spelling is not based only on sound–symbol correspondences.**

➢ **Visual, etymological and morphemic strategies are useful to achieve correct spelling.**

➢ **Fluent letter formation is more important than accuracy in size or alignment.**

➢ **Joined writing should be taught as soon as possible to ensure fluency, and possibly help spelling development.**

M-LEVEL EXTENSION > > M-LEVEL EXTENSION > > M-LEVEL EXTENSION

Collect some samples of early writing from children in Nursery or the Reception year. Analyse which sounds each child has been able to discriminate and consider whether there seems to be a relationship between the fluency of their letter formation and the accuracy of their spelling. Compare these aspects with samples of writing from other children in other year groups. If you can gain access to the work of one particular child over time, track the development of their understanding of sound–symbol correspondence, spelling patterns and the fluency of their handwriting.

FURTHER READING   FURTHER READING   FURTHER READING   FURTHER READING

DfE (2013) *Teachers' Standards*. London: DfE. **(www.gov.uk/government/uploads/system/uploads/ attachment_data/file/208682/Teachers__Standards_2013.pdf)**

DfE (2013) *The 2014 National Curriculum.* London: DfE.

(www.gov.uk/government/collections/national-curriculum)

Jager Adams, M. (1990) *Beginning To Read: Thinking And Learning About Print*. Cambridge, MA: Massachusetts Institute of Technology.

Medwell, J., Strand, S. and Wray, D. (2007) 'The Role of Handwriting in Composing for Y2 Children'. *Journal of Reading, Writing and Literacy*, 2 (1): 18–36.

Medwell, J., Strand, S. and Wray, D. (2009) 'The Links between Handwriting and Composing for Y6 children'. *Cambridge Journal of Education*, 39 (3).

Peters, M. (1967) *Spelling: Caught Or Taught?* London: Routledge and Kegan Paul.

Peters, M. and Smith, B. (1993) *Spelling In Context: Strategies For Teachers And Learners*. Windsor: NFER-Nelson.

Rose, J. (2006) *Independent Review of the Teaching of Reading*. London: DfES.

Sassoon, R. (1990) *Handwriting: The Way To Teach It*. Cheltenham: Stanley Thornes.

5
Words, vocabulary and morphology

Curriculum context

National Curriculum programmes of study

This knowledge is designed to underpin the teaching of the Key Stage 1 and Key Stage 2 programmes of study for English, which state, for example, that pupils should be taught

in spoken language to:

- use relevant strategies to build their vocabulary

in reading to:

- apply their growing knowledge of root words, prefixes and suffixes (etymology and morphology) both to read aloud and to understand the meaning of new words they meet
- develop pleasure in reading, motivation to read, vocabulary and understanding by

  - discussing word meanings, linking new meanings to those already known
  - using dictionaries to check the meaning of words that they have read
  - discussing words and phrases that capture the reader's interest and imagination

- understand both the books they can already read accurately and fluently and those they listen to by:

  - drawing on what they already know or on background information and vocabulary provided by the teacher

and in writing to:

- add prefixes and suffixes to spell longer words
- use knowledge of morphology and etymology in spelling and understand that the spelling of some words needs to be learnt specifically
- draft and write by:

  - composing and rehearsing sentences orally, progressively building a varied and rich vocabulary
  - selecting appropriate grammar and vocabulary, understanding how such choices can change and enhance meaning

- evaluate and edit by:

  - proposing changes to grammar and vocabulary to improve consistency, to enhance effects and clarify meaning
  - recognising vocabulary and structures that are appropriate for formal speech and writing.

Early Years Foundation Stage

The Early Learning Goals specify that, by the end of the Early Years Foundation Stage, children should:

- extend their vocabulary, exploring the meanings and sounds of new words;
- hear and say sounds in words in the order in which they occur;
- use their phonic knowledge to write simple regular words and make phonetically plausible attempts at more complex words.

Introduction

The sheer breadth of English vocabulary gives it great richness and flexibility. In teaching children to use and improve their use of English, one of our concerns is to improve their range of words, and the flexibility and appropriateness with which they use them. It is also useful to study words and their origins so that children can understand the language they use. To do this you need to know something about the development, change and selection of English vocabulary. The formation of words is also a part of the grammar of English so that, although grammar is often considered at 'sentence level', parts of grammar are concerned with what happens within words.

The origins of English vocabulary

It is important that teachers know something about the history of English for two reasons; first, so that they have the background knowledge to do some word study with children and, second, so that they can understand why English is such a complicated and at times seemingly illogical language.

English is part of the Germanic branch of the Indo-European family of languages (along with German, Dutch, Icelandic and the Scandinavian languages). Evidence for the relationship between English and other languages can be seen just by looking at simple names for numbers – the sort of activity you might do with children.

PRACTICAL TASK PRACTICAL TASK PRACTICAL TASK PRACTICAL TASK PRACTICAL TASK

Look at these number names:

English	German	Danish	French	Norwegian	Urdu
one	eins	en	un	en	ek
two	zwei	to	deux	to	do
three	drei	tre	trois	ter	teen
four	vier	fire	quatre	fire	char
five	fünf	fem	cinq	fem	paanch
six	sechs	seks	six	seks	chhe
seven	sieben	syv	sept	sju	saat
eight	acht	otte	huit	atte	aath
nine	neun	ni	neuf	ni	nau
ten	zehn	ti	dix	ti	das

What evidence do you find for a common original language?
Which languages would you identify as closest to English?
Which languages do you think might have influenced English?

English has been shaped by invasion and settlement of the British Isles and this is evident in its vocabulary, which has benefited from three broad influences:

* Anglo-Saxon and Old Norse (the language of the Vikings);
* French;
* Latin (with words from Greek coming through Latin).

The following chart gives a rough chronology of English:

Dates	Historical events	Language influence	Stages of English
900–700BC	Celts settle in British Isles	Celtic	Pre-English
55BC–43AD	Roman raids and settlement	Latin but little preserved in modern English	
Early 5th century	Romans leave		
449	Germanic tribes invade	Anglo-Saxon	Old English (450–1100)
600	England converts to Christianity	Latin (via the church) Words borrowed include: altar, cup, abbot, hymn, pear, cook, rue	
750	Beowolf composed		
9th–11th century	Vikings invade	Scandinavian (borrowings: dyke, skirt, kin, take, disk)	
1066	Battle of Hastings Normans invade	Norman French. Latin, through Norman. French for legal or learned vocabulary	Middle English (1100–1450)
1200	Normandy and England separated		
13th–14th century	Growing sense of Englishness	London becomes dominant. Migration to London from Midlands converges dialects	
1337–1450	Hundred Years War (Chaucer)		
1476	First English book published. Spelling standardised		Early Modern English (1450–1700)
1564–1616	Shakespeare	Latin and Greek through the influence of the Renaissance and printing (borrowings: anachronism, allusion, capsule, dexterity, exist)	
16th–19th century	Imperialism	Swahili, Hindi, Chinese, etc. (borrowings: rajah, safari, loot)	Modern English (1700–present)
19th–21st century	Varieties of Standard English	Technical and local vocabularies	

Anglo-Saxon and Norse influences on English vocabulary

When the Celtic inhabitants of Britain were driven back by Angles, Saxons and Jutes around 450AD very few Celtic words entered the language of the invaders. In modern English a few river names such as *Dart, Exe* and *Nene* and the element *coombe* in place names (Ilfracombe) remain as the only evidence of the Celtic past. The dialects of the Angles, Saxons and Jutes gave rise to Anglo-Saxon, or **Old English**, the language of England between about 450 and 1100.

PRACTICAL TASK PRACTICAL TASK PRACTICAL TASK PRACTICAL TASK PRACTICAL TASK

Look at these versions of the Lord's Prayer. Use of written English was quite different in Old English times so few comparable texts exist. This is one text which can be used for comparison.

Old English (eleventh century)

> *Fæder ure þu þe eart on heofonum; Si þin nama gehalgod to becume þin rice gewurþe ðin willa on eorðan swa swa on heofonum. urne gedæghwamlican hlaf syle us todæg and forgyf us ure gyltas swa swa we forgyfað urum gyltendum and ne gelæd þu us on costnunge ac alys us of yfele soþlice.*

(Corpus Christi College MS 140, ed. Liuzza (1994))

Middle English (1400AD)

> *Oure fadir that art in heuenes, halewid be thi name, thi kyngdoom come to, be thi wille don in erthe as in heuene, gyue to vs this dai oure breed ouer othir substaunce*
>
> *and forgyue to vs oure detis, as we forgyen to oure dettouris,*
>
> *and lede vs not in to temptacioun, but delyuere vs from yuel, amen.*

(Bodleian Library MS Rawlinson C.751, cited in Lollard Sermons, ed. Cigman (1989, p. xxiv))

Early Modern English (The King James Bible, 1611)

> *Our father which art in heauen, hallowed be thy name.*
>
> *Thy kingdome come. Thy will be done, in earth, as it is in heauen.*
>
> *Giue vs this day our daily bread.*
>
> *And forgiue vs our debts, as we forgiue our debters.*
>
> *And lead vs not into temptation, but deliuer vs from euill: For thine is the kingdome, and the power, and the glory, for euer, Amen.*

(Holy Bible, 1611)

Modern English (Book of Common Prayer, 1928)

> *Our Father, who art in heaven, Hallowed be thy Name. Thy kingdom come. Thy will be done, On earth as it is in heaven. Give us this day our daily bread. And forgive us our trespasses, As we forgive those who trespass against us. And lead us not into temptation, But deliver us from evil. For thine is the kingdom, the power, and the glory, for ever and ever. Amen.*

- What letters can you identify that have not come into Modern English?
- Which words can you identify in the Old English version? Are they particular types of word?

Old English words exist in most important word categories in Modern English. Many of the main content words have Anglo-Saxon origins:

Nouns: father (faeder), king (cynig), sun (sunne), day (daeg), wife (wif), heaven (heofonum), Monday (monandaeg)

Adjectives: evil (yfele), cold (cald), busy (bisig)

Verbs: fight (feohtan), forgive (forgyf), live (libban)

These structure words, which hold sentences together, are also Anglo-Saxon originally:

Personal pronouns: I, you, he, she, we, us

Demonstrative pronouns: this, that, these, those

Auxiliary verbs: can, shall

Conjunctions: as, and, but, so, then

Prepositions: in, on, under, over, down, by

Adverbs: when, while, where

Finally, although most rude words related to the body and bodily functions come from Anglo-Saxon (arse, shit and fart, for instance), they were originally acceptable words and we have no evidence that speakers of Old English swore or used profanities!

PRACTICAL TASK PRACTICAL TASK PRACTICAL TASK PRACTICAL TASK PRACTICAL TASK

- Sort the Old English words below into food, questions and prepositions. A version of this activity could be used with children.

- What is it that allows you to translate the words into Modern English? What does that tell you about the relationship between speech and writing?

Hunig, bread, hwy, aefter, hwaet, butere, haer, mete, milc, hwaenne, behindan, beforan.

The Vikings, who raided England from about 780 to 1014, then conquered and ruled for 14 years, brought Old Norse to England. It was quite similar to English and the inhabitants on both sides of the Danelaw line could converse with one another. The languages eventually became one and English acquired a range of new words and word parts from Old Norse. These exist in many modern English words – for instance, the words window, fellow, leg, loan, skill, skin, skirt, get and thrive. Some of the more harsh sounds in spoken English originate from Norse: **sk**irt, **k**id, **g**et, e**gg**.

Norman French influences on English

The Norman invasion of 1066 brought with it a French-speaking ruling class. French dominated the judicial, legal, church and military systems for 300 years but did not obliterate the English language, unlike Anglo-Saxon which had marginalised the Celtic languages. Although the kings of England spoke French for 200 years after the invasion, within a few generations it was the dominant, but second, language for the middle classes. The peasants and many of the middle classes spoke English. This meant that there was a long period (150 years) from which little written English literature remains, but it was also a time when the language itself underwent significant changes. It is estimated that 10,000 French words and phrases passed into English, over 70 per cent of them nouns, including the following: authority, bailiff, chancellor, peasant, prince, realm, reign, jail, jury, judge, priory, religion, repent, heresy, archer, army, captain, combat, enemy, garrison, appetite, bacon, clove, supper, toast, veal, art, beauty, chess, fur, rhyme, romance, vellum, volume, alkali, arsenic, copy, gender, cellar, curtain, pantry, amorous, allow, to have mercy on, to do justice to, to hold one's peace, and to make a complaint. The words here should give you some idea of the social spheres of influence of the Norman rulers!

Although many Old English (OE) words disappeared, many new French (F) forms exist alongside older alternatives and taking slightly different meanings – for example, doom (OE) and judgement (F), hearty (OE) and cordial (F). In this way, the resulting language, Middle English, which was spoken and written from 1100 to 1450, was more extensive, richer and far closer to Modern English than Old English. You can see this clearly by revisiting the Middle English version of the Lord's Prayer that we looked at earlier.

Three major changes in the Middle English period have affected all Modern English spellers. First, Norman scribes introduced French spellings of English sounds. For example, qu- for cw-, queen for cwen. Norman scribes also used c before e instead of s, so sircle became circle and sell became cell. New letters appeared – k, z and j came into much more common use. v began to be used either to represent the phoneme /v/ (*haue* for have) or the modern English vowel sound /u/ (*vnder* for under). The resulting mixture of French and old English spelling conventions is one reason why English spelling is such a trial today.

Second, Middle English lost its inflections (mostly endings). Those of you who have studied German or Latin will remember that words in different positions in a sentence have different endings. This was true of Old English. For example:

Nominative (subject)	cyning	king
Accusative (object)	cyninge	king
Genitive (possessive)	cyninges	king
Dative (doing or giving)	cyninge	king

Loss of inflections made Middle English much easier to spell. The few inflected endings that remain in English (plurals and verb tenses) were very much simpler than Old English. These inflections, many of them using suffixes, may seem diverse and complicated but there are actually very few when compared with languages like French and German. The essential inflections in English are:

- -s for the third person singular of a present tense verb or plural noun;
- -ed for the past tense;
- -t, -en or -ed for a past participle (spelt, eaten, reserved);
- -ing added to verbs to make the present participle;
- different forms of the verb to be: am, are, is, was, were, (have/has/had) been, (will) be;
- irregular noun plurals like sheep, children;
- the dozen or so strong verbs (which change a vowel for the past tense, rather than add -ed. For example, swim–swam.).

The relative neglect of English as a language of power during Norman domination gave the language a chance to become simpler and more user-friendly. In terms of current day spelling we have this to be grateful for.

PEDAGOGICAL LINK PEDAGOGICAL LINK PEDAGOGICAL LINK PEDAGOGICAL LINK

These inflections can present young children with particular difficulties in everyday use so you may wish to pay particular attention to teaching children the rules for using them.

Many phonics schemes include the spelling of inflected endings at the higher levels, although they are not really a phonics issue. However, these inflections are important spelling patterns, so the patterns, exceptions and use should be taught.

Third, towards the end of the Middle English period, there was a very significant change in the pronunciation of all seven long vowels, which was not fully completed for 200 years. This meant that English was pronounced very differently in Chaucer's time to Shakespeare's time, and this is reflected in how English is written down.

By the end of the Middle English period, English was a strong language used throughout the country (although in many different dialects) with all the factors in existence that would lead to a standard English for the first time. London had emerged as the political and commercial capital with a large number of chancery scribes (the forerunner of the civil service) standardising government and commercial copying. The central midlands dialect (written by Chaucer) was not only influenced by the London dialect but was widely spread through the Wycliff bible and the preaching of the Lollards (see Cigman, 1989). Moreover, mass migration from the midlands had a definite effect on the London dialect. When Caxton set up his printing press in 1476 it is not surprising that he chose Westminster and the London speech as his norm – it ensured his popularity with his chancery neighbours and began the spread of a standard form of English in Britain.

Standardisation and Latin and Greek influences on English

The Early Modern English period, from 1400 to 1800, saw an explosion of literature and printing. It has been estimated that 20,000 books were published. This led printers like Caxton to make decisions about language – spelling, word choice and expression. For instance, Caxton wrote of his difficulties in deciding between egges (a northern form from Old Norse) and eyren (a southern form from Old English). In this case the northern word won. Caxton and other printers, many of Dutch origins, made these decisions on a pragmatic basis and a consensus eventually arose. But examination of early printed manuscripts shows that Caxton and other printers were extremely inconsistent in their spelling (broke and boke, axed and axyd, on the same page, and final -e used haphazardly and intermittently throughout the publication), punctuation and use of capital letters. Indeed, much later, Shakespeare still used four different spellings of his own name.

PRACTICAL TASK PRACTICAL TASK PRACTICAL TASK PRACTICAL TASK PRACTICAL TASK

Look at the Early Modern English version of the Lord's Prayer that we considered earlier.

- How are v and u used?
- What are the rules for capital letters?
- How would commas be used differently today?

Shakespeare's work alone had a huge impact on the lexicon (words) of the English language. Some of the words first recorded by Shakespeare have survived into Modern English: *accommodation, fancy-free, lack-lustre, laughable, submerged*. His idiomatic expressions are common today: 'what the dickens' (*The Merry Wives of Windsor*), 'a foregone conclusion' (*Othello*), 'hoist with his own petard' (*Hamlet*), 'cold comfort' (*King John*), 'love is blind' (*Merchant of Venice*), 'a tower of strength' (*Richard III*) and 'it's Greek to me' (*Julius Caesar*) are all everyday expressions. We would expect any educated citizen to use or understand these phrases and yet such citizens are often unaware of their literary origins. Of course, many words Shakespeare used have not passed into Modern English. We can be pretty sure no one uses *tortive* or *unplausive* today because they are not in our dictionary or spell-checker. We must also remember that Shakespeare did not spell words in the same way as we do now.

PRACTICAL TASK PRACTICAL TASK PRACTICAL TASK PRACTICAL TASK PRACTICAL TASK

Around 1600 Shakespeare used these words. What are modern equivalents and which letters are used differently?

dutie, vs, greeuously, vpon, enuy, outliue, thou, villaine

Shakespeare's contribution to English is immeasurable not only in literary terms, but also as a linguistic innovator. It would be worth researching Shakespeare's English with Year 6 children on language study grounds alone.

PRACTICAL TASK PRACTICAL TASK PRACTICAL TASK PRACTICAL TASK PRACTICAL TASK

Below is probably one of the most popular pieces of Shakespeare's work for study with Year 6 children because it is interesting in quite clear rhythmic and rhyming ways. Look at the vocabulary and identify the archaic words. Then look up their meanings in a dictionary or etymological dictionary. With a class you would want to consider how words were added together to make words like hedge-pig, and their subsequent development.

Enter the three Witches.

FIRST WITCH: Thrice the brinded cat hath mew'd.

SECOND WITCH: Thrice and once the hedge-pig whined.

THIRD WITCH: Harpier cries, "Tis time, 'tis time.'

FIRST WITCH: Round about the cauldron go; In the poison'd entrails throw. Toad, that under cold stone Days and nights has thirty-one Swelter'd venom sleeping got, Boil thou first i' the charmed pot.

ALL:	Double, double, toil and trouble; Fire burn and cauldron bubble.
SECOND WITCH:	Fillet of a fenny snake, In the cauldron boil and bake; Eye of newt and toe of frog, Wool of bat and tongue of dog, Adder's fork and blind-worm's sting, Lizard's leg and howlet's wing, For a charm of powerful trouble, Like a hell-broth boil and bubble.
ALL:	Double, double, toil and trouble; Fire burn and cauldron bubble.
THIRD WITCH:	Scale of dragon, tooth of wolf, Witch's mummy, maw and gulf Of the ravin'd salt-sea shark, Root of hemlock digg'd i' the dark, Liver of blaspheming Jew, Gall of goat and slips of yew Sliver'd in the moon's eclipse, Nose of Turk and Tartar's lips, Finger of birth-strangled babe Ditch-deliver'd by a drab, Make the gruel thick and slab. Add thereto a tiger's chawdron, For the ingredients of our cauldron.
ALL:	Double, double, toil and trouble; Fire burn and cauldron bubble.
SECOND WITCH:	Cool it with a baboon's blood, Then the charm is firm and good.

(Macbeth, Act 4, Scene 1, Lines 1–38)

The vocabulary of English underwent great change in the Early Modern period of English. From the start of the Renaissance around 1430 to the seventeenth and eighteenth centuries when writers modelled their writing on classical literature, words were borrowed from Latin and Greek at an amazing rate. Some scholars wrote books entirely in Latin (Sir Isaac Newton, for instance) and teachers tried to teach grammar school children in Latin. Shakespeare mocked the pedantry of those who talked in Latin in *Love's Labours Lost*.

English changed constantly throughout the Early Modern period and a great deal was written about the changes. Capital letters were debated and although authors such as Butler and Pope used capitals for most nouns, eventually a standard (proper nouns, important nouns and the start of sentences) was established. Punctuation developed a near modern form at this time. Changing from the virgule (/), point (.) and colon (:) used by Caxton in the fifteenth century, the semi-colon emerged and was used interchangeably with the colon. Turned double commas (speech marks) emerged and the use of apostrophes changed. At the end of the sixteenth century lists of correct spellings were produced (Mulcaster's contained 7000 words) and vowels came to be spelled more predictably. The Middle English use of v and u was sorted out in relation to sound quality, rather than position in the word. By the end of the eighteenth century notions of correctness were current and incorrect spelling was stigmatised for the first time. This is very significant for you as a teacher. Correct spelling is, even today, taken as a mark of an educated person, but learning to spell correctly involves learning a very inconsistent system.

Until around 1650 there were some Latin borrowings in English literature but in the second half of the eighteenth century there was an explosion of Latin words. Latinisms were used as fashionable, sophisticated, educated and generally 'better' than older, indigenous words. When Wordsworth stood up for 'Language such as men do use' and wrote his poetry in quite ordinary words he was criticised by contemporary critics for not using words of sufficient dignity. The result of this period has been the inclusion of many words of Latin (L) and Greek (G) origins. There are also parts of words, including prefixes and roots of words (discussed below in the formation of words). Because these prefixes are so common it is quite important that children learn about them. They give children another key to understanding and so help reading and comprehension.

Prefixes:

a, an (G) *a-, an-*, not *un*, *-less*, without (agnostic, amorphous)
ad, a (L) *ad*, towards, against, at: (adhere, adjacent, admire)
amb(i) (L) *ambo, ambi*, both, around (ambidexterous, ambiguous)
ante (L) *ante,* before (antecedent, antediluvial, antenatal, anteroom)
ant(i) (G) *anti*, against, opposite (Antarctic, antibiotic, antidote)

PRACTICAL TASK PRACTICAL TASK PRACTICAL TASK PRACTICAL TASK PRACTICAL TASK

What is the difference between the prefix ant- in anteroom and Antarctic?

What is the difference between the prefix hom- in homogeneous and homicidal?

You will need to consult an etymological dictionary or a large dictionary such as the *Concise Oxford Dictionary*.

Here are some more Latin and Greek prefixes you might want to study with children.

Look up the word of origin, whether the origin is Latin or Greek, and add some words in which the prefix is used.

bene-	bi-, bin-, bis-	circum-	com-, con-, co-	de-	dis-, di-
dys-	en-, em-	iniqui-	eu-	ex-	hyper-
in-, im-	orth(o)-	par(a)-	poly-	post-	pre-
re-	quasi-	sub-	tri-		

What prefixes can you identify that indicate the numbers one to ten? Complete the list:

uni-: unicycle, uniform
bi-:

Roots derived from Latin or Greek:

acer(b), acid, acri, acu, (L) *acer*, sharp, bitter (acerbic, acrimony)
amic, amor, imic, (L) *amor*, love (amateur, amicable, inimicable)
anim, (L) *animus*, mind (animated, animosity, magnanimous)

PRACTICAL TASK PRACTICAL TASK PRACTICAL TASK PRACTICAL TASK PRACTICAL TASK

Here are some more roots. Use a dictionary to look up the origins (Latin or Greek) and origin word, a modern meaning and some example words for each of these roots.

arch	astro	aud(io)	bio	capit	chron(o)
cosm(o)	cred	cur	dem(o)	exter(n)	extrem
fac(t), fect, fic	fin	hetero	(h)omo	hydr(o)	labor
mal(e)	medi	mon(o)	nom(ic)	nom(in)	omni
oper	pass	photo	sci	spir	super
tel	the(o), thus	tract	urb		

The following words are of particular use to you in the study of literature. Look them up and note them.

	Origin word	Meaning
bath(y)	bathos	depth
cris, crit	krisis	judgement
gram		
loc, loq		
log		
morph		
onomato, onomast		
phras		
romanc, romant		
thes(is), thet		
verb		

If homicide is the killing of a person, what are fratricide, parricide, suicide and matricide?

If bigamy means being married to two people at one time, what is meant by monogamy, polygamy and hypergamy?

In doing these activities you may notice that the last two, which require reasoned investigation, are more memorable than simply looking up words. This should influence you when setting tasks for children.

Other influences on English vocabulary

English has continued to develop since the eighteenth century and Modern English has not always been the English of today. A look at Austen's novels, for instance, shows us how English words have continued to change in meaning and use. For instance, 'A supposed inmate of Mansfield Hall' was not detained at Her Majesty's Pleasure as 'inmate' did not signify imprisonment as it does now. Some additions to the lexicon of English reflect Britain's imperial past:

India	*bungalow, chutney, dungaree, jungle, pyjamas, shampoo, gymkhana*
Australia	*kangaroo, boomerang, dingo*
Africa	*apartheid, trek, safari, voodoo*
Scotland	*slogan, clan*
Native American	*caucus, pecan, muskrat, terrapin, igloo, pow-wow*
Ireland	*blarney, brat, whiskey*

Others simply reflect the spread of people and influence:

Scandinavian languages	*fiord, krill, ski, slalom, floe, geyser, sauna*
Chinese	*mandarin, tea, yen*
Spanish	*adobe, armada, mosquito, plaza, cockroach, canyon, rodeo*
German	*delicatessen, noodle, kindergarten, spiel*
Russian	*vodka, sputnik*

It must be remembered that the formation and spelling of these words is quite arbitrary. They have entered English through the (sometimes incorrect) pronunciation of many people and contain letter combinations that can be unusual in English spelling. In doing so, these words (and there are thousands of them) add to the rich mix of spelling conventions that make English so hard to spell.

The study of the origins of words – **etymology** – is included as a useful part of language study. To work with children on this you need a good etymological dictionary (see Further reading). These are not easy to use and you need to make sure you understand the conventions and abbreviations. In practice you may find a good (large) dictionary such as the *Concise Oxford Dictionary* provides enough etymological information for the sort of study you will do with children. The *Oxford English Dictionary* online is a counsel of perfection for teachers but might overwhelm children. It contains more information about each word and its origins and use than you could ever want. As a teacher you will find two specialist dictionaries useful: a dictionary of place names and a dictionary of proper names. These are fascinating fields of interest for children. Study of names and places is an important way of making language study personal for children. Some medieval names told a great deal about the owners: John Rex (a king), William Neuman (a newcomer to the area), William de Paris. These names have often survived in different forms. De Paris has become Parish, Neuman is usually Newman, Walsh comes from the Saxon word for foreigner, or Welsh. Brown, Green and Red tell us about a personal characteristic of our ancestors. Cooper, Butler, Clark, Smith and Thatcher tell us about professional groups. Palmer refers to someone who has made a pilgrimage.

Place names are even more interesting because they tell us about social structures, people, landscape and history. Most place names have an Old English element, which might be a word borrowed from the Roman usage or Celtic place name, a saint or deity's name, a person's name or a reference to the landscape, as shown in the following table.

Feature	Elements in place names
Valleys and hollows	bottom, clough, combe, dale, den, ditch, glen, hope, slade
Woods	bear, carr, derry, fen, frith, heath, holt, rise, moor, oak, shaw, tree, well, with, wold, wood
Routes and places	bridge, ford, gate, mark, path, stead, stoke, stow, stree, sty, way
Buildings (and stones)	brough, burton, caster, cross, kirk, mill, minster, stain, ston, wark
Fields and clear places	combe, croft, den, ergh, field, ham, haugh, lease, land, lock, meadow, rick, rode, shot, side, thwaite, worth, worthy
Farms and dwellings	barton, berwick, biggin, bold, by, cote, ham, hampsted, house, stett, stall, thorpe, ton, toft, wick
Hills	bank, barrow, breck, cam, cliff, crook, down, edge, hill, how, hurst, ley, ling, lith, mond, over, pen, ridge, side, tor
Rivers	beck, brook, stream, burn, ey, font, ford, keld, lade, mere, mouth, ord, pool, rith, wade, water, well
Coastline	ey, holme, hythe, naze, ness, port, sea

PRACTICAL TASK PRACTICAL TASK PRACTICAL TASK PRACTICAL TASK PRACTICAL TASK

Look up the place names on the map below. What do they tell you about the settlement and history of the area? This sort of activity is interesting in most areas.

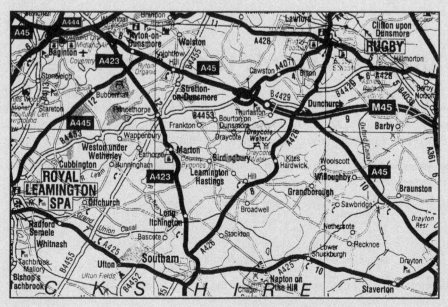

Despite the commonness of Old English origins, place names tell us something of the history of the places because they contain parts of words from different times:

- Roman – -cester, caster, chester (fort or town), strat, street, port (gate or harbour);
- Saxon – -borough, -bury, -burgh (fortified place), -hooe, hough, how (rounded hill), -ing (people or family of), wic (farm), ham (homestead or village), ey, y, ea (river), leigh, ley (clearing), tun, ton (farmstead);
- Viking – -by (farm or village), thorpe (village or hamlet), fell (hill), kirk (church), garth (yard);
- Norman French – additions of castle, abbey, bishop's, King's, tower, forest, mount, market;
- eighteenth and nineteenth centuries – spa (referring to a town with a spring).

On the map on the previous page, notice that there are lots of villages, and some towns, with the -ton ending. This is a Saxon place-name element, and originally meant 'enclosure' or 'farmstead'. Thus 'Leamington' meant 'the farmstead of the Leamings (a family)'. You will also find 'Southam' = 'homestead in the South', and 'Wappenbury' = 'Wappa's burgh' (fortified place). These are all Saxon name elements, suggesting that this area was largely populated by Saxons. Yet amongst these names, you will also find names ending in '-thorpe' (e.g. Eathorpe), a Viking place-name element meaning 'village', and '-by' (Rugby), a Viking element meaning 'farm'. This mixture of place-name origins makes sense when you learn that this part of the country (Warwickshire) was very much border country after 886AD, when King Alfred agreed a treaty with the Danes that fixed the boundary between England and the Danelaw along a line roughly the same as the course of the old Roman road, Watling Street (the modern A5 follows this line today). So, part of the history of the area is embedded in its place names.

REFLECTIVE TASK

Think about some place names in the area where you live. Can you spot any clues in these names to the history of the area? The following website will help you to investigate these names:

www.localhistories.org/names

Adding new words to the language

This chapter has considered the origins of words in the English language and two principal ways in which words have entered the English language: borrowing from other languages and sound changes. There are also some other processes that have caused new words to enter English and you may want to investigate some of these with children.

- *Back formation* is a very common way of using the formation of one word and applying it to other words to make new words.

work (verb)	+	er (noun suffix)	=	worker (agent noun)
burglar (agent noun)	–	ar (noun suffix)	=	burgle (verb)

So we had television before to televise, glazing before to double-glaze.

- **Folk etymology** is a sort of mis-analysis, where obscure morphemes are misinterpreted in terms of more familiar morphemes. For instance, salt-cellar comes from the French word **salier** (salt box), but when the use of **salier** was lost, people started to use the form sellar, which became cellar. Salt-cellar has no connection with basements. Other examples are sparrow-grass for asparagus, nephew-tism for nepotism and helpmate from helpmeet, in which meet meant 'suitable'.
- **Function-shift** is a process whereby one part of speech (word class) is shifted to become a different type of word. So, today, laugh, run, buy and steal have become nouns as well as verbs. Likewise, position, process and contrast have become verbs as well as nouns.
- **Acronyms** are quasi-words formed using the initial letters or sounds from a phrase to make a word. NATO means the **N**orth **A**tlantic **T**reaty **O**rganisation. Laser is **l**ight **a**mplification through the **s**timulated **e**mission of **r**adiation.
- **Blending** is a very common practice of combining two parts of a word. **Smoke** and **fog** make **smog**. **Breakfast** and **lunch** make **brunch**. **Chuckle** and **snort** make **chortle**. Not all of these words remain popular and **skort – skirt** and **shorts** – has not really displaced culottes!
- **Clipping** is the practice of shortening words. Dormitory, advertisement, laboratory, examination and taxi-cab are obvious examples, having become dorm, advert, lab, exam and taxi.

All these processes of vocabulary change usually incur some resistance, with people denouncing new words as 'wrong' or 'ugly'. This is a normal reaction to linguistic change. It has been recorded in discussion of Old English, Middle English and Early Modern English and continues to occupy newspaper space today. We may find the expression 'patently obvious' an unnecessary repetition (it is patent or obvious, it need not be both) but we also know that it is common, accepted and, therefore, correct usage. The Latinate use of patent (from *pateo* – I lie open) is uncommon and rather pedantic. This is the way of English language change. It is inexorable, despite the natural conservatism of English speakers. It is the work of teachers to recognise and teach accepted English usage and to encourage children to look at the origins and formation of English words.

The structure of English words

Morphology, the study of the structure of words, goes hand in hand with work on word origins. Children need to learn to break down and assemble words because this helps them to read and understand words and to be able to understand the grammar of sentences. To teach this you need to understand basic morphology.

Morphology cuts across the study of words and the study of grammar because **morphemes,** the smallest units of meaning in words, may indicate meaning and may also indicate how a word functions in a sentence.

In English, morphology includes ways of describing the structure of words as diverse as an, books, get, unexceptional, ironing board and antidisestablishmentarianism. The function of the parts of the words in these examples varies. Some morphemes are used to build up the words and some are used to indicate grammatical contrast. Linguists study two fields of morphology:

- **lexical or derivational morphology** studies how words are built up out of new elements (un ex cep tion al, for instance);
- **inflexional morphology** studies the way words vary through form to express grammatical function (the -s, in books, for instance).

For this reason, morphology has an important part to play at the grammatical or sentence levels of language as well as in spelling.

Morphemes

Some words cannot be broken down into smaller grammatical parts and consist only of a single morpheme: car, a, person. These words have only a root (sometimes called a stem or base part). Although we can say how many syllables or vowels and consonants they have, these words have only one morpheme because a **morpheme** is the smallest unit of meaning in a word. In English there are two main types of morphemes. **Free morphemes** are those that can stand alone (cat). **Bound morphemes** are those that never exist on their own, but are only attached to another word (-s, -ed, -ing). Although you might use the term morpheme with children, you would not usually distinguish between free and bound morphemes. However, in English we often add meaningful units (morphemes) at the beginning or end of a morpheme – **affixes. Prefixes** go before the root (or stem) and **suffixes** go after. These affixes mean we can create hundreds of words, including the word often said to be the longest in the dictionary: antidisestablishmentarianism.

PRACTICAL TASK PRACTICAL TASK PRACTICAL TASK PRACTICAL TASK PRACTICAL TASK

Divide the words below into their component morphemes:

Comfortable   *environmentally*

senseless   *thickeners*

Prefixes and suffixes have different roles in English. Prefixes simply allow the creation of new words (a lexical function) and you can see that even the prefixes in the list of Latin and Greek prefixes above contribute to thousands of words. Suffixes have two different roles. Some suffixes have the lexical role of allowing the creation of new words and changing the function of the word (-ness, -ship, -ism). You may hear these called derivational suffixes, but this is not a term you would use in a Key Stage 2 class. Other suffixes are grammatical in function, such as the plural -s, past tense -ed and comparative -er. These inflexional suffixes (inflection, inflected endings) show what a word does in a sentence.

RESEARCH SUMMARY RESEARCH SUMMARY **RESEARCH SUMMARY** RESEARCH SUMMARY

The research team led by Terezhina Nunes and Peter Bryant has established through a series of research studies that explicit knowledge (and teaching) of the morphemic structure of words can have many benefits for aspects of children's literacy, both in terms of their reading fluency and comprehension, and in terms of their spelling accuracy. In their book (Nunes and Bryant, 2006), they outline the research studies they carried out and discuss the implications for teachers of their work.

The teaching strategies which they found to be productive included:

- Analogy tasks, in which children were given one pair of words (for example, 'read' –'reader') and asked to produce the missing word to complete the pair 'magic' –'?'.

- Counting the number of morphemes in particular words. E.g. How many morphemes are in 'unforgettable'?
- Putting morphemes into categories, e.g. sorting words into those that contain suffixes that form 'person words' (act-or, hunts-man, spokes-person, art-ist) and those with suffixes that form 'other words'.
- Subtracting morphemes from pseudowords. E.g. What jobs do these people do on Mars? – 'spamters', 'montists'.

Derivational suffixes

The 322 derivational suffixes are added to words to change the function of the word in a sentence. Some of the most common are listed below. It is important for children to study the way these suffixes work and the spelling conventions that they use.

- Suffixes to make adjectives from nouns:
  -ed, blurred, pointed
  -esque, Kafkaesque
  -ful, beautiful, useful
  -ic, Celtic, dynamic
  -al, accidental, operational
  -ish, foolish
  -less, careless, feckless
  -ly, friendly
  -y, sandy
- Suffixes to make nouns from adjectives:
  -ity, stupidity
  -ness, carelessness
- Suffixes to make nouns from verbs:
  -age, wastage
  -al, denial
  -ee, payee, employee
  -er, adviser
  -or, executor
- Verb makers:
  -ate, orchestrate
  -en, chasten
  -ify, beautify
- Adverb makers:
  -ly, happily
  -ward(s), homeward
- Concrete noun makers:
  -eer, racketeer
  -er, teenager
  -ette, usherette
- Abstract noun makers:
  -dom, serfdom
  -ery, drudgery
  -hood, sainthood
  -ing, farming

To what categories do these suffixes belong? Use examples to find out.

-ise(-ize)   *-wise*   *-ship*   *-let*

-ling   *-ocracy*   *-ant*

Inflexional suffixes and formations

Although most inflections (inflectional suffixes, inflected words) were lost in English after the Norman Conquest, the few that remain are an extremely important part of our grammar and it is vital that children can form them correctly and use the correct word so that it has the right person, number and gender for the sentence. In this section we outline the inflections still used in English, including inflexional suffixes. Studying inflections and looking at the conventions governing them helps children to get them right.

In **nouns**, only two inflections have survived to the present day:

- the -s marking the possessive (genitive case) (the girl's hat)
- the -s marking the plural (hats)

These inflections survive but are not always necessary for meaning and in some English variants they are dropped (*two pound fifty* is as comprehensible as *two pounds fifty*). However, standard written English requires the -s. There are spelling conventions governing the addition of inflected -s.

Sort these plurals into groups based on spelling. What 'rules' can you derive?

fishes	horses	cows	birds	crows	boxes
oranges	stories	leaves	glasses	noses	cases
fairies	halves	foxes	lives	glasses	parties
lasses	sheep				

It is important to note that spelling rules can relate to the position of vowels and consonants and also to other **sounds**, not just writing conventions.

For **adjectives**, English has inflected suffixes relating to the comparative (-er) and superlative (-est) forms. Adjectives with three or more syllables are preceded by more and most.

	Comparative	*Superlative*
big	bigger	biggest
fast	faster	fastest

near	nearer	nearest
beautiful	more beautiful	most beautiful
interesting	more interesting	most interesting

There are a few exceptions but these are very common words: good, better, best; bad, worse, worst. For children, it is important to get these right in written English; when there is any doubt, children will find the comparative and superlative forms are given in the entries of most good dictionaries.

Some English **pronouns**, the personal and relative pronouns, are also inflected. They do not change form just by a change of ending, but have different forms depending on the use of the pronoun in sentences.

- Personal pronouns:

  Subject (nominative case): I, you, he, she, it, we, they
  Object (accusative case): me, you, him, her, it, us, them
  Possessive (genitive case): mine, yours, his, hers, its, ours, theirs

- Relative pronouns:

  Subject (nominative case): who
  Object (accusative case): whom
  Possessive (genitive case): whose

The grammatical issue for children is choosing the correct pronoun to agree with the noun in terms of function in the sentence (case), person (first, second, third) and number (singular and plural).

PEDAGOGICAL LINK PEDAGOGICAL LINK PEDAGOGICAL LINK PEDAGOGICAL LINK

It is important to show children how verbs are customarily set out, as this makes it easier to remember the idea of first, second and third person and singular and plural forms.

Verbs in Modern English retain few inflections. When set out in the customary way to show person and number (singular and plural) we can see only the -s of the present third person singular remains (replacing the -eth in telleth, sayeth, doeth of Chaucer's day).

Person	Singular	Plural
First	(I) run	(we) run
Second	(you) run	(you) run
Third	(he, she, it) runs	(they) run

Some verbs are, of course, irregular and are inflected not through suffixes but through changes of consonant.

Person	Singular	Plural
First	(I) have	(we) have
Second	(you) have	(you) have
Third	(he, she, it) has	(they) have

Others have a more irregular formation. Of course, these are the most commonly used verbs and present an important challenge to young users, who need to get them right in person and number. This requires an implicit understanding of person that is quite sophisticated and many teachers find it much harder to discuss subject– or object–verb agreement than to exemplify it because of the very abstract nature of the concepts.

Person	Singular	Plural
First	(I) am	(we) are
Second	(you) are	(you) are
Third	(he, she, it) is	(they) are

The past tense and past participle of many English verbs (called **weak verbs**) take an inflected -ed suffix. When adding this suffix, again there are spelling conventions which as adults we take for granted but which children benefit from considering explicitly.

Person	Singular	Plural
First	(I) jumped	(we) jumped
Second	(you) jumped	(you) jumped
Third	(he, she, it) jumped	(they) jumped

PRACTICAL TASK PRACTICAL TASK PRACTICAL TASK PRACTICAL TASK PRACTICAL TASK

Group these words by spelling group for their past tense forms. What is the 'rule' governing double letters?

jumped	*hopped*	*raced*
skipped	*lounged*	*plopped*
thumped	*flopped*	*skidded*

Some verbs (called **strong verbs**) form their past tense and past participle by changing a vowel in the stem (or base): ride – rode, break – broke, do – did – done, see – saw – seen.

Most verbs form their present participle using the inflected suffix -ing: running, jumping, being, etc. Again the addition of -ing is governed by spelling conventions.

PRACTICAL TASK ~~PRACTICAL TASK~~ PRACTICAL TASK ~~PRACTICAL TASK~~ PRACTICAL TASK

What 'rules' for adding -ing can you infer from these words?

running, jumping, being, holding, planning, saving, waiting, smiling

These inflections are an important part of the grammar of English and when you teach them to children it is essential that they understand how each word indicates meaning in the sentence, how the words change depending on function in a sentence and how to spell the words. This means that teaching inflections is a sentence-level activity because it is teaching grammar, but it is also a word-level activity because you need to teach the spelling conventions that accompany many inflections.

A SUMMARY OF **KEY POINTS**

> There are a great many words in English, with new ones entering the language all the time. This change is inevitable and adds flexibility and variety to language.

> Historical change, particularly due to the invaders and settlers of the British Isles, has had a huge influence on English words. Etymological dictionaries can be used to trace the origins of English words.

> Standard English, including standard spelling and punctuation, is a relatively recent development and correct spelling was not established until the eighteenth century.

> The origins of proper nouns are a particularly rich source of information about language, people and places in English.

> English words are built up from morphemes, including prefixes, suffixes and roots (or stems).

> Derivational suffixes change the function of a word in a sentence and children need to learn the spelling conventions governing the addition of these suffixes.

> Although largely lost from Old English, a few inflections remain in suffixes and spellings. Children need to learn these and the spelling conventions governing the addition of -s, -ed, -er, -est and -ing.

M-LEVEL EXTENSION > > M-LEVEL EXTENSION > > M-LEVEL EXTENSION

English is acquiring new words all the time. Here are just a few words that are now an accepted part of English but that were unknown 30 years ago:

- internet;
- spyware;
- memory stick;
- blog.

These obviously relate to new technologies. Other words, such as twitter and tweet, now have different and very specific meanings in their technological usage.

A useful way of raising your own awareness of new words in English is to make a note of words as you come across them which seem unusual to you. Technology is a good place to begin, but another, very easy place to start is in your local coffee franchise! *Frappuccino, tazo,* or *latte* may be new words to you, and *tall* and *grande* may be familiar words used in different ways.

FURTHER READING · FURTHER READING · FURTHER READING · FURTHER READING

Bryson, B. (2009) *Mother Tongue: The Story of the English Language*. London: Penguin. This book is a light-hearted look at the English language.

Crystal, D. (2nd edn) (2003) *The Cambridge Encyclopaedia of The English Language*. Cambridge: Cambridge University Press. This volume is a truly superb mix of sound information about English and linguistic trivia. It is accessible, good value and beautifully illustrated.

DfE (2013) *Teachers' Standards*. London: DfE. **(www.gov.uk/government/uploads/system/uploads/attachment_data/file/208682/Teachers__Standards_2013.pdf)**

Hoad, T. (ed.) (1993) *The Concise Oxford Dictionary of English Etymology*. Oxford: Oxford University Press.

Mills, A.D. (ed.) (2003) *The Oxford Dictionary of British Place Names*. Oxford: Oxford University Press.

Newby, M. (1987) *The Structure of English: A Handbook of English Grammar*. Cambridge: Cambridge University Press.

Nunes. T. and Bryant, P. (2006) *Improving Literacy by Teaching Morphemes*. Abingdon: Routledge.

6
The grammar of the sentence in Standard English

Curriculum context

National Curriculum programmes of study

This knowledge is designed to underpin the teaching of the Key Stage 1 and Key Stage 2 programmes of study for English, which state, for example, that pupils should be taught

in spoken language to:

- speak audibly and fluently with an increasing command of Standard English

and in writing to:

- develop their understanding of the concepts set out in English appendix 2 by:
  o learning the grammar in English appendix 2 Y1/2/3/4/5/6
- learning how to use:
  o sentences with different forms: statement, question, exclamation, command Y2
  o expanded noun phrases to describe and specify [for example, the blue butterfly] Y2
  o the present and past tenses correctly and consistently, including the progressive form Y2

- o subordination (using when, if, that, or because) and co-ordination (using or, and, or but) Y2
- o some features of written standard English Y2
- o extending the range of sentences with more than one clause by using a wider range of conjunctions, including: when, if, because, although Y3/4
- o using the present perfect form of verbs in contrast to the past tense Y3/4
- o choosing nouns or pronouns appropriately for clarity and cohesion and to avoid repetition Y3/4
- o using conjunctions, adverbs and prepositions to express time and cause Y3/4
- o using fronted adverbials Y3/4
- o recognising vocabulary and structures that are appropriate for formal speech and writing, including subjunctive forms Y5/6
- o using passive verbs to affect the presentation of information in a sentence Y5/6
- o using the perfect form of verbs to mark relationships of time and cause Y5/6
- o using expanded noun phrases to convey complicated information concisely Y5/6
- o using modal verbs or adverbs to indicate degrees of possibility Y5/6
- o using relative clauses beginning with who, which, where, when, whose, that or with an implied (ie omitted) relative pronoun Y5/6

- indicate grammatical and other features by:

- o using commas after fronted adverbials Y3/4
- o indicating possession by using the possessive apostrophe with plural nouns Y3/4
- o using and punctuating direct speech Y3/4
- o using commas to clarify meaning or avoid ambiguity in writing Y5/6
- o using hyphens to avoid ambiguity Y5/6
- o using brackets, dashes or commas to indicate parenthesis Y5/6
- o using semicolons, colons or dashes to mark boundaries between independent clauses Y5/6
- o using a colon to introduce a list Y5/6
- o punctuating bullet points consistently Y5/6

- use the grammatical terminology in <u>English appendix 2</u> in discussing their writing Y1/2/3/4
- make simple additions, revisions and corrections to their own writing by:

- o rereading to check that their writing makes sense and that verbs to indicate time are used correctly and consistently, including verbs in the continuous form Y2
- o proposing changes to grammar and vocabulary to improve consistency, including the accurate use of pronouns in sentences Y3/4
- o selecting appropriate grammar and vocabulary, understanding how such choices can change and enhance meaning Y5/6
- o ensuring the consistent and correct use of tense throughout a piece of writing Y5/6
- o ensuring correct subject and verb agreement when using singular and plural, distinguishing between the language of speech and writing and choosing the appropriate register Y5/6
- o proofreading to check for errors in spelling, grammar and punctuation (for example, ends of sentences punctuated correctly) Y2/3/4/5/6.

Early Years Foundation Stage

The Early Learning Goals specify that, by the end of the Early Years Foundation Stage, children should:

- use past, present and future forms accurately when talking about events that have happened or are to happen in the future;
- write simple sentences which can be read by themselves and others.

Introduction

The ways in which sentences can be structured and the analysis of the various parts of a sentence together make up what is usually referred to as '**grammar**'. Grammar is actually a good deal broader than this. In the previous chapter, for example, we described the grammar of word structures, and later we will discuss the grammar of whole texts. Nevertheless, when we talk about grammar to people who are not professional linguists or professional teachers, what is usually understood is sentence grammar. Many people, of course, have memories of being taught this kind of grammar, usually in a fairly dull way, while at school, and many also admit to some confusion over concepts such as adverb, prepositions, relative clauses, etc.

No one, apart from a few pedants, would suggest nowadays that knowledge of sentence grammar should be taught and learned as an end in itself. There is little point in knowing about the ways adverbs work, for instance, unless this knowledge in some way helps the learner become a more effective user of spoken and written English. Grammatical knowledge can help to put speakers and writers more in control of their use of language. It can aid them in their attempts to communicate and thus make them more effective language users. For this reason it is worth teaching in school, and therefore worth being studied by intending teachers of English, at whatever level.

The purpose of this and the following chapter is to help you become familiar with the ways sentences work in Standard English. By this, we mean the many possible ways sentences can be structured and adapted to meet particular purposes and create particular effects. In the process of looking at sentence structure we will also help you to understand the component parts of the English sentence, that is, word classes such as nouns, verbs and prepositions, and sentence parts such as phrases and clauses.

You should bear in mind that, in these chapters, we refer to the sentence grammar of Standard English. You will know that there are many varieties of English (dialects), which differ in various respects from Standard English grammar. So several of the sentence patterns we discuss with reference to Standard English are handled differently in other dialects.

The structure of the chapter

The chapter will be organised around the following topics:

- **What is a sentence?** In this section, we will offer a definition of a sentence and examine two common ways in which this structure is misused: the use of sentence fragments and of run-on sentences.

Working far into the night in an effort to learn the new material.	*This chapter has a lot of difficult information in it, you should start studying right away.*	*Having prepared himself well for his subject knowledge final audit and having exhausted everyone in the family with his requests that someone help him by testing his knowledge, Jeffrey, who had never been a particularly good student at school, knew he was ready to take on the greatest challenge of his life.*

Are these sentences or not sentences?

- **What kinds of sentences are there?** Here, we will look at key sentence types such as statements, questions and commands.

What kind of sentence?
This book makes a number of things clearer.
Did I really leave school without having learnt all of this?
Make sure you read this very carefully.
You cannot possibly find this sort of thing difficult!

Sentences also vary from the very simple to the much more complex. We will explore the mechanisms by which this complexity can be achieved and the sentence remain grammatically acceptable.

A simple sentence
The cat sat on the mat

A complex sentence.

Mistress Cholmondely, the very superior Persian who was gracing us with her presence while her real owners were abroad, delicately perched her silken rear on the rather worn rag rug my grandmother had left us as a doormat and I have to admit that I was struck by the incongruity of this act.

- **The component parts of a sentence**. Here, we will examine the parts of a sentence such as subject and predicate, clauses and phrases. The concept of word classes, and the key characteristics of these classes, will be described in the following chapter.

Analysing sentences
Students who are conscientious will always be careful to note in their books the ideas they have been thinking about.

Subject	*Students who are conscientious*
Predicate	*will always be careful to note in their books the ideas they have been thinking about.*
Dependent clause	*Students who are conscientious*
Adverbial phrase	*Students who are conscientious will always be careful to note in their books the ideas they have been thinking about.*
Noun	*Students*
Adjective	*conscientious*
Preposition	*will always be careful to note <u>in</u> their books the ideas they*
Verb	*have been thinking about.*

What is a sentence?

Before we look at the parts of a sentence, we need to define a sentence itself. A sentence is a group of words containing a subject and predicate (defined below). Sometimes, however, the subject is 'understood', as in a command: '[You] Read this book and learn what it says'. That probably means that the shortest possible complete sentence is something like 'Go!'

A sentence ought to express a thought that can stand by itself, but you will occasionally find examples of groups of words that are punctuated like sentences (capital letter at the beginning, full stop at the end) but which cannot stand by themselves. These are sentence fragments (see below), which are normally incorrect (but see below for one exception to this rule, the 'stylistic fragment').

Because of difficulties like these in defining a sentence, some people resort to defining it simply by its punctuation:

'A sentence begins with a capital letter and ends with a full stop.'

This is fine until you come to teach children how to punctuate, when usually the first thing they are taught is to use a capital letter at the beginning of a sentence and a full stop at the end! Circular definitions such as this are not much use in trying to understand grammatical principles.

Problems with sentences

There are two main problems in sentence formation that children (and adults too for that matter) often show. The first we will refer to as a **sentence fragment** and the second as a **run-on sentence**.

A **sentence fragment** fails to be a sentence because it cannot stand by itself. It does not contain even one independent clause. There are several reasons why a group of words may seem to act like a sentence but do not meet the criteria for being a complete sentence.

- It may locate something in time and place with a prepositional phrase or a series of such phrases, but it still lacks a proper subject–verb relationship within an independent clause:

  In Germany, during the last war and just before the final ceasefire.

This sentence accomplishes a great deal in terms of placing the reader in time and place, but there is neither a subject nor a verb.

- It describes something, but contains no subject–verb relationship:

  Working far into the night in an effort to learn the material for her examination.

This is a verbal phrase that wants to modify something, that is, the real subject of the sentence. In this case we can assume the subject is the 'she' who was working so hard but the sentence fragment does not tell us.

- It may have most of the makings of a sentence but still be missing an important part of a verb string:

  Some of the footballers playing in the England team last year.

Remember that an *ing* verb form without an auxiliary form to accompany it can never be a verb. This fragment could be made into a sentence just by adding an auxiliary, such as *were*, before the participle *playing*.

- It may even have a subject–verb relationship, but it has been subordinated to another idea by a dependent word or phrase and so cannot stand by itself:

  Even though he was the better player.

This sentence fragment has a subject, he, and a verb, was, but it cannot stand by itself because of the dependent phrase *even though*. We need an independent clause to follow up this dependent clause:

> *Even though he was the better player, he lost the game because <u>he failed to use his opportunities</u>.*

Sometimes sentence fragments can be used for a particular stylistic purpose and might be called '**stylistic fragments**'. Look at the following example from a child's diary:

> *I like being at camp, apart from the sausages. We have sausages for breakfast and sometimes for tea as well. When I get home I'm going to have a really big plate of chips for my lunch. With no sausages!*

The final three words clearly make sense here and the way they are written adds a stylistic punch to the piece. However, they do not meet the normal definition of a sentence in that they could not make sense alone.

As long as the writer is in control of this, it is allowed, but in general sentence fragments are not used for deliberate effect like this, but through error.

A **run-on sentence** has at least two parts, either one of which can stand by itself (in other words, two independent clauses), but the two parts have been run together instead of being properly joined with a connective.

> *You should not find this material difficult, it should be just common sense.*

This could be rewritten correctly in three ways;

- By making it into two separate sentences:

> *You should not find this material difficult. It should be just common sense.*

- By using a semicolon in place of the comma:

> *You should not find this material difficult; it should be just common sense.*

- By inserting a linking connective between the two clauses:

> *You should not find this material difficult because it should be just common sense.*

It is important to realise that the length of a sentence has nothing to do with whether a sentence is a run-on or not; being a run-on is a structural flaw that can affect even a very short sentence.

> *The sun is hot, put on some sun block.*

An extremely long sentence, on the other hand, might be unwieldy, but it can be structurally sound.

> *Knowing better than anyone else how the previous government had ignored the needs of teacher training students and created a crisis characterised by a demoralised trainee group that were panicking at the thought of what was expected of them and realising*

that someone had to do something about the situation or the country would suffer even more from a shortage of teachers, the Secretary of State for Education began to lay plans for education legislation that took into consideration the needs of the country's schools and the students who would teach in them.

When two independent clauses are connected by only a comma, they make a run-on sentence that is referred to as a *comma-splice*. The example above (about the sun block) is a comma-splice. When you use a comma to connect two independent clauses, it must be accompanied by a conjunction (and, but, for, nor, yet, or, so).

The sun is hot, so put on some sun block.

Run-on sentences typically happen in the following circumstances:

- When an independent clause gives a direction based on what was said in the preceding independent clause:

This next chapter has a lot of difficult information in it, you had better start studying it straight away.

We could put a full stop in place of the comma and start a new sentence. We could also replace the comma by a semicolon.

- When two independent clauses are connected by a connective such as however, moreover, nevertheless.

I have spent hours reading this chapter, however, I am still not sure I fully understand it.

Again, in place of the first comma, we could use either a full stop (and start a new sentence) or a semicolon.

- When the second of two independent clauses contains a pronoun that connects it to the first independent clause.

This chapter does not make any sense to me, it seems rather difficult.

Although these two clauses are quite brief, and the ideas are closely related, this is a run-on sentence. We need a full stop in place of the comma.

PRACTICAL TASK PRACTICAL TASK PRACTICAL TASK PRACTICAL TASK PRACTICAL TASK

In each of the following groups of sentences, only one is written correctly. Identify the correct sentence in each case. You should also give reasons for rejecting the remaining sentences.

Group 1

(a)   *The committee makes a decision on the matter, then the Director either accepts or rejects the decision.*

(b)   *The committee makes a decision on the matter then the Director either accepts or rejects the decision.*

(c)   *First the committee makes a decision on the matter, then the Director either accepts or rejects the decision.*

(d)   *The committee makes a decision on the matter, and then the Director either accepts or rejects the decision.*

Group 2

(a)   *Police began to comb the area for the missing child in an intensive search, they knew that in cases of missing children, they had to act as quickly as possible.*

(b)   *Police began to comb the area for the missing child in an intensive search; they knew that in cases of missing children, they had to act as quickly as possible.*

(c)   *Police began to comb the area for the missing child in an intensive search, they knew that in cases of missing children; they had to act as quickly as possible.*

(d)   *Police began to comb the area for the missing child in an intensive search, they knew that in cases of missing children. They had to act as quickly as possible.*

Group 3

(a)   *Thinking that the sale of tickets began at 8.00 a.m., many people spent the night outside the ticket office they were quite upset when they learned that the tickets would not go on sale until 1.00 p.m.*

(b)   *Thinking that the sale of tickets began at 8.00 a.m. Many people spent the night outside the ticket office they were quite upset when they learned that the tickets would not go on sale until 1.00 p.m.*

(c)   *Thinking that the sale of tickets began at 8.00 a.m., many people spent the night outside the ticket office, so they were quite upset when they learned that the tickets would not go on sale until 1.00 p.m.*

(d)   *Thinking that the sale of tickets began at 8.00 a.m., many people spent the night outside the ticket office they were quite upset when they learned; that the tickets would not go on sale until 1.00 p.m.*

Group 4

(a)   *Because people disagreed with many of the prime minister's policies on tax, especially on small businesses, and many of them were dissatisfied with the prime minister's performance in general, he knew his chances of re-election were quite slim, so he launched an aggressive campaign of false promises and mud-slinging that the voters, no doubt, saw right through.*

(b)   *Because people disagreed with many of the prime minister's policies on tax, especially on small businesses, and many of them were dissatisfied with the prime minister's performance in general. He knew his chances of re-election were quite slim, so he launched an aggressive campaign of false promises and mud-slinging that the voters, no doubt, saw right through.*

(c)   *Because people disagreed with many of the prime minister's policies on tax, especially on small businesses, and many of them were dissatisfied with the prime minister's performance in general, he knew his chances of re-election were quite slim, so he launched an aggressive campaign of false promises and mud-slinging. That the voters, no doubt, saw right through.*

(d)   *Because, people disagreed with many of the prime minister's policies on tax, especially on small businesses, and many of them were dissatisfied with the prime minister's performance in general, he knew his chances of re-election were quite slim, so he launched an aggressive campaign of false promises and mud-slinging that the voters, no doubt, saw right through.*

Group 5

(a)   *After travelling through Europe, Mark plans to finish his studies at the university his parents are not too happy about his travelling before he finishes college, but Mark is determined to take his trip now.*

(b)   *After travelling through Europe, Mark plans to finish his studies at the university. His parents are not too happy about his travelling before he finishes college, but Mark is determined to take his trip now.*

(c)   After travelling through Europe, Mark plans to finish his studies at the university, his parents are not too happy about his travelling before he finishes college, but Mark is determined to take his trip now.

(d)   After travelling through Europe, Mark plans to finish his studies at the university his parents are not too happy about his travelling before he finishes college. But Mark is determined to take his trip now.

What kinds of sentences are there?

Sentences have a number of purposes, which influence their structures.

Statements

At a basic level, sentences offer statements.

The cat sat on the mat.

The man with the starting pistol fired it to begin the race.

Students who work carefully through the material in this chapter should develop an extensive understanding of sentence structures.

Notice how these sentences, although each containing a statement at their heart, vary according to the complexity with which they convey this statement. Sentence complexity is an important issue, which we will discuss below. Sentences that make statements are often referred to as 'declarative' sentences.

Questions

In addition to statements, sentences can be used to express questions. Each of the statements above could be reworked to ask several questions, depending on what the questioner wished to know.

Did the cat sit on the mat?
Where did the cat sit? What did the cat do on the mat?
Who fired the starting pistol?
What did the man fire?
Why did the man fire the starting pistol?
What do students need to do to develop an extensive understanding of sentence structures?
How should students work through the material in this chapter?
What will students develop if they work through this material?

Perhaps the two most important things to learn about the ways in which these questions are structured are the importance of question words such as what, how and why, and the use of auxiliary verbs in transforming statements into questions.

It would not, of course, be true to say that all questions begin with one of the question words: what, when, who, where, why and how. Many do, however, and an understanding of how sentence structure changes following one of these words is important in helping learners of English to avoid errors such as, 'Why the cat sat on the mat?', 'Where sat the cat?' Crucial to this structural change is the auxiliary verb. Both of these sentences need the auxiliary 'did', which then changes the form of the main verb from 'sat' to 'sit'.

The most common auxiliary verbs are 'be', 'do' and 'have' and these are used in conjunction with main verbs to express shades of time and mood. The combination of auxiliary verbs with main verbs creates what are called verb phrases. In the following sentence, 'will have been' are auxiliary verbs and 'studying' is the main verb; the whole verb phrase is underlined:

As of next August, I will have been studying English for ten years.

English is unlike many other languages in that it cannot form questions without the use of auxiliary verbs. In French, for example, the simple statement:

Il veut le faire. (He wants to do it.)

can be transformed into a question by simply reversing the subject and verb:

Veut-il le faire?

In English this could only be accomplished by adding an auxiliary verb:

Does he want to do it?

One form of question, which very commonly occurs in non-standard varieties of English, is the tag question. Here the sentence is declarative until the very end when it is transformed into a question by the addition of a tag such as 'isn't it?', 'does she?'

She ate all her breakfast, didn't she?

We don't want to miss the start, do we?

The use of contractions (isn't, didn't) in tag questions is normal, indicating their more conversational use. Sometimes the tag is fully spelt out.

You left the party early, did you not?

There were several reasons for what you did, were there not?

This suggests a much greater formality, such as would be found in, for example, legalistic contexts.

Commands

Sentences can also be used to give commands, in the course of which they enter what is known as the imperative mood:

Sit down.

Don't do that.

Come over here this minute.

These are all examples of command sentences and you should notice that in these sentences the verbs have all lost their personal pronouns. This is normal in commands, although it is possible in some varieties of English to produce sentences such as:

You sit down. Don't you do that.

You come over here this minute.

Obviously, it is impossible to command someone to do something in the past, so the imperative mood refers to actions in the present or immediate future.

Exclamations

A fourth purpose for sentences is to express an emotion. The term 'exclamation' refers to any expression used to communicate a strong attitude towards some individual, situation or event. This type of sentence is usually indicated by the use of the exclamation mark at the end and often this mark is the only way of distinguishing an exclamation from a statement.

Many exclamations, however, do not consist of fully formed sentences, and usually lack a main verb. They are a special kind of sentence fragment known as 'interjections':

For goodness sake!

Good gracious!

Oh no!

and many others that cannot be printed here!

Because they do not conform to the requirements of full sentences, sentence fragments such as these can be referred to as 'minor sentences'.

Simple and complex sentences

Sentences also vary in their levels of complexity, with four main types being apparent, depending on the number and type of clauses they contain.

- Simple sentences contain one independent clause.

  We drove from London to Edinburgh in six hours.

- Compound sentences contain more than one independent clause, joined by a connecting word or phrase known as a conjunction.

  We were exhausted, but we arrived in time for my mother's birthday party.

- Complex sentences contain one independent clause and at least one dependent clause.

  Although he is now 79 years old, he still claims to be 65.

- Compound-complex sentences contain more than one independent clause and at least one dependent clause.

  After it was all over, my dad claimed he knew we were planning something, but we think he was really surprised.

The component parts of a sentence

To understand the ways in which such variations in complexity are achieved, we need to understand the building blocks of the English sentence, clauses and phrases.

Subjects, objects and predicates

Every complete sentence contains two parts: a subject and a predicate. **The subject** is what (or whom) the sentence is about, while **the predicate** tells something about the subject. In the following sentences, the predicate is enclosed in braces ({ }), while the subject is <u>underlined.</u>

<u>Joanne</u> {*runs*}.

<u>Joanne and her dog</u> {*run on the beach every morning*}.

To determine the subject of a sentence, first isolate the verb and then make a question by placing 'who?' or 'what?' before it. The answer is the subject.

The crowd littered the terraces with empty paper cups and discarded newspapers.

The verb in the above sentence is *littered*. Who or what littered? The crowd did. *The crowd* is therefore the subject of the sentence. The predicate (which always includes the verb) goes on to relate something about the subject. What about the crowd? It *littered the terraces with empty paper cups and discarded newspapers* – this is therefore the predicate.

Imperative sentences (sentences that give a command or an order) differ from conventional sentences in that their subject, which is always 'you', is understood rather than expressed.

Stand on your head. ('You' is understood before stand.)

Every subject is built around one noun or pronoun (or more) that, when stripped of all the words that modify it, is known as the simple subject. Look at the following example:

A piece of pepperoni pizza would satisfy his hunger.

The subject is built around the noun *piece*, with the other words of the subject (*a* and *of pepperoni pizza*) modifying the noun. *Piece* is the simple subject.

Likewise, a predicate has at its centre a simple predicate, which is always the verb or verbs that link up with the subject. In the example above, the simple predicate is *would satisfy*.

A sentence may have a compound subject – a simple subject consisting of more than one noun or pronoun, as in these examples where the subjects are <u>underlined</u>:

<u>*Football scarves, rock posters and family photographs*</u> covered the boy's bedroom walls.

<u>*My uncle and I*</u> walked slowly through the art gallery and admired the paintings which were hanging there.

The second sentence above also features a compound predicate, a predicate that includes more than one verb pertaining to the same subject (in this case, *walked* and *admired*).

As well as its central verb, the predicate may also contain **an object** that completes the verb's meaning. Two kinds of objects follow verbs: **direct objects** and **indirect objects**. To determine if a verb has a direct object, isolate the verb and make it into a question by placing 'whom?' or 'what?' after it. The answer, if there is one, is the direct object. Look at the examples:

The footballer kicked the ball into the net.

The verb here is *kicked* so the question becomes, 'what did he kick?' The answer *the ball* is the object.

John's teacher gave him an excellent mark in the test.

The verb here is *gave* so the question becomes, 'what did he give?' The answer *an excellent mark* is the object.

This sentence also contains an indirect object. An indirect object (which, like a direct object, is always a noun or pronoun) is, in a sense, the recipient of the direct object. To determine if a verb has an indirect object, isolate the verb and ask 'to whom?', 'to what?', 'for whom?', or 'for what?' after it. The answer is the indirect object. In the sentence above, therefore, the answer to the question, 'To whom did the teacher give the excellent mark?' is *him*, i.e. John, who is the indirect object.

Not all verbs are followed by objects. Look at the verbs in the following sentences:

The speaker rose from her chair to protest.

After work, Winston usually jogs around the canal.

There is no answer to the questions, 'What did she rise?' and 'What did he jog?' These verbs do not have objects. Verbs that take objects are known as **transitive verbs**. Verbs not followed by objects are called **intransitive verbs**.

In addition to the transitive verb and the intransitive verb, there is a third kind of verb called a **linking verb**. The word (or phrase) that follows a linking verb is called not an object, but a **subject complement**. The most common linking verb is 'be'. Other linking verbs are 'become', 'seem', 'appear', 'feel', 'grow', 'look', and 'smell', among others. Note that some of these are sometimes linking verbs, sometimes transitive verbs, or some-times intransitive verbs, depending on how you use them. The subject complements are underlined in the following sentences:

> He was a _radiologist_ before he became a _full-time yoga instructor._

> Your home-made apple pie smells _delicious._

Note that a subject complement can be either a noun (*radiologist, instructor*) or an adjective (*delicious*).

An **object complement** is similar to a subject complement, except that (obviously) it modifies an object rather than a subject. Consider this example of a subject complement:

> The driver seems tired.

In this case, as explained above, the adjective *tired* modifies the noun *driver*, which is the subject of the sentence. Sometimes, however, the noun will be the object, as in the following example:

> I consider the driver tired.

In this case, the noun *driver* is the direct object of the verb *consider*, but the adjective *tired* is still acting as its complement.

In general, verbs that have to do with perceiving, judging or changing something can cause their direct objects to take an object complement. In the following examples the object complements are underlined:

> Paint it _black._

> The judge ruled her _out of order._

> I saw the Prime Minister _sleeping._

In every case, you could reconstruct the last part of the sentence into a sentence of its own using a subject complement:

> It is black.

> She is out of order.

> The Prime Minister is sleeping.

PRACTICAL TASK   PRACTICAL TASK   PRACTICAL TASK   PRACTICAL TASK   PRACTICAL TASK

In the following sentences, identify the subjects and predicates and say whether the main verb is transitive or intransitive.

The boy quickly jumped over the barbed wire fence.

I thought there would be something to pay.

> The teacher finally finished his marking at 11.30 that night.
>
> The day you realise that new clothes cost money will be the day you start dressing sensibly.
>
> By accident, the girl broke three pieces of pottery while she was in the antique shop.

The clause

A clause is a group of related words containing a subject and a verb. A clause can be usefully distinguished from a phrase, which is a group of related words that does not contain a subject–verb relationship, such as 'in the morning' or 'running down the street' or 'having grown used to the noise'. Sometimes a phrase will contain a verb form and a noun:

He wrote a letter suggesting that the teacher was to blame.

The underlined phrase still contains no subject–verb relationship, so does not qualify as a clause.

Clauses can be categorised into independent and dependent clauses. This simply means that some clauses can stand by themselves, as separate sentences, and some cannot. Another term for dependent clause is subordinate clause: this means that the clause is subordinate to another element (the independent clause) and depends on that other element for its meaning.

Independent clauses could stand by themselves as discrete sentences. The ability to recognise a clause, and to know when a clause is capable of acting as an independent unit, is essential to good writing and is especially helpful in avoiding sentence fragments and run-on sentences.

It is important to understand how to combine independent clauses into larger units of thought. Look at the following sentence, for example:

Jill didn't mean to do it, but she did it anyway.

This is made up of two independent clauses: 'Jill didn't mean to do it' and 'she did it anyway'. These are connected by a comma and a co-ordinating conjunction ('but'). If the word 'but' was missing from this sentence, the sentence would be called a *comma-splice*: two independent clauses would be incorrectly connected with only a comma between them.

Clauses can be combined in three different ways: co-ordination, subordination, and by means of a semicolon.

Co-ordination involves joining independent clauses with a co-ordinating conjunction such as 'and', 'but', 'or', 'nor', 'for' and 'yet'. Clauses connected like this are usually well balanced both in length and importance.

James arranged to join the local youth club, but he forgot to tell his parents about this.

Subordination involves turning one of the clauses into a subordinate element (one that cannot stand on its own) through the use of a subordinating conjunction ('although', 'because', etc.) or a relative pronoun ('which', 'who', 'that', etc.). When the clause begins with a subordinating word, it is no longer an independent clause; it is called a dependent or subordinate clause because it depends on something else (the independent clause) for its meaning.

Although James arranged to join the local youth club, he forgot to tell his parents about this.

James did not tell his parents about joining the youth club, because he was afraid they might stop him.

Semicolons can connect two independent clauses, although this is less common in modern English.

James has an outgoing personality; many of his friends think he would be an excellent member of the youth club.

Dependent clauses cannot stand by themselves and make good sense. They must be combined with an independent clause so that they become part of a sentence that can stand by itself. Dependent clauses can perform a number of functions within a sentence. They can act either in the capacity of some kind of noun or as some kind of modifier. There are three basic kinds of dependent clauses, categorised according to their function in the sentence.

- **Adverbial clauses** provide further information about what is going on in the main (independent) clause: where, when, or why. (The dependent clauses in the following sentences are underlined.)

  When the film is over, we'll go for a meal.

  We wanted to write this book because we think it will be useful to teachers.

Notice that these adverbial clauses might come before or after the main clause. When they come before the main clause, they are known as 'fronted adverbials', that is, they 'front' the sentence. We will discuss this phenomenon in more detail in the next chapter but, for now, it would be worth considering whether the meaning is changed at all by the order in which the adverbial and the main clause come in the sentence. So, if both orders are possible, does the order chosen make a difference? Look at the following two sentences:

Unless you study carefully, you will never learn this material.

You will never learn this material unless you study carefully.

You will probably agree that the difference between these two meanings is very subtle, if there is one at all. As we will see in the next chapter, however, fronted adverbials can sometimes have a more dramatic effect on meaning than this.

- **Adjectival clauses** work like multi-word adjectives.

  My brother, who is a teacher, told me about this book.

  The examination that I took last summer was dreadfully difficult.

- **Noun clauses** can do anything that nouns can do.

What he does with his life is no concern of mine. [The noun clause here is the subject of the sentence.]

Do you understand <u>what he is talking about</u>? [Here the noun clause is the object of the verb.]

Dependent clauses can also be classified as restrictive and non-restrictive. A **non-restrictive clause** is not essential to the meaning of the sentence; it can be removed from the sentence without changing its basic meaning. Non-restrictive clauses are usually set apart from the rest of the sentence by a comma or a pair of commas (if they are in the middle of a sentence).

The teacher, <u>who used to be a secretary</u>, could type very competently.

Notice the difference in meaning that is caused when a clause is changed to **a restrictive clause**, a change that is signalled purely by punctuation.

The students, who were penniless, could not afford to buy books.

The students who were penniless could not afford to buy books.

In the first sentence of this pair, the non-restrictive clause 'who were penniless' clearly applies to all of the students referred to in this sentence. Its omission from the sentence would result in less information but would not significantly change the meaning.

In the second sentence, however, 'who were penniless' acts as a limiting modifier of the students; it only applies to some of them and it is this subset who are the subject of the sentence. This restrictive clause could not be omitted from the sentence without severe disruption to the meaning.

Relative clauses are dependent clauses that are introduced by a relative pronoun (that, which, whichever, who, whoever, whom, whose, etc.). Relative clauses can be either restrictive or non-restrictive.

Phrases

A **phrase** is a group of related words that does not include a subject and verb. There are several different kinds of phrases. Basically, any of what were traditionally called 'parts of speech' (nouns, verbs, adjectives, etc.) can consist of single words or groups of words. These groups are phrases and they take their type from their grammatical function in a sentence. (In the following sentences, the phrases being described are <u>underlined</u>.)

- **A noun phrase** comprises a noun and any associated modifying words.

  The long and winding road leads to your door.

  Children sometimes make fun of people with glasses.

- **A prepositional phrase** consists of a preposition, a noun or pronoun that serves as the object of the preposition, and, sometimes, an adjective that modifies the object.

  The boy jubilantly kicked the ball <u>into the gaping net</u>.

  He clearly heard his mother's cheers <u>from across the vast field</u>.

Prepositional phrases usually tell when or where, for example 'in forty minutes', 'in the sun' and 'against the side'; that is, they are adverbial or adjectival.

- **An adjectival phrase** consists of a group of words that do the job of an adjective in modifying a noun.

  The children were afraid of the teacher <u>with the loud laugh</u>.

  Students <u>with long memories</u> will remember their first reading books.

- **An adverbial phrase** consists of a group of words that modify a verb. They usually provide answers to questions such as when, where, how, why and for how long.

  The game was played <u>in one half of the pitch</u>.

  The politician resigned his seat <u>for personal reasons</u>.

A SUMMARY OF **KEY POINTS**

- ➢ **A sentence is a group of words containing a subject and a predicate.**
- ➢ **A sentence has a capital letter at the start and a full stop at the end; usually, it will express a thought that can stand by itself.**
- ➢ **There are two common ways in which this structure is misused: the use of sentence fragments and of run-on sentences.**
- ➢ **Sentences can have different purposes, including statements, questions, commands and exclamations, and can vary in length and complexity.**
- ➢ **Sentences are made up of different components, such as a subject, an object and a predicate.**
- ➢ **Clauses are groups of related words containing a subject and a verb. They can be independent (i.e. they could stand by themselves as discrete sentences) or dependent (i.e. they cannot make sense by themselves).**
- ➢ **Phrases are groups of related words that do not include a subject and a verb.**

M-LEVEL EXTENSION > > M-LEVEL EXTENSION > > M-LEVEL EXTENSION

A useful way of checking your understanding of the construction of sentences in English is to play the expanding sentence game (you can try this with children too).

Begin by thinking of a simple sentence.
The cat sat on the mat.

Change the articles in this sentence.
A cat sat on a mat.

Change common nouns to proper nouns
Tibbles sat on the Isfahan.

Change the nouns and the verb
The feline squatted on the rug.

Add adjectives to the nouns
The dirty, flea-ridden cat sat on the pristine, silk mat.

Add adverbs
The cat sat prissily and disdainfully on the mat.

Add adjective phrases
The cat with the squint sat on the mat in the corner.

Add an adverb phrase
The cat sat with undue caution on the mat.

Add relative clauses
The cat, who really wanted his dinner, sat on the mat, which he then proceeded to chew.

Make a compound sentence
The cat sat on the mat and began to growl menacingly.

Make a complex sentence
The rather aloof cat, having recovered from the earlier blow to its delicate ego, sat gingerly on the very soft mat, against which it purred in a whining manner.

Combine any of these changes
Mistress Cholmondely, the very superior Persian who was gracing us with her presence while her real owners were abroad, delicately perched her silken rear on the rather worn rag rug my grandmother had left us as a doormat and I have to admit I was struck by the incongruity of this act.

When using the expanding sentence game with children, consider which year groups you feel would be appropriate for each expansion type.

FURTHER READING   FURTHER READING   **FURTHER READING**   FURTHER READING

Chalker, S. and Weiner, E. (1998) *The Oxford Dictionary of English Grammar*. Oxford: Oxford University Press. A comprehensive resource for queries about grammar.

DfE (2013) *Teachers' Standards*. London: DfE. **(www.gov.uk/government/uploads/system/uploads/ attachment_data/file/208682/Teachers__Standards_2013.pdf)**

Hughes, A. (2011) *Online English Grammar*. **(www.edufind.com/english/grammar)**. An excellent online resource.

Newby, M. (1987) *The Structure of English: A Handbook of English Grammar*. Cambridge: Cambridge University Press. Well-written and engaging account of English grammar.

University College London (2011) *The Internet Grammar of English*. **(www.ucl.ac.uk/internet-grammar/ home.htm)**. An excellent online resource.

7
The components of sentences

Curriculum context

National Curriculum programmes of study

This knowledge is designed to underpin the teaching of the Key Stage 1 and Key Stage 2 programmes of study for English, which state, for example, that pupils should be taught

in spoken language to:

- speak audibly and fluently with an increasing command of Standard English

and in writing to:

- develop their understanding of the concepts set out in English appendix 2 by:
  - learning the grammar in English appendix 2 Y1/2/3/4/5/6
- learning how to use:
  - sentences with different forms: statement, question, exclamation, command Y2
  - expanded noun phrases to describe and specify [for example, the blue butterfly] Y2
  - the present and past tenses correctly and consistently, including the progressive form Y2
  - subordination (using when, if, that, or because) and co-ordination (using or, and, or but) Y2

- o some features of written standard English Y2
- o extending the range of sentences with more than one clause by using a wider range of conjunctions, including: when, if, because, although Y3/4
- o using the present perfect form of verbs in contrast to the past tense Y3/4
- o choosing nouns or pronouns appropriately for clarity and cohesion and to avoid repetition Y3/4
- o using conjunctions, adverbs and prepositions to express time and cause Y3/4
- o using fronted adverbials Y3/4
- o recognising vocabulary and structures that are appropriate for formal speech and writing, including subjunctive forms Y5/6
- o using passive verbs to affect the presentation of information in a sentence Y5/6
- o using the perfect form of verbs to mark relationships of time and cause Y5/6
- o using expanded noun phrases to convey complicated information concisely Y5/6
- o using modal verbs or adverbs to indicate degrees of possibility Y5/6
- o using relative clauses beginning with who, which, where, when, whose, that or with an implied (ie omitted) relative pronoun Y5/6

- indicate grammatical and other features by:

- o using commas after fronted adverbials Y3/4
- o indicating possession by using the possessive apostrophe with plural nouns Y3/4
- o using and punctuating direct speech Y3/4
- o using commas to clarify meaning or avoid ambiguity in writing Y5/6
- o using hyphens to avoid ambiguity Y5/6
- o using brackets, dashes or commas to indicate parenthesis Y5/6
- o using semicolons, colons or dashes to mark boundaries between independent clauses Y5/6
- o using a colon to introduce a list Y5/6
- o punctuating bullet points consistently Y5/6

- use the grammatical terminology in English appendix 2 in discussing their writing Y1/2/3/4
- make simple additions, revisions and corrections to their own writing by:

- o rereading to check that their writing makes sense and that verbs to indicate time are used correctly and consistently, including verbs in the continuous form Y2
- o proposing changes to grammar and vocabulary to improve consistency, including the accurate use of pronouns in sentences Y3/4
- o selecting appropriate grammar and vocabulary, understanding how such choices can change and enhance meaning Y5/6
- o ensuring the consistent and correct use of tense throughout a piece of writing Y5/6
- o ensuring correct subject and verb agreement when using singular and plural, distinguishing between the language of speech and writing and choosing the appropriate register Y5/6
- o proofreading to check for errors in spelling, grammar and punctuation (for example, ends of sentences punctuated correctly) Y2/3/4/5/6.

Early Years Foundation Stage

The Early Learning Goals specify that, by the end of the Early Years Foundation Stage, children should:

- use past, present and future forms accurately when talking about events that have happened or are to happen in the future;
- write simple sentences which can be read by themselves and others.

Introduction

The words in a sentence can be classified according to the role they play in that sentence. Such a classification produces a number of word classes which, in traditional Latinate grammar, are often referred to as *parts of speech*. The major word classes are: nouns, pronouns, determiners, adjectives, verbs, adverbs, conjunctions and prepositions.

REFLECTIVE TASK

It will undoubtedly be the case that you feel confident you already know the meaning of some of the above **parts of speech**. It would be useful for you to review this knowledge before you embark on a reading of each of the sections of the chapter. Make a list of the parts of speech: nouns, pronouns, determiners, adjectives, verbs, adverbs, conjunctions and prepositions.

For each, think about what you already know. Then read the section of the chapter that deals with this part of speech. Has anything surprised you?

Our aim in this chapter is to present as full a description as we can of the nature and function of each of these word classes. You should be aware, however, that the classification system we are using here is traditional and rather unsatisfactory in that, as it is derived from the study of the static ancient languages Latin and Greek, it is often a challenge to apply it to modern English usage. In many ways it has been superseded by alternative grammars, such as Halliday's functional grammar (2004), which better represent the dynamic, meaning-centred nature of our language. From a functional perspective, grammar is concerned with what language is doing, or being made to do. The concept of *rules*, which is how most of us can remember being taught grammar at school, is replaced by the concept of *possibilities*. In other words, it is about what language can be made to do, and what the constraining factors are in this.

Although functional grammar, and other analysis systems sharing its attention to the ways language represents meaning, are more useful tools for enhancing language users' control of the systems they use, they are not yet widely used in educational contexts. The National Curriculum for English relies on traditional descriptions of sentence grammar, and it is these which form the focus of the Y6 Spelling, Punctuation and Grammar (SPAG) test. For that reason, this is the system we focus on in this chapter.

RESEARCH SUMMARY RESEARCH SUMMARY **RESEARCH SUMMARY** RESEARCH SUMMARY

The value of 'traditional' grammar instruction in terms of improving children's use of language, especially in writing, has long been questioned by research. Braddock, Lloyd-Jones and Schoer (1963) in their review of research on the teaching of writing concluded that *The teaching of formal grammar has a negligible effect on the improvement of writing* (pp37–8), and this conclusion has since been reiterated many times by research findings and reviews, for example Hillocks (1986). Modern approaches

---

to grammar teaching no longer stress formal drills but tend to focus on grammar in the context of the reading and writing of whole texts. In the Effective Teachers of Literacy project, Medwell *et al.* (1998) found that teachers who were effective at teaching literacy did teach grammar explicitly but always within the context of a text they shared with their pupils. More recently, research (Jones, Myhill and Bailey, 2013) has shown the positive impact of contextualised grammar instruction on secondary school pupils' writing performance.

Nouns

Nouns refer to people, places or things. There are a number of types of nouns.

- *Common nouns* refer to things that are not unique:
  dog, country, freedom, hope, bird

They can be divided into categories in several ways, for example: concrete/abstract or countable/uncountable.

1. **Concrete** nouns refer to things that can be touched, seen, smelt or heard:
   door, cat, wind, ground

2. **Abstract** nouns refer to feelings or qualities:
   love, warmth, despair, beauty

3. **Countable** nouns denote things we can count:
   one dog, a horse, sixteen men, the shop

They usually have a singular and plural form:
   two dogs, ten horses, a man, the shops

4. **Uncountable** nouns denote things that we do not usually count:
   tea, sugar, water, air, rice

They also include abstract ideas or qualities:
   knowledge, beauty, anger, fear, love

These do not usually have a plural form. Some examples of common uncountable nouns are:

   money, advice, information, furniture, happiness, sadness, news, research, evidence, safety, beauty, knowledge

- *Proper nouns* are indicated by capital letters and include:

1. Names and titles of people, e.g. *Winston Churchill, the Headmaster of Eton*
2. Titles of works, books, etc., e.g. *War and Peace, The Merchant of Venice*
3. Months of the year, e.g. *January, February*
4. Days of the week and seasons, e.g. *Sunday, Winter*
5. Holidays, e.g. *Christmas, May Day*
6. Geographical names, including:
   a) names of countries and continents, e.g. *England, Europe*
   b) names of regions and districts, e.g. *Sussex, the Costa Brava*
   c) names of cities, towns and villages, e.g. *London, Cape Town*

d) names of rivers, oceans, seas and lakes, e.g. *the Atlantic, Lake Victoria, the Rhine*

e) names of geographical formations, e.g. *the Himalayas*

f) names of streets, buildings and parks, e.g. *Park Lane, Hyde Park, the Empire State Building*

7. Nationalities, e.g. *English, French, Chinese*

- **Compound nouns** are formed from the combination of two or more other words, neither of which is necessarily a noun itself. The meaning of the word they create together is different from the meaning of the constituent words on their own.

head + ache = headache (noun + verb)
girl + friend = girlfriend (noun + noun)
work + man = workman (verb + noun)
hair + cut = haircut (noun + verb)
break + down = breakdown (verb + preposition).

PRACTICAL TASK PRACTICAL TASK PRACTICAL TASK PRACTICAL TASK PRACTICAL TASK

Identify the ten nouns in this passage:

High above the city, on a tall column, stood the statue of the Happy Prince. He was gilded all over with thin leaves of fine gold, for eyes he had two bright sapphires, and a large red ruby glowed on his sword-hilt. He was very much admired indeed.

Pronouns

Pronouns can be thought of as a subclass of nouns. They act in place of a noun in a sentence:

Noun

John has a new car.

People should try to watch less television.

Pronoun

He has a new car.

They should try to watch less television.

In these examples the pronouns have the same reference as the nouns they replace. In each case, they refer to people, and so can be called **personal pronouns**. Although the pronoun *it* does not usually refer to a person, it is also included in this group. There are three personal pronouns, each with a singular and a plural form:

Person	Singular	Plural
First	I	we
Second	you	you
Third	he/she/it	they

These pronouns also have another set of forms:

Person	Singular	Plural
First	me	us
Second	you	you
Third	him/her/it	them

The first set of forms (I, you, he ...) can replace nouns that are the subject of a sentence, and the second set (me, you, him...) nouns that are the object of a sentence.

As well as personal pronouns, there are many other types, as summarised below:

Pronoun type	Examples	An example sentence
Possessive	mine, yours, his, hers, ours, theirs	The white car is <u>mine.</u>
Reflexive	myself, yourself, himself, herself, itself, oneself, ourselves, yourselves, themselves	He injured <u>himself</u> playing football.
Reciprocal	each other, one another	They really hate <u>each other.</u>
Relative	that, which, who, whose, whom, where, when	The book <u>that</u> you gave me was really boring.
Demonstrative	this, that, these, those	<u>This</u> is a new car.
Interrogative	who, what, why, where, when, whatever	<u>What</u> did he say to you?
Indefinite	anything, anybody, anyone, something, somebody, someone, nothing, nobody, none, no one	There's <u>something</u> in my shoe.

The subject/object and singular/plural distinctions only apply to personal, possessive and reflexive pronouns. It is only in these types, too, that gender differences are shown (personal *he/she*, possessive *his/hers*, reflexive *himself/herself*).

Many of the pronouns listed above also belong to another word class – the class of determiners. They are pronouns when they occur independently, that is, without a noun following them, as in *This is a new car*. But when a noun follows them – *This car is new* – they are determiners.

Determiners

Nouns are often preceded by the words *the, a* or *an*. These words are called *determiners*. They indicate the kind of reference that the noun has. The determiner *the* is known as the **definite article** because it pinpoints the noun to a particular instance. It is used before both singular and plural nouns and is invariable:

Singular	Plural
the taxi	*the taxis*
the paper	*the papers*
the apple	*the apples*

The determiner *a* (or *an*, when the following noun begins with a vowel) is known as the **indefinite article** and is more open-ended in its reference. It is used only when the noun is singular:

a taxi   *a paper*   *an apple*

The articles *the* and *a/an* are the most common determiners, but there are many others:

any taxi   *that* question
those apples   *this* paper
some apples   *whatever* taxi
whichever taxi

Many determiners **express quantity**:

all examples   *both* parents
many people   *each* person
every night   *several* computers
few excuses   *enough* water
no escape

Numerals are determiners when they appear before a noun. Here, **cardinal numerals** express quantity:

one book
two books
twenty books

In the same position, **ordinal numerals** express sequence:

first impressions
second chance
third prize

There is also a set of determiners that are not directly related to numbers, which include *last, latter, next, previous and subsequent*:

next week   *last orders*
previous engagement   *subsequent developments*

As we mentioned earlier, there is considerable overlap between determiners and pronouns. Many words can be both:

Pronoun	**Determiner**
This is a very boring book.	*This book is very boring.*
That's an excellent film.	*That film is excellent.*

Determiners always come before a noun, but pronouns are more independent than this. They function in much the same way as nouns, and they can be replaced by nouns in the sentences above. On the other hand, when these words are determiners, they cannot be replaced by nouns.

The words underlined in the following sentences are either pronouns or determiners. Decide which is which.

1. *One day I'll manage to beat you.*
2. *One really finds it hard to understand that kind of behaviour.*
3. *I didn't have any bread so I had to go and buy some.*
4. *Some people were standing by the gateway.*
5. *Any old rubbish will do.*
6. *We were looking for items for the jumble sale and wondered if you had any.*

Adjectives

Adjectives are used to give more information about a noun. They:

- describe feelings or qualities:

  He is a lonely man.
  They are honest people.

- give nationality:

  Pierre is French.
  Siegfried is German.

- tell more about a thing's characteristics:

  That is a wooden table.
  The knife is sharp.

- tell us about age:

  He is a young man.
  She is a teenager.

- tell us about size and measurement:

  John is a tall man.
  This is a very long film.

- tell us about colour:

  Paul wore a red shirt.
  The sunset was crimson and gold.

Adjectives are generally invariable in English. They do not change their form depending on the gender or number of the noun.

A hot potato.

The hot potatoes.

They can occur in front of the noun or after a verb such as 'to be'.

A beautiful girl.

The girl is beautiful.

If we need to emphasise or strengthen the meaning of an adjective, we use 'very' or 'really'.

A very hot potato.

The really hot potatoes.

If we need to compare nouns we can achieve this through the use of comparative or superlative adjectives.

My Dad is tall, but Billy's Dad is even taller (comparative). *Jenny's Dad is the tallest of all* (superlative).

There are some general rules for the formation of comparatives and superlatives, dependent on the number of syllables an adjective has. As with all 'rules' in English grammar, however, there are a number of exceptions. Common rules are summarised in the following table. Examples:

Number of syllables in the adjective	Comparative form	Superlative form
one syllable tall	+ -er taller	+ -est tallest
two syllables (ending in 'y') noisy happy	+ -ier noisier happier	+ -iest noisiest happiest
two syllables (not ending in 'y') modern famous	more more modern more famous	most most modern most famous
three syllables or more important expensive	more more important more expensive	most most important most expensive

A cat is fast, a tiger is faster but a cheetah is the fastest.

A car is heavy, a truck is heavier, but a train is the heaviest.

A park bench is comfortable, a restaurant chair is more comfortable, but a sofa is the most comfortable.

There are a number of irregular comparatives and superlatives, for example:

good	*better*	*best*
bad	*worse*	*worst*
little	*less*	*least*
much	*more*	*most*

Verbs

Verbs are words that indicate the occurrence or performance of an action, or the exist-ence of a state. The most common definition of a verb – a doing word – is only partially correct. Some verbs do indicate actions:

jump, fall, run, march

Others indicate feelings or mental states:

love, believe, trust, hope

Perhaps the three most commonly used verbs in English, however, generally do neither of these. Be, have and do indicate states or actions:

I am happy.

That man has two very powerful cars.

We did sixteen lengths during our swimming lesson.

They are also widely used as auxiliaries to other verbs:

We were running along the street.

He had ridden that horse several times before.

Although it was difficult, we did manage to start the car this morning.

Unlike nouns and adjectives, which in English (unlike in other languages) generally do not change their forms, verbs are variable depending on the person they are linked with and on their tense.

Regular verbs change their forms only in the third person, i.e. the *he/she* form. Thus:

First person singular	*I jump*	*I hope*	*I discover*
Second person singular	*You jump*	*You hope*	*You discover*
Third person singular	*He jumps*	*He hopes*	*He discovers*
First person plural	*We jump*	*We hope*	*We discover*
Second person plural	*You jump*	*You hope*	*You discover*
Third person plural	*They jump*	*They hope*	*They discover*

Some irregular verbs, on the other hand, change in different ways:

	By changing in more than the first person	**By not changing at all**	**Some irregular verbs do change in the regular way**
First person singular	*I am*	*I can*	*I feel*
Second person singular	*You are*	*You can*	*You feel*
Third person singular	*She is*	*She can*	*She feels*
First person plural	*We are*	*We can*	*We feel*

| Second person plural | *You are* | *You can* | *You feel* |
| Third person plural | *They are* | *They can* | *They feel* |

In English, verb tense is indicated by changing the form of the verb. All verbs, whether regular or irregular, have five forms. These are:

- the infinitive to + the verb stem – e.g. <u>to jump</u>;
- the simple present – e.g. I <u>jump</u>;
- the simple past – e.g. I <u>jumped</u>;
- the past participle – e.g. I have <u>jumped</u>;
- the present participle – e.g. I am <u>jumping</u>.

The difference between a regular and an irregular verb is the formation of the simple past and the past participle. Regular verbs are dependably consistent – the simple past ends in -ed as does the past participle. The chart below shows these five forms for regular verbs.

Infinitive	Simple present	Simple past	Past participle	Present participle
to laugh	laugh(s)	laughed	laughed	laughing
to start	start(s)	started	started	starting
to wash	wash(es)	washed	washed	washing
to wink	wink(s)	winked	winked	winking

Irregular verbs, on the other hand, can end in a variety of ways, with no consistent pattern. Here are some examples:

Infinitive	Simple present	Simple past	Past participle	Present participle
to drive	drive(s)	drove	driven	driving
to feel	feel(s)	felt	felt	feeling
to put	put(s)	put	put	putting
to swim	swim(s)	swam	swum	swimming

PEDAGOGICAL LINK PEDAGOGICAL LINK PEDAGOGICAL LINK PEDAGOGICAL LINK

Young children (and learners of English) make two frequent errors with irregular verbs. They either add an incorrect -ed to the end of an irregular verb, or they mix up the simple past and past participle. Read this sentence and identify the errors.

Olivia feeled like exercising yesterday, so she putted on her bathing suit and drived to the swimming pool, where she swum so far that only an extra large pepperoni pizza would satisfy her hunger.

PRACTICAL TASK PRACTICAL TASK PRACTICAL TASK PRACTICAL TASK PRACTICAL TASK

There are a great many irregular verbs in English. Some are listed in the table below. Try to complete the table before comparing your version with that given in the Appendix at the back of the book.

Infinitive	Simple present	Simple past	Past participle	Present participle
to arise	arise(s)	arose	arisen	arising
to bear	bear(s)		borne	
to beat	beat(s)	beat		beating
to become	become(s)		become	
to begin	begin(s)		begun	beginning
to bend	bend(s)	bent		bending
to blow	blow(s)	blew		blowing
to break	break(s)		broken	
to catch	catch(es)		caught	catching
to do	do(es)	did		
to eat	eat(s)		eaten	
to fall	fall(s)	fell		falling
to fly	flies, fly		flown	
to give	give(s)		given	
to go	go(es)	went		going
to hide	hide(s)		hidden	
to know	know(s)		known	knowing
to rise	rise(s)		risen	
to see	see(s)	saw		
to sing	sing(s)		sung	singing
to speak	speak(s)		spoken	speaking
to steal	steal(s)	stole		stealing
to stride	stride(s)			striding
to take	take(s)		taken	
to wear	wear(s)		worn	
to write	write(s)	wrote		writing

Information about verb tense in English is also given by the use of auxiliary verbs, particularly *be* and *have*. These accompany verb forms, either infinitives or participles, to form tenses such as past and present continuous, and future. The table below shows this:

Infinitive	Present continuous	Past continuous	Future
to become	I am becoming	I was becoming	I will become
to eat	I am eating	I was eating	I will eat
to fall	I am falling	I was falling	I will fall
to rise	I am rising	I was rising	I will rise
to see	I am seeing	I was seeing	I will see
to write	I am writing	I was writing	I will write

The auxiliary verb *be* is also used to form the **passive**, as in the following:

> *We keep the butter in the fridge.*
> *The butter is kept in the fridge.*
> *The teacher punished the boy for bad behaviour.*
> *The boy was punished by the teacher for bad behaviour.*

The auxiliary verb *do* is used to form the **interrogative** and **negative**.

> *Do you speak English?*
> *Did Peter live in Hong Kong?*
> *Does Helen know Peter?*
> *I don't speak English.*
> *Peter did not live in Hong Kong.*
> *Helen does not know Peter.*

A special group of auxiliary verbs are known as **modal auxiliary verbs**. These are used to indicate degrees of certainty in the verb they accompany. The following verbs can function as modal auxiliaries:

> *will, shall, may, might, can, could, must, ought to, should, would*

Will and *shall* are used to form the future but can also indicate an obligation or a promise:

> *He shall go to school!*
> *I will do your homework!*

Notice the use of the exclamation mark in these sentences to indicate the way that *shall* and *will* used like this are stressed in their pronunciation.

May and *might* are used to express permission or possibility:

> *You may stay up later tonight to watch the football. (permission)*
> *It may rain today. (possibility)*
> *It might snow today. (possibility)*

Can and *could* are used to express capability, permission or possibility.

> *She can speak English. (capability)*
> *He realised that he could swim after all. (capability)*
> *Can I park my car here? (permission)*
> *Could you help me? (permission)*
> *A car can be a useful means of transport or a dangerous weapon. (possibility)*
> *Ali could play the piano when he was a boy. (possibility)*

Must, ought to and *should* express obligation or advice:

> *You must leave immediately.*
> *You must try to drink less.*
> *You ought to thank them.*
> *You ought to exercise every day.*
> *They should be happy.*
> *You shouldn't eat too much.*

Would is used in conditional sentences:

> *I would ask her if she was here.*
> *They would have gone but it rained.*

It is also used as a polite form to ask someone to do something or to ask someone a question.

Would you mind looking after my children tonight?
Would you like something to drink?

Beyond the regular/irregular distinction, verbs also differ according to their mood.

A verb may be in one of three moods: the indicative mood, the imperative mood, and the subjunctive mood.

The indicative mood is the most common and is used to express facts and opinions or to make inquiries. Most of the statements you make or you read will be in the indicative mood. The highlighted verbs in the following sentences are all in the indicative mood:

Joe <u>picks up</u> the boxes.
The Alsatian dog <u>fetches</u> the stick.
Charles <u>closes</u> the window.

The imperative mood is also common and is used to give orders or to make requests. The imperative is identical in form to the second person indicative. The highlighted verbs in the following sentences are all in the imperative mood:

<u>Pick up</u> those boxes.
<u>Fetch</u>.
<u>Close</u> the window.

The subjunctive mood has almost disappeared from everyday language and is therefore more difficult to use correctly than either the indicative mood or the imperative mood. The subjunctive mood rarely appears in everyday conversation or writing and is used in a set of specific circumstances. You form the present tense subjunctive by dropping the 's' from the end of the third person singular, except for the verb *be*.

paints
present subjunctive: *paint*
walks
present subjunctive: *walk*
thinks
present subjunctive: *think*
is
present subjunctive: *be*

Except for the verb *be*, the past tense subjunctive is indistinguishable in form from the past tense indicative. The past tense subjunctive of *be* is *were*.

painted
past subjunctive: *painted*
walked
past subjunctive: *walked*
thought
past subjunctive: *thought*
was
past subjunctive: *were*

The subjunctive is found in a handful of traditional circumstances. For example, in the sentence 'God save the Queen', the verb *save* is in the subjunctive mood. Similarly, in the sentence 'Heaven forbid', the verb *forbid* is in the subjunctive mood.

The subjunctive is usually found in complex sentences. It is most often used in dependent clauses to following verbs of wishing or requesting.

It is urgent that Fiona <u>attend</u> Monday's meeting.

The teacher ordered that Kevin <u>scrub</u> his desk clean.

We suggest that Mr. Smith <u>move</u> his car out of the no parking zone.

I wish that this book <u>were</u> still in print.

Parliament recommended that the bill be <u>passed</u> immediately.

Adverbs

Adverbs usually modify, or add to the meaning of, verbs. They describe how, where, why or when an action was done. They can also modify an adjective, or another adverb.

Mary sings <u>beautifully</u>.
David is <u>extremely</u> clever.
This car goes <u>incredibly</u> fast.

In the first example, the adverb beautifully tells us how Mary sings. In the second, extremely tells us the degree to which David is clever. Finally, the adverb incredibly tells us how fast the car goes.

The adverb may follow the verb, as in:

He broke the news as <u>gently</u> as possible.

Or it may precede the verb, as in:

She <u>slowly</u> handed him the important document.

From the examples above, you can see that many adverbs end in -ly. More precisely, they are formed by adding -ly to an adjective:

Adjective	Adverb
slow	*slowly*
quick	*quickly*
soft	*softly*
sudden	*suddenly*
gradual	*gradually*

Because of their distinctive endings, these adverbs are known as -ly adverbs. However, by no means all adverbs end in -ly. Note also that some adjectives also end in -ly, including *costly, deadly, friendly, kindly, likely, lively, manly* and *timely.*

Like adjectives, many adverbs are gradable, that is, we can modify them using very or extremely:

softly	*very softly*
suddenly	*very suddenly*
slowly	*extremely slowly*

The modifying words *very* and *extremely* are themselves adverbs. They are called **adverbs of degree** because they specify the degree to which an adjective or another adverb applies. Adverbs of degree include *almost, barely, entirely, highly, quite, slightly, totally* and *utterly*. They are not gradable; you could not have, for example, *entirely almost*, or *barely very*.

Many adverbs give information about the manner, time or place of an event or action.

Adverbs of manner tell us how an action is performed:

> She sang <u>loudly</u> in the bath.
> The sky <u>quickly</u> grew dark.

Adverbs of time indicate not only specific times but also frequency:

> I'll come back <u>tomorrow</u>.
> I <u>sometimes</u> watch television at the weekend.

Adverbs of place indicate where something has occurred, or should occur:

> I've left my gloves <u>somewhere</u>.
> Put the box <u>there</u>, on the table.

Additive adverbs add two or more items together, emphasising that they are to be considered equal:

> We did French at school today. We <u>also</u> did English.
> The French was rather boring. The English was boring <u>too</u>.

In contrast, **exclusive adverbs** focus attention on what follows them, to the exclusion of other possibilities:

> It's <u>just</u> a question of how we organise it.
> School exists <u>solely</u> for the purpose of educating our children.

Particularising adverbs also focus attention on what follows them, but do not exclude other possibilities:

> These animals are <u>particularly</u> found in East Africa.
> This book is <u>mostly</u> about the English language.

A special subclass of adverbs includes a set of words beginning with wh-. The most common are *when, where* and *why*, though the set also includes *whence, whereby, wherein* and *whereupon*. To this set we can add the word *how*, but the whole set is usually referred to as wh- adverbs. Some of these can introduce a question:

> <u>When</u> are you going to London?
> <u>Where</u> did you leave the car?

They can also introduce various types of clause:

> This is the town <u>where</u> Shakespeare was born.
> I have no idea <u>how</u> it works.

Adverbs (and adverbial phrases and clauses) are normally put after the verb they modify.

> *He spoke <u>angrily</u>.*
> *They live <u>just here</u>.*
> *We will go <u>in a few minutes</u>.*

or after the object or complement:

> *He opened the door <u>quietly</u>.*
> *She left the money <u>on the table</u>.*
> *We saw our friends <u>last night</u>.*
> *You are looking tired <u>tonight</u>.*

But adverbials of frequency (how often) usually come in front of the main verb:

> *We <u>usually</u> spent our holidays with our grandparents.*
> *I have <u>never</u> seen William at work.*

But if we want to emphasise an adverbial we can put it at the beginning of a clause or sentence:

> *<u>Last night</u> we saw our friends.*
> *<u>In a few minutes</u> we will go.*
> *<u>Very quietly</u> he opened the door.*

These are known as fronted adverbials and their position makes a difference not to the exact meaning of the sentence but to the style and emphasis. After all, *We saw our friends last night* has a very similar meaning to *Last night we saw our friends.* The only difference is stylistic.

Conjunctions

Conjunctions are grammatical connectors that link words, phrases or clauses. A conjunction can indicate the relationship between the elements that it connects in the sentence. Without these, we would not see the relationship. There are three types of conjunctions:

- *A **co-ordinating conjunction*** connects words, phrases and clauses that have equal or the same grammatical functions, for example nouns, verbs, adjectives, prepositional phrases, adverb clauses, etc. The co-ordinating conjunctions include: ***and, but, or, yet, nor, for*** and ***so***. Examples are:

Connecting nouns:	*I will buy a coat <u>and</u> a hat.*
Connecting verbs:	*I did not call <u>nor</u> write to my mother.*
Connecting adjectives:	*The boy was nice <u>but</u> weird.*
Connecting dependent clauses:	*If the team are on form <u>and</u> they have their fair share of luck, it will be a great game.*
Connecting independent clauses:	*Ten thousand students applied to this university, <u>but</u> only six thousand were admitted.*

- *A **correlative conjunction*** is a co-ordinating conjunction that works in pairs to connect elements in a sentence. The correlative conjunctions include: ***both ... and, not ... but, not only ... but also, either ... or, neither ... nor, although ... yet, whether ... or***. Examples are:

Connecting nouns:	*The name of my teacher was <u>not</u> Miss Smith <u>but</u> Miss Smithers.*
Connecting adjectives:	*Schools should provide <u>both</u> a safe <u>and</u> an interesting environment.*
Connecting prepositional phrases:	*Orange juice is made <u>either</u> by squeezing oranges <u>or</u> by mixing orange concentrate.*
Connecting independent clauses:	*<u>Not only</u> did Joanne pass the examination, <u>but</u> she <u>also</u> scored the highest mark.*

- **A *subordinating conjunction*** connects elements with different grammatical functions, usually a dependent and an independent clause. The subordinating conjunctions include: ***after, in case, unless, although, in that, until, as, now that, when, as if, once, whenever, as though, since, where, because, so, whereas, before, so that, whether, even though, than, which, except that, that, while, however, though, who/whom, if.*** Examples are:

He was acting <u>as though</u> he had done something wrong.
I am sure <u>that</u> the teacher will let you finish your painting today.
<u>When</u> the bell rings, the children have to come into the classroom.
<u>Since</u> her cat ran away, Jenny has been very sad.

PRACTICAL TASK PRACTICAL TASK PRACTICAL TASK PRACTICAL TASK PRACTICAL TASK

Take these pairs of sentences and suggest possible ways of combining them to make single sentences. The first, for example, might be combined as:

The boy has a red coat and a blue coat.

This boy has a red coat but that boy has a blue coat.

This boy has a red coat whereas that boy has a blue coat.

1. *The boy has a red coat. The boy has a blue coat.*

2. *The teacher was ill. The children did not have to go to school.*

3. *The boy went to school. The boy was late.*

4. *The dog ran across the street. The dog did not run in front of a car.*

5. *The teacher failed me. I did not pass my examination.*

Prepositions

A preposition is a word or group of words that shows the relationship – in time, space or some other sense – between its object (the <u>noun</u> or <u>pronoun</u> that follows the preposition) and another word in the sentence:

Alison put the bag <u>in</u> her locker.

(Here, *in* shows the spatial relationship between the verb *put* and the object of the preposition *locker*.)

Jamie kicked the ball <u>through</u> the goalposts.

(Here, *through* indicates the direction in which the ball travelled.)

Here are some of the common prepositions in English:

about, above, according to, across, after, against, along, alongside, along with, among, apart from, around, at, away from, because of, before, behind, below, beneath, beside, besides, between, beyond, by, by means of, concerning, considering, despite, down, during, except, from, in, in addition to, in front of, in place of, inside, instead of, into, near, of, off, on, on account of, on behalf of, onto, on top of, out, out of, outside, over, owing to, prior to, round, round about, since, through, throughout, till, to, towards, under, underneath, until, unto, up, up to, upon, with, within, without

---

A SUMMARY OF **KEY POINTS**

➤ The words in a sentence can be classified according to the role that they play.

➤ The main word classes or 'parts of speech' are nouns, pronouns, determiners, adjectives, verbs, adverbs, conjunctions and prepositions.

➤ There are four types of common noun: concrete, abstract, countable and uncountable.

➤ Proper nouns are indicated by capital letters and include the names of a wide range of things.

➤ Compound nouns are formed from two or more other words.

➤ Pronouns act in place of a noun and include personal pronouns for use in the first, second and third person, with versions for the subject and object of a sentence.

➤ Determiners include the definite and indefinite articles, and those that express quantity.

➤ Adjectives give more information about a noun, and some are used in a comparative or superlative form.

➤ Verbs indicate the occurrence or performance of an action or the existence of a state. They can be regular or irregular in form.

➤ Adverbs modify or add to the meaning of verbs; some are formed from adjectives.

➤ Conjunctions are grammatical connectors that link words, phrases or clauses. There are three types: co-ordinating, correlative and subordinating.

➤ Prepositions are words or groups of words that show the relationship between their object (the noun or pronoun that follows them) and another word in the sentence.

M-LEVEL EXTENSION > > M-LEVEL EXTENSION > > M-LEVEL EXTENSION

Consider whether children should be taught the 'parts of speech' in a particular order. Can some components of sentences be taught discretely or would they all benefit from being taught in the context of the reading and writing of whole texts? Make a list of texts that could be used for this purpose with the particular year group(s) that you work with.

FURTHER READING   FURTHER READING   **FURTHER READING**   FURTHER READING

DfE (2013) *Teachers' Standards*. London: DfE. (**www.gov.uk/government/uploads/system/uploads/ attachment_data/file/208682/Teachers__Standards_2013.pdf)**

Jones, S., Myhill, D. and Bailey, T. (2013) 'Grammar for Writing? An investigation of the effects of contextualised grammar teaching on students' writing'. *Reading and Writing*, 26 (8): 1241–63.

University College London (2011) *The Internet Grammar of English*. (**www.ucl. ac.uk/internet-grammar/ home.htm**). Probably the best online reference source for queries about English grammar.

8
Punctuation

Curriculum context

National Curriculum programmes of study

This knowledge is designed to underpin the teaching of the Key Stage 1 and Key Stage 2 programmes of study for English, which state, for example, that pupils should be taught

in reading to:

- read words with contractions [for example, I'm, I'll, we'll], and understand that the apostrophe represents the omitted letter(s) Y1

and in writing to:

- develop their understanding of the concepts set out in English appendix 2 by:
  o leaving spaces between words Y1
  o beginning to punctuate sentences using a capital letter and a full stop, question mark or exclamation mark Y1
  o using a capital letter for names of people, places, the days of the week, and the personal pronoun 'I' Y1
  o learning how to use both familiar and new punctuation correctly, including full stops, capital letters, exclamation marks, question marks, commas for lists and apostrophes for contracted forms and the possessive (singular) Y2

- indicate grammatical and other features by:
  - using commas after fronted adverbials Y3/4
  - indicating possession by using the possessive apostrophe with plural nouns Y3/4
  - using and punctuating direct speech Y3/4
  - using commas to clarify meaning or avoid ambiguity in writing Y5/6
  - using hyphens to avoid ambiguity Y5/6
  - using brackets, dashes or commas to indicate parenthesis Y5/6
  - using semicolons, colons or dashes to mark boundaries between independent clauses Y5/6
  - using a colon to introduce a list Y5/6
  - punctuating bullet points consistently Y5/6.

Early Years Foundation Stage

The Early Learning Goals specify that, by the end of the Early Years Foundation Stage, children should:

- write simple sentences which can be read by themselves and others.

Introduction

Punctuation is an art, not a science, and a sentence can often be punctuated correctly in more than one way. It may also vary according to style: formal academic prose, for instance, might make more use of colons, semicolons and brackets and less of full stops, commas and dashes than conversational or journalistic prose.

In earlier periods of English, punctuation was often used rhetorically – that is, to represent the rhythms of the speaking voice. Writers in the seventeenth century, for example, often wrote with a delightful clarity and simplicity, and their prose was close to that of today. Their punctuation, however, clung to an older rhetorical system, which has now disappeared. Take, for example, the following two sentences from Sprat's History of the Royal Society (1667):

> *They have therefore been most rigorous in putting in execution, the only Remedy, that can be found for this extravagance: and that has been, a constant Resolution, to reject all the amplifications, digressions, and swellings of style: to return back to the primitive purity, and shortness, when men deliver'd so many things, almost in an equal number of words. They have exacted from all their members, a close, naked, natural way of speaking; positive expressions; clear senses; a native easiness: bringing all things as near the Mathematical plainness, as they can: and preferring the language of Artisans, Countrymen, and Merchants, before that, of Wits, or Scholars.*

REFLECTIVE TASK

Sprat's text is not punctuated in the way that would be normal today. Try to rewrite this text using modern punctuation.

Each time you use a punctuation device, try to justify to yourself why you are using it.

The extract contains 106 words, all of them still current, but it is cluttered with an outdated use of punctuation: 18 commas, three semicolons, four colons, one apostrophe, ten capital letters and two full stops – nearly one punctuation symbol to every three words, on average.

The main function of modern English punctuation, on the other hand, is logical: it is used to make clear the grammatical structure of the sentence, linking or separating groups of ideas and distinguishing what is important in the sentence from what is subordinate. It can still be used to break up a long sentence into more manageable units, but this may only be done where a logical break occurs. Jane Austen's sentence: 'No one who had ever seen Catherine Morland in her infancy, would ever have supposed her born to be a heroine' would now lose its comma, since there is no logical break between subject and verb (compare: 'No one would have supposed').

The importance of punctuation can be illustrated by comparing the two following letters. In both cases, the text is the same. It is the punctuation that makes all the difference!

> *Dear John: I want a man who knows what love is all about. You are generous, kind and thoughtful. People who are not like you admit to being useless and inferior. You have ruined me for other men. I yearn for you. I have no feelings whatsoever when we're apart. I can be forever happy – will you let me be yours? Gloria*

> *Dear John: I want a man who knows what love is. All about you are generous, kind and thoughtful people, who are not like you. Admit to being useless and inferior. You have ruined me. For other men, I yearn. For you, I have no feelings whatsoever. When we're apart, I can be forever happy. Will you let me be? Yours, Gloria*

In the following examples, punctuation changes meaning in more subtle ways:

> *They did not go, because they were lazy.*

is not the same as:

> *They did not go because they were lazy.*

The following sentences indicate the different weights of commas, brackets and dashes:

> *People in the north are more friendly and helpful than those in the south.*
> *People in the north are more friendly, and helpful, than those in the south.*
> *People in the north are more friendly (and helpful) than those in the south.*
> *People in the north are more friendly – and helpful – than those in the south.*

In this example, the difference is merely a hyphen:

> *twenty-odd people*

is very different from:

> *twenty odd people*

You might have a go at punctuating the following. Two very different meanings will emerge!

> *woman without her man is a monster*

The above should have convinced you that punctuation is important. It should also have alerted you to an important feature of punctuation – one which hundreds of teachers regularly fail to emphasise sufficiently to their children. The traditional way of explaining punctuation to children is by emphasising its role as an indicator of the intonation present in speech: the prosody in linguistic terms. This produces such advice as 'When you come to a comma, take a short breath; when you meet a full stop, take a longer breath'. This advice does have an element of truth, although there are many sentences that can be read perfectly sensibly with no pauses at all at commas. (The advice-giving sentence just quoted is a good example of this.) What is underplayed in such advice is the crucial role that punctuation plays in indicating meaning in written text. Look at the following examples:

Children who like pizza often eat very few vegetables.

Children, who like pizza, often eat very few vegetables.

The only difference between these two sentences is the use of commas to mark off the adjectival clause who *like pizza*. Yet the sentences mean completely different things. In the first, the adjectival clause is restrictive – the predicate *often eat very few vegetables* only refers to those children who meet the criterion of liking pizza. In the second, it is non-restrictive – the claim is that all children like pizza and all *often eat very few vegetables*. The punctuation indicates the meaning.

Notice also that, while the commas in the second sentence will tend to produce pauses when the sentence is read aloud, it would also be quite natural to pause slightly in the first sentence after *pizza*, where there is no comma. Punctuation is often an imperfect indicator of intonation and we mislead children if we stress this aspect.

PRACTICAL TASK PRACTICAL TASK PRACTICAL TASK PRACTICAL TASK PRACTICAL TASK

In the following sentences, decide what effects, on both intonation and meaning, the use of punctuation has.

However stressed the teacher, children are not allowed to talk in class.
'However,' stressed the teacher, 'children are not allowed to talk in class.'
Cheese, which is very smelly, is still good to eat.
Cheese which is very smelly is still good to eat.

Punctuation marks

We can define punctuation as marks beyond the normal, lower-case letters and numerals that accompany written text and indicate aspects of its meaning. There are 12 main punctuation marks in English, and we will describe the use of each of the following:

- capital letters;
- full stops;
- commas;
- semicolons;
- colons;

- apostrophes;
- inverted commas;
- question marks;
- exclamation marks;
- hyphens;
- dashes;
- brackets.

You should note that languages other than English use different punctuation marks. Even languages that use the same script system as English, such as French and Spanish, have slightly different punctuation: French has its accents, é, è, c¸ and â largely indicating variations in pronunciation; Spanish has a slightly different collection of accents, é and ñ, which indicate pronunciation and stress, as well as two unique marks, ¿, ¡ (like upside down ? and !), which are used before questions and exclamations.

Capital letters

There are a number of rules for using capital letters.

1. A sentence should always begin with a capital letter.
2. A capital letter should always be used for the pronoun 'I'.
3. Proper nouns always begin with a capital letter. These include:

> forenames – Anna
> surnames – Patel
> titles – Doctor Brown
> salutations in letters – Dear Sir
> countries – Poland
> continents – Europe
> nations – French
> races – Arabs
> towns and cities – London
> streets – Acacia Avenue
> houses – Rose Cottage
> geographical features – Mount Everest
> days of the week – Tuesday
> months of the year – February
> special festivals – Easter
> historical periods – The Renaissance
> organisations – The Amateur Athletics Association
> companies – Tate and Lyle
> political parties – The Green Party

4. Always use a capital letter with deities, religions and sacred books: God, Christ, Buddha, Allah, Christianity, Islam, The Bible, The Koran.
5. Always use capital letters for the main words of a title, but not for the articles and prepositions, unless they begin the title: e.g. 'Have you seen *Gone with the Wind*?'
6. Capital letters are usually used at the beginning of each line of poetry, even if this is not quoted in verse form: e.g. 'Now is the winter of our discontent Made glorious summer …'There are some poets, such as e.e.cummings, who omit capitals deliberately.

7. Capital letters are used to begin sentences in direct speech: She said, 'This is the way it should be.'
8. Always use a capital letter for the first word after the greeting in a letter:
    Dear Peter,
    We are sorry

Full stops

There are two main uses of full stops. The first, and most common, is to signal the end of sentences, unless these are exclamations or questions. As we discussed in Chapter 6, there is a tendency for commas to be used where there should be a full stop:

> *I am tired, I want to go to bed.*

This is known as a comma-splice and should be avoided. The example above is clearly two separate statements, which must be separated by a semicolon, a conjunction or a full stop.

> *I am tired; I want to go to bed.*
> *I am tired and I want to go to bed.*
> *I am tired. I want to go to bed.*

PRACTICAL TASK PRACTICAL TASK PRACTICAL TASK PRACTICAL TASK PRACTICAL TASK

Which of the following sentences is correctly written? Suggest changes to repair those which are incorrect.

1. John was feeling bored during the holiday, his cousin was invited to stay with him.
2. On the first morning of his visit they went fishing.
3. They had both had fishing rods as birthday presents.
4. By the end of the morning they had caught no fish, John suggested a walk along the bank.
5. A long line of stepping-stones stretched across the river.
6. The stones were wet and slippery.
7. John went first, his cousin followed.
8. John fell and knocked his cousin into the water with him.
9. The boys walked damply home.

The second use of full stops is to show when words have been shortened. These are called **'abbreviations'**:

> *B.C. – Before Christ*
> *Mr. – Mister*
> *Mrs. – Mistress*
> *a.m. – ante meridiem (before noon)*
> *p.m. – post meridiem (after noon)*
> *Dr. – Doctor*

You should note that, where such abbreviations have become very common, there is a tendency to omit the full stops. Few people nowadays would write BBC or FBI with their full stops. Some abbreviations have also lost their full stops because they have become words in their own rights. We call these **acronyms** and often no longer remember quite what the abbreviations stood for, for example radar (radio detecting and ranging) and NATO (North Atlantic Treaty Organisation).

If a sentence ends with an abbreviation, there is no need for an extra full stop.

They arrived at 8 p.m.
NOT They arrived at 8 p.m..

If abbreviations occur in a list or clause that would normally require a comma, then one should be used as well as the full stop.

At 3 p.m., nevertheless, we had to leave.

Commas

Commas are perhaps the most difficult punctuation mark to get right, largely because there is a degree of optionality about their use. The exhortation considered above, that a comma indicates a short breath, has also caused a good deal of confusion about the correct use of commas. The comma-splice is probably a direct result of this. There are nine main uses for commas, and additional optional uses.

1. Commas are used to **separate items in a list:**

    I bought bacon, eggs, butter and bread.

It is not usual to place a comma before the 'and' but this can be appropriate.

The two couples who went were Peter and Sarah and John and Jackie.

Here there is some confusion about the pairings and a comma after 'Sarah' would avoid this problem. Similarly:

For dinner I had fish and chips, bread and butter, and a cup of tea.

2. Commas are also used **to indicate a change of subject** in long sentences. In a short sentence such as the following, a comma is not needed.

    He was hiding but I could see him.

In a sentence with a similar basic construction, but much longer, the comma can be useful:

He could have tried harder to get on the train standing at the station, but his luggage was very heavy.

3. Commas are used **to mark off names and titles** of people spoken to:

    'Good morning, Mr. Harrison.'
    'David, can you lend me some money?'
    'Shut up, Bob, and sit down.'

4. Commas are used in direct speech **to mark the change from narrative to speech** and vice versa:

    'Mary,' he said, 'I think you had better go.'

Notice that the comma to signal the change from direct speech to narrative goes inside the inverted commas, whereas the comma signalling the switch back to speech is outside the inverted commas.

5. Commas are used **to mark a word or phrase in apposition**:

    Danny, Champion of the World, crept through the undergrowth.
    Joe, red in the face, ran out of the room.
    He rejected Gordon, the only boy who could have helped him.

The word or phrase in apposition could be removed from these sentences without destroying the sense of each.

6. Commas are also used **to mark off short asides**:

    I hate children, don't you?
    You are coming, aren't you?
    Well, it's not my fault.
    You know, you're not so bad after all.

7. Commas are used **to mark off phrases beginning with participles**:

    Crouching as still as possible, he watched the gateway like a hawk.
    The dead man, lying still on the ground, blocked the road.
    She marched ahead, beaming from ear to ear.

8. Commas are **used with non-restrictive adjectival clauses, as discussed earlier:**

    The class, who were very noisy, were not allowed to go to play.
    The class who were very noisy were not allowed to go to play.

The first sentence suggests we are talking about only one class, who happen to be being noisy. The adjectival clause adds information about this class but does not restrict the reference at all. The second sentence suggests there is more than one class, and it is the one which were noisy who are the subject. The second adjectival clause, therefore, restricts the reference. It is essential to the meaning and thus no comma is required.

9. Commas are **used with some subordinate adverbial clauses:**

    Although it was sunny, he took the bus home.
    He took the bus home although it was sunny.

In the first example, the main clause comes second and the reader needs to be alerted by the comma to the importance of what is coming. In the second example, the main clause has been passed when the conjunction is reached, so no comma is needed.

10. There are some **optional uses** of commas. For example, although we stressed earlier that saying that a comma indicates a short pause in a sentence was too simplistic, it is occasionally possible to use a comma **to create a pause** when you wish to emphasise a word or phrase:

    He took on the dangerous task, without hesitation.

The comma is not strictly necessary here but it does have the effect of emphasising the final phrase.

Again, even though it is not usual to **use a comma before 'and' or 'but'**, this can sometimes be helpful.

I went to see the new car and the old car broke down on the way.

The reader may momentarily think the writer was going to see both the new and the old car. A comma would prevent any niggling confusion here.

11. Commas can also be used after a fronted adverbial.

Disappointingly, the team was well beaten in the match on Saturday. (Adverb)
In spite of the weather, we will still be going to the beach tomorrow. (Adverbial phrase)
Although he knew it was hopeless, the soldier made one last effort. (Adverbial clause)

Semicolons

The semicolon has two uses.

1. To separate items in a list when the items are long:

There are three people I admire: my mother, for putting up with me for so long; my father, for putting up with both my mother and me; and my cat, for affecting not to notice any of us.

If this had been simply, *'There are three people I admire: my mother, my father and my cat'*, commas would have sufficed to demarcate the list items.

2. To link statements that are closely related:

Young men can play any game; older men have less choice. Birds can fly great distances; 200 kilometres is little to them.

The semicolons here are replacing full stops but are permissible when the two separate sentences are very closely linked. In the first example, the second sentence offers an idea that contrasts with the first. In the second example, the second sentence expands on the first.

Colons

The colon has three uses.

1. It is used **to introduce a list**:

You will need the following ingredients: eggs, flour, milk, cheese and bacon.

2. It is used **to introduce a statement that explains or exemplifies** what has just been said in the previous sentence:

Our cat is easily frightened: he always jumps at the sound of our doorbell. Crewe Alexandra will win the match: they have the better team.

3. It is used **when a complete sentence develops or explains another** complete sentence. In this case the colon takes the place of a full stop:

He wanted to go to bed: he was tired.
There were no eggs left: James had eaten them all.

PRACTICAL TASK PRACTICAL TASK PRACTICAL TASK PRACTICAL TASK PRACTICAL TASK

Try to punctuate these sentences correctly, using commas, semicolons and colons.

1. They were enemies nevertheless they loved each other.

2. The car was old and unreliable it was also rather uncomfortable.

3. The Mafia has one important unwritten law loyalty to the family.

4. My brother can't be trusted he told me it was Wednesday today.

5. The West prospers the Third World suffers.

6. I like her she makes me laugh.

7. Brutus dies at the end of the play however Antony does not forget the noble motives from which he acted.

8. There are several arrogant figures in the play Caesar who habitually refers to himself in the third-person Brutus who is so convinced of his own rectitude that he spares no thought for the feelings of others and perhaps Cicero who will not follow what other men begin.

Apostrophes

The apostrophe is probably one of the most misused punctuation marks. The following, genuine, notices were seen in a typical British High Street:

POTATOE'S – £2 A KG

The Sport's Store

The best burger in town – you'll love it's taste

The apostrophe has three uses, although the third is not universally accepted as correct.

1. The first use is to **show possession**: *The car belonging to the man = The man's car.*

   Though the use of the possessive apostrophe can look confusing, there is a simple rule (with only two exceptions).

   ### The apostrophe rule: add an 's on to the end of the possessor

   > *Mike = Mike's*
   > *children = children's*
   > *dog = dog's*

   The exceptions are as follows:

   ### Exception 1: if the possessor ends in a single s (not ss) just add an apostrophe.

   > *James =James'*
   > *boys = boys'*

   Note that words that end in a double s, conform to the first rule.

   > *boss = boss's*
   > *glass = glass's*

Exception 2: its (meaning 'belonging to it').

This possessive pronoun has no apostrophe. Only use an apostrophe when it's means 'it is':

> *The dog left its muddy footprints on the carpet.*
> *The dog always reminds us when it's hungry.*

Many expressions to do with time require apostrophes:

> *a day's work*
> *two days' sleep*
> *a week's holiday*

There is an assumption of possession in these phrases – 'the work of the day'.

Also, it is possible for the thing that is possessed to be understood without being stated. The apostrophe is still needed:

> *Let's go to Ben's (house).*
> *It's my father's (wallet).*

Note the following, however:

> *He is a friend of my dad's. WRONG*
> *He is a friend of my dad. RIGHT*
> *He is my dad's friend. RIGHT*

2. The second use of apostrophes is **to indicate omissions**, and apostrophes are used to mark the places where letters have been missed out, for a number of reasons.

Contraction	I do not – I don't
	he would – he'd
	who has – who's
	six of the clock – six o'clock
Shortening	telephone – 'phone
	omnibus – 'bus

Although correct, this type is rarely used now

To indicate pronunciation	'E 'ad an 'ard life'.
Dates	'76 was a hot summer.

3. Although they are often misused to **indicate plural forms** (see the notices above) apostrophes can some-times be used to do this.

> *Dot your i's and cross your t's.*
> *There are three 9's in 999.*
> *There are over 600 M.P.'s.*

Such usage does not command universal acceptance, however, although sometimes the alternative (e.g. *Dot your is and cross your ts*) does not look correct.

Inverted commas (speech marks)

Inverted commas are also known as '**speech marks**' or '**quotation marks**'. They are used to indicate direct speech. This is a term used to define words which are actually spoken by a character in a story or anybody else's speech that the writer needs to record. Of course, it has to be made clear to the reader when the person is speaking and when the writer is narrating. There are sentences within sentences that have to be marked off. There are four patterns possible with direct speech:

1. Speech first, narrative second: *'We are not amused,' she said.*

2. Narrative first, speech second: *She said, 'We are not amused.'*

3. One sentence of speech interrupted by narrative: *'We are not,' she said, 'amused.'*

4. Two or more sentences of speech divided by narrative: *'We are not amused,' she said. 'You couldn't make me laugh if you tried.'*

1. Speech first, narrative second: There is always a mark between speech and narrative. Only commas, question marks and exclamation marks can be used at this point in the sentence pattern. The inverted commas enclose both the spoken words and the punctuation that goes with them. A small letter follows the question mark and the exclamation mark as well as the comma, because the sentence as a whole has still not been finished.

2. Narrative first, speech second: There is a comma between the narrative and the speech. The inverted commas enclose the words spoken and the final full stop, which marks the end of the direct speech and of the whole sentence. The first word of the direct speech begins with a capital letter: the words spoken are a sentence in their own right.

3. One sentence of speech interrupted by narrative: This puts the above two sets of instructions together. The second part of the direct speech begins with a small letter because it is a continuation of the sentence.

4. Two or more sentences of speech divided by narrative: The direct speech is two separate sentences, so there is a capital letter and a full stop for each.

Inverted commas show where direct speech begins and ends. You do not need new inverted commas for each sentence within the speech:

'You're wrong,' she said. 'That's mine. Get your own. You're not short of money.'

Use a new line for a new speaker and for the next sentence of narrative following speech:

'Hello,' she said. 'What are you doing here?'
'Killing time,' he said.
Judy looked out of the window. She mumbled, 'And that's not all.'
Tom stared at her, boiling with anger.

Double inverted commas are sometimes used for direct speech and single inverted commas for all the other occasions when they are required:

"Have you read 'Harry Potter and the Goblet of Fire'? It's a brilliant book," she said.

This can sometimes produce interesting typographical entanglements:

"Have you seen 'Who's Afraid of Virginia Woolf?'?"

Single or double inverted commas are also used to pick out words and phrases that an author wants to particularise:

You have used 'emergent' in the wrong sense here.
'How do you spell "commitment"?' he asked.

Question marks

The question mark comes at the end of a sentence that asks a question. There is sometimes confusion stemming from lack of awareness of the difference between a direct and an indirect question. Look at these two sentences:

Are you confused?
He asked me if I was confused.

The first one is called a **direct question** because it actually expects an answer. The second is called **an indirect question** because it does not ask a question but reports the occurrence of one. The first requires a question mark. The second does not.

Exclamation marks

Exclamation marks are used when a special note of urgency is required:

'Shut up back there!' shouted the teacher.
'Help!'
'How brave you are!'

Remember that the exclamation mark has a built-in full stop so you cannot use another element of punctuation with it and must use a capital letter after it.

Hyphens

Hyphens are used for a number of purposes:

- Continuation of a word between two lines. In word-processed text this is usually done automatically, yet there are several rules that pertain.

Firstly, a hyphenated word must be divided between syllables. The break must be convenient and must not interfere with the pronunciation of either half of the word. Look at the following:

It is the first time in the history of this competition that someone has achieved a perf-
ect score.
It is the first time in the history of this competition that someone has achieved a per-
fect score.

The first of these sentences is more uncomfortable to read than the second because of the awkward hyphenation.

Single-syllable words cannot be divided.

- Making one word out of two or more other words. Many nouns that are now one word were once two words. Many phrases that are now two words will one day be one word. Many words are at an intermediate stage and require hyphenation. All of this is debatable. Which of the following are correct, for example?

  post box
  post-box
  postbox

Sometimes the choice is more obvious:

> *walking stick*
> *walking-stick*
> *walkingstick*

Hyphens can be used to form 'compound' adjectives out of two or more words (green-eyed, bow-legged, old-fashioned, etc.). Often they are vital to meaning:

> *a hard working person/a hard-working person*
> *a little used path/a little-used path*

- For some combinations of numbers. For example:

> *twenty-one*
> *forty-seven*
> *ninety-six*
> *twenty-seventh*
> *fifty-eighth*
> *seventy-seventh*

- To indicate range in dates and figures as well as routes and destinations. For example:

> *the 1914-18 war*
> *a car in the £20,000-£30,000 range*
> *the London-Bristol road*
> *the Dover-Calais ferry*

Dashes

A dash can be used to indicate a dramatic pause or a hesitation, or a pair can function rather like brackets in separating a clause or phrase from the rest of the sentence. Look at the examples:

> *'The man was lying on the floor, gun in hand – dead.'*
> *'What do you – no, you must – it's not my – where are you go–'*
> *'I went to town this afternoon – I know I shouldn't have done – and spent all this month's salary on clothes.'*

Brackets

Brackets can mark off additional information in a similar way to commas and dashes. Look at the following sentences, for example:

> *Melanie Jones, the team leader, gave last-minute orders before the game.*
> *Melanie Jones – the team leader – gave last-minute orders before the game.*
> *Melanie Jones (the team leader) gave last-minute orders before the game.*

All these are possible, but the phrase 'the team leader' becomes increasingly isolated from the rest of the sentence. Brackets are the most powerful of the three elements of punctuation above. Very often they are too powerful for the writer's purpose and should be used sparingly.

Bullet points

There are several different punctuation styles for bullet-pointed lists. It is very important to be consistent and use the same style throughout a document.

Most lists are introduced with a colon (:), not a semicolon (a common mistake). Occasionally, a list will be introduced by a sentence ending in a full stop rather than a colon. The writer needs to decide whether to make the first-level bullet points flushed to the left or indented in from the left. You also need to use the same type of bullet point throughout. The most common is the round black bullet point. For second-level bullet points, the most common are dashes or round hollow circles.

With lists that are made up of full sentences, use normal sentence punctuation, as in the following list.

Here are some tips for editing your writing:

- *Read your document the next day with fresh eyes.*
- *Read your headings separately to see if they are consistent.*
- *Ask someone else to read your document.*

Semicolons were traditionally used in lists to separate each bullet point, but although this is still correct, they are not used as often now. If you do use semicolons, the accepted practice, as in this list, is to:

- put a semicolon at the end of each point;
- use 'and' after the second-to-last point; and
- finish with a full stop.

Normally lower case is used for the first letter in each bullet point, and a full stop after the last bullet point.

Before you travel abroad, remember to:

- *make sure your passport is valid;*
- *find out if you need any vaccinations;*
- *check you have all your tickets.*

Microsoft Word has a different default setting to this, in which all lists begin with initial capitals, and this is becoming a widely used style. As always, consistency is important.

When the lists consist of single word or very short items, it is now usual not to use any punctuation marks at the end of each item.

In punctuating sentences, it is important to be:

- *accurate*
- *consistent*
- *careful*

A SUMMARY OF **KEY POINTS**

➢ **A sentence can often be punctuated in more than one way but the meaning of the sentence may vary with different punctuation.**

➢ **There are 12 main punctuation marks in the English language.**

➢ **Capital letters have many uses. A sentence always begins with a capital letter and the personal pronoun 'I' is always capitalised.**

> ➢ Full stops signal the end of a sentence and may also be used in abbreviations.
> ➢ There are nine main uses for commas and additional optional uses.
> ➢ Semicolons either separate longer items in a list or link closely related statements.
> ➢ Colons introduce a list or a statement that explains or exemplifies what has just been said, or is used when a complete sentence develops another complete sentence.
> ➢ The two main uses of apostrophes are to show possession and to indicate omissions.
> ➢ Inverted commas, also known as speech or quotation marks, are used to indicate directly reported speech.
> ➢ Question marks and exclamation marks indicate sentences that are not simple statements.
> ➢ Hyphens can be used to continue a word between two lines, to join two or to combine two or more words or numbers, or to indicate a range.
> ➢ Dashes can be used to indicate a dramatic pause or hesitation or used instead of brackets to separate parts of a sentence.
> ➢ Brackets can mark off additional information in a similar way to commas and dashes but are the most powerful of the three elements.
> ➢ Bullet-pointed lists can be punctuated in a variety of ways and a consistent approach is very important.

M-LEVEL EXTENSION > > M-LEVEL EXTENSION > > M-LEVEL EXTENSION

Having familiarised yourself with the 'rules' of punctuation, it would be useful at this point to examine some pieces of children's writing.

- What punctuation mistakes, if any, can you spot in these pieces?
- What misunderstandings about punctuation do these mistakes seem to suggest?

In particular, you might consider whether the children are using punctuation as a way of indicating intonation and phrasing or whether they have a more grammatical sense of its use. Devise a programme of activities to address any misconceptions.

FURTHER READING   FURTHER READING   FURTHER READING   FURTHER READING

DfE (2013) *Teachers' Standards*. London: DfE. (**www.gov.uk/government/uploads/system/uploads/attachment_data/file/208682/Teachers__Standards_2013.pdf**)

King, G. (2000) *Punctuation*. London: Collins Wordpower. A comprehensive and very humorous guide to English punctuation.

Truss, L. (2003) *Eats, Shoots and Leaves.* London: Fourth Estate. The best-selling book about punctuation. The fact that this description is not a simple oxymoron indicates something about the readability of the book.

Vandyck, W. (2005) *The Punctuation Repair Kit*. London: Hodder. A humorous guide aimed at Key Stage 2 children.

9
Cohesion: grammar at the level of the text

Curriculum context

National Curriculum programmes of study

This knowledge is designed to underpin the teaching of the Key Stage 1 and Key Stage 2 programmes of study for English, which state, for example, that pupils should be taught

in reading to:

- develop pleasure in reading, motivation to read, vocabulary and understanding by:
  - discussing the sequence of events in books and how items of information are related Y2
  - identifying main ideas drawn from more than one paragraph and summarising these Y3/4/5/6

and in writing to:

- draft and write by:
  - using a wide range of devices to build cohesion within and across paragraphs Y5/6
- evaluate and edit by:
  - assessing the effectiveness of their own and others' writing and suggesting improvements Y3/4/5/6
  - proposing changes to grammar and vocabulary to improve consistency, including the accurate use of pronouns in sentences Y3/4/5/6.

Early Years Foundation Stage

The Early Learning Goals specify that, by the end of the Early Years Foundation Stage, children should:

- follow instructions involving several ideas or actions;
- develop their own narratives and explanations by connecting ideas or events;
- write simple sentences which can be read by themselves and others.

Introduction

As we pointed out earlier, the popular view of grammar is that it is largely concerned with sentence structures. Grammar, however, operates at a wider level than this and includes the rules and expectations concerning how groups of sentences work together to form texts or discourse. In this chapter, we will look at the ways in which texts cohere and illustrate the importance of understanding this to provide appropriate help to learner readers and writers as they interpret and create texts.

The differences between spoken and written language

One of the mistakes often made when thinking about language is to assume that speech and writing are just two forms of the same thing, differing only in the medium of expression. Written language, however, is much more than spoken language that has been 'written down'. The differences between these media are historic in origin and mean that, in order to be a successful user of written text, one needs to have some understanding, albeit perhaps implicit, about how written language works.

Writing emerged to satisfy new communicative needs at a particular period of history. As societies became more and more complex, their organisational systems began to go beyond the here-and-now interchanges of speech. There was a need for permanent records, which could be referred to again and again, and writing developed principally as a means of satisfying this need. The contexts, therefore, in which written language tends to be used are very different from those in which spoken language is used. The reader is, in most cases, removed in both time and space. They read the text at a different time from when it was written, and in a different place. As a result, the language of the written text has to make greater allowances for the reader in order to facilitate understanding.

Written language does, in fact, perform many of the same functions as spoken language: to get things done (e.g. public signs, product labels), to inform (e.g. newspapers, advertisements), to entertain (e.g. fiction books, comic strips). These various functions of the written language are reflected in the characteristics of the texts themselves, observable within the sentences at the level of grammar, and beyond the sentences at the level of text structure. This creates the idea of 'style', which includes such areas as choice of vocabulary, layout, etc.

The characteristics associated with written text can sometimes occur in spoken language and vice versa. In other words, some spoken texts will be more like written texts than others, and some written texts will be more like spoken texts than others, depending on the purpose and the context. Look at the following two written texts. The first is a written note left for a parent and the second is from an academic text:

Mum,
Please can you make sure my blue T-shirt is clean? I need it for the disco tonight.
Thanks,
Kate xx

With so much emphasis on pair and group work in classrooms today, trust, openness,
and relationships between members of the group have become of vital importance.
Many classroom activities require students to reveal information about themselves,
their work, their private lives, their friends and family, and for many this may be a new
and somewhat alarming experience.

It is obvious that the second text is less like spoken language than the first. But how?
What are the features that make written discourse different from spoken language?

Linguistically, written text tends to be more complex, with longer sentences, more complex clauses and greater information load. There are good reasons for this. As mentioned
earlier, unlike spoken interaction, with written discourse there is no common situation:
the situation has to be inferred from the text. The words themselves must carry all the
shades of meaning that in spoken discourse could be conveyed by non-verbal behaviour.
The writer must make assumptions about the reader's state of knowledge. If incorrect
assumptions are made, then communication may be hindered.

These extra layers of understanding affect both readers and writers. Readers have to
be able to interpret the systems by which information is carried through written texts,
and writers have to be able to use these systems to create meaningful texts. By analysing written text, we are able to see the decisions that the writer has made, with regard
to how sentences are formed internally and combined with others externally, and how
assumptions regarding the reader's knowledge of the subject and ability to interpret the
text will play an important part in this process.

What makes a text a text?

PRACTICAL TASK PRACTICAL TASK PRACTICAL TASK PRACTICAL TASK PRACTICAL TASK

Below are ten sentences, but they are placed in the wrong order. Can you reorder them so that they
read as a piece of coherent written text?

(a) Eventually, he came to the rescue.

(b) A door led from the cells to the dock.

(c) The magistrates arrived at Warwick's No. I Court.

(d) It was jammed and nobody could open it.

(e) The court started its proceedings 20 minutes late.

(f) Jim Glossop, 39, was a defendant on a charge of assault.

(g) They were faced with an embarrassing problem.

(h) The police tried and an engineer tried.

(i) Still the lock would not open,

(j) He kicked the door open.

What helped you to reorder this text? You will probably agree that certain words helped, e.g. pronouns like *it, he, they,* conjunctions like still, *eventually.* Also, you had an expectation that the text would relate the events in chronological order.

Now try this one. Reorder the sentences:

(a) *A British Aerospace spokesman said: 'We are just very grateful that Mrs. Fuller was not more seriously injured.'*

(b) *'When I spoke to her later in hospital, she could only remember the dazzling lights.'*

(c) *Roy, 31, said: 'I was first on the scene and it was a terrible shock.'*

(d) *And last night, as air chiefs began an inquiry, concussed Julie was making a good recovery in hospital.*

(e) *Julie swerved around the tractor, but slammed into the plane's wing.*

(f) *She was about to pick up Roy when she was dazzled by the light of an oncoming tractor towing a Hawk training jet.*

(g) *Julie's fireman husband Roy raced to the crash scene to find her injured in the wreckage.*

(h) *Bruised motorist Julie Fuller was nursing her dented pride yesterday after smashing into a five-million-pound plane.*

(i) *'The car was badly damaged and she had head injuries.'*

(j) *Their car was a write-off and the jet's wing was damaged.*

(k) *Julie, 27, had been driving along the perimeter road of Surrey's Dunford airfield.*

(l) *But the couple's baby son Bryn luckily escaped unharmed.*

Which of these two reordering activities did you find more difficult to do? Why do you think this was the case?

You probably found the second reordering activity considerably more difficult than the first. Why? Once again, there were words/phrases that could help: the use of a full name followed by the use of a first name only; words like *she, he, their;* conjunctions like *and* or *but;* definite and indefinite articles, e.g. *a (five-million-pound plane)* and *the (plane);* the use of different tenses *(had been driving);* and the use of related vocabulary, e.g. *plane, jet* and *wing.*

You may have found that you had groups of sentences but were not sure how to order the groups. One of the reasons for this may be that the facts are not included in chronological order. The second text is a newspaper report and typical of newspaper reports is that they begin with the main fact – in this case that Julie smashed into a plane and is now in hospital – and then describe the details – the damage to the plane and the people involved, and how the crash happened – before finishing with comments – both personal and official. In this case, knowledge of the information structure of newspaper reports of this type, as part of an awareness of the genre, helps reconstruction of the text.

From these activities it seems clear that there are certain rules or regularities that people follow when creating written text. These rules depend on the context, or the situation that gives rise to the discourse, and within which the discourse is embedded. But there are two different types of context: the linguistic context –the language that surrounds or accompanies the piece of discourse under analysis – and the non-linguistic context within which the discourse takes place, for example the type of communicative event (newspaper report, letter or note); the topic; the purpose; the participants and the relationships between them; and the background knowledge and assumptions underlying the communication. Roughly speaking, we can refer to the linguistic elements of discourse as **cohesive** items, and the interpretation that the reader brings based on non-linguistic context as the establishment of **coherence**.

Texts contain text-forming devices – words or phrases that enable the writer to establish relationships between the clauses and sentences of a text, and which help to tie the sentences together. These devices may be grammatical or lexical. They are clues or signals as to how to interpret the text, but not absolutes. In the first text, 'they' could refer either to the magistrates or to the police and engineer, but our interpretation of the text, based on our own knowledge that magistrates are probably less likely than the police to put their shoulders to the task of knocking down a door, guides us to the correct interpretation. In other words, cohesive devices are guides to coherence. Coherence is something created by the reader in the act of reading the text and is the feeling that a text hangs together, that it makes sense, and is not just a jumble of sentences. Take, for example, the following two sentences:

Clare loves potatoes.
She was born in Ireland.

These are cohesive (the 'she' in the second sentence links to 'Clare' in an obvious way), but they are only coherent if one already shares the stereotypical ethnic association between being Irish and loving potatoes, or is prepared to assume a cause-effect relationship between the two sentences. Cohesion and coherence in written texts are not, therefore, the same thing. We will come back to this point later in the chapter.

What is cohesion?

Cohesion, as defined by Halliday and Hasan (1989, p4), *occurs where the interpretation of some element in the discourse is dependent on that of another.* In other words, it is the linguistic glue that makes parts of a text stick together. Cohesion operates both within and across sentence boundaries and texts generally consist of chains of cohesive links forming a complex web of meaning relationships. As an example of this complexity, look at the following, relatively simple, extract from a children's novel.

'Let's start at once,' said Roger, but at that moment the kettle changed
its tune. It had been bubbling for some time, but now it hissed quietly
and steadily, and a long jet of steam poured from its spout. The water
was boiling. Susan took the kettle from the fire and emptied into it a small
packet of tea.

The links within this text that are most obvious are, as with most texts, the noun-pronoun sequences. The 'its' in lines 2 and 3, and both occurrences of 'it' in line 2 refer back to the kettle and understanding these references is crucial to understanding this text. The 'it' in line 4 also, most probably, refers back to the kettle, repeated immediately before in the same sentence. It could, however, also refer to 'water' in line 3. Such ambiguous reference will not matter here since, even if a reader 'reads' the 'water – it' reference, this will not make an appreciable difference to their understanding of the text overall. There are, however, texts in which such ambiguity *could* make a difference to understanding.

There are other, more subtle, links here. 'Tune' in line 2 leads to 'bubbling' and then 'hissed', both exemplifications of the changing nature of this tune. All these then link to 'jet of steam', which explains the origin of these phenomena. 'The water was boiling' then provides further explanation and 'fire' adds to the sequence. Neither of these items makes full sense by itself, but only in the context of the others.

Cohesive ties

Halliday and Hasan (1976) offer a comprehensive analysis of cohesion and identify four broad categories, which may be further subdivided:

Categories of cohesive ties	Reference	Substitution and ellipsis	Conjunction	Lexical
Subdivisions	Personal Demonstrative Comparative	Nominal Verbal Clausal	Additive Adversative Causal Temporal	Reiteration Collocation

Reference

These are the cohesive devices in a text that can only be interpreted with reference either to some other part of the text or to the world experienced by the sender and receiver of the text. Reference items include pronouns (personal reference), demonstratives and the article 'the' (demonstrative reference), and items like 'such as', 'more' and 'as much' (comparative reference).

Here are some examples:

- *Personal reference* is achieved by means of personal pronouns, possessive pronouns and possessive adjectives.

  ... she has knitted together folk, pop and country in her songs.
  It will be released in the New Year.

Who do 'she', 'her' and 'it' refer to?

If we have access to the context in which the sentences appear, we can answer these questions with no problems.

  Since Nanci Griffith began recording 16 years ago, she has knitted together strands of folk, pop and country in her songs. She is about to hit 40, divorced and nomadic. And so for her twelfth album she has focused on personal reflection and made a work of striking beauty. The album was recorded in Tennessee with the help of other renowned country musicians. It will be released in the New Year.

In this example, 'she' and 'her' and 'it' all refer back to something previously mentioned in the text: to Nanci Griffith and to the twelfth album. These are cases of personal reference referring **anaphorically** (i.e. backwards) to something previously mentioned.

Now look at the following examples. Who do 'he' and 'her' refer to in the following sentences and in what way do these reference items differ from those in the previous sentences?

He was called 'The Voice Beautiful' when a student at drama school, and Ralph Fiennes, on the phone to me, certainly lived up to the name.

In her tight blue dress and red high heels, Kate Moss stepped out of the taxi and walked towards the door of The Nitecap Club in downtown Chicago.

'He' refers to Ralph Fiennes and 'her' to Kate Moss, but notice how in these examples the reference items point the reader forwards – they draw us further into the text to find the elements to which the reference items refer. This is **cataphoric** reference and is sometimes used by authors for dramatic effect, to heighten the suspense, conveying a message of 'read on and find out'.

- **Demonstrative reference** is expressed through demonstratives *(this, that),* the definite article and the adverbs *here, there, now,* and *then*. For example:

One section of the book that seems weaker than others concerns establishing trust. <u>This</u> is, indeed, an important area, as a negative group atmosphere is often the result of feelings of insecurity.

On the way out she dropped her wallet near the door. Fortunately the shop assistant saw it lying <u>there</u> and picked it up.

Here, 'this' refers back to 'establishing trust', and 'there' to 'near the door'.

- **Comparative reference** is expressed through adjectives and adverbs and serves to compare items within a text in terms of similarity or difference.

'Circle Time' is an activity designed to change the relationship between the teacher and the children. It involves asking those children who have something to say to contribute. <u>Such</u> an activity has therefore a dual purpose.

Three hours is insufficient for this amount of work. You will have to allocate <u>more</u> time.

'Such' and 'more' are examples of comparative reference.

In all the above examples of reference, the reference items all referred (anaphorically or cataphorically) to a referent mentioned in the text: that is, they were text-internal. But it is also possible to refer 'outwards' from texts to identify the referent, in cases when backward reference does not supply the necessary information. Such outward, or **exophoric,** reference often directs us to the immediate context, such as when someone says 'leave it on the table please' about a parcel you have for them. Sometimes the referent is not in the immediate context but is assumed by the speaker/writer to be part of a shared world, in terms either of knowledge or experience. In English the determiners often act in this way:

The government is to blame for unemployment.

It would be odd if someone then asked the question 'Which government?' as it is assumed by the speaker that the hearer will know which one, usually 'our government' or 'that of the country we are in'. Exophoric references like these will often be culture bound and outside the experience of those not belonging to the culture.

Substitution and ellipsis

Whereas reference indicates a semantic relationship between two items, substitution is more grammatical in nature. A word, phrase or clause is substituted in a following sentence for one with a similar grammatical function. Look at the following short text:

Car <u>tyres</u> eventually wear out, of course. New <u>ones</u> have to be fitted.

'Ones' here is used as a substitute for 'tyres'. In this case, because it is a noun that is substituted, this is referred to as **nominal substitution.** In English this kind of substitution is often achieved by the use of 'one' (or 'ones') or 'the same', and, as with reference, these can be anaphoric or cataphoric. Look at the following examples:

> *My school was in the next village, over two miles away, and, although we could afford <u>one</u>, we didn't have <u>a car</u>.* (cataphoric – the substitution occurs before the noun)

> *There were <u>ghosts</u> in that old house. I had to admit I'd never seen <u>one</u>, but I knew they were there.* (anaphoric – the substitution occurs after the noun)

In the next example, it is a verb phrase that is substituted, and this is referred to as **verbal substitution**:

> *Some animals <u>feed their young with milk</u>. Animals that <u>do this</u> are called mammals.*

Various forms of the verb 'do' frequently substitute for other verbs in English.

Sometimes, much more extensive sections of text are substituted, as in these examples:

> *The teacher said to me, 'Well, now <u>you should be able to complete this exercise by yourself</u>.' 'I hope <u>so</u>,' I replied rather uncertainly.*

> *Has everyone <u>gone home</u> already? Surely <u>not</u>.*

Such **clausal substitution** often uses 'so' or 'not' as the substitute.

Another type of cohesive tie that operates in very similar ways to substitution is **ellipsis**. Look at the following example:

> *They walked slowly along the path that wound between the rocky outcrops. On one side they could trace the course of a dried-up stream, and on the other a broken wall rose from time to time.*

Most readers will have no problem recognising that the second sentence could read:

> *On one side of the path they could trace the course of a dried up stream, and on the other side of the path a broken wall rose from time to time.*

To avoid the inelegance of repetition, words have been omitted in the first version of this sentence. This phenomenon is known as **ellipsis** and, as can be seen in this example, appreciating how it works is crucial to understanding the text. The reader has to be able to supply, almost subconsciously, the missing words to make sense of the sentence. When ellipsis occurs, something is presupposed and, as the words are not physically present, they have to be supplied by the reader.

Conjunction

Conjunction differs from reference, substitution and ellipsis in that it does not set off a search backward or forward for its referent. It is not anaphoric or cataphoric. However, it is a linguistic cohesive device in that it signals a relationship between segments of the text. Halliday (1985) suggests four broad categories:

- *Additive conjunctions* simply add on a sentence or clause as if it were additional information or an after-thought – *in addition, furthermore, for instance, besides.*
- *Adversative conjunctions* draw a contrast between the clause or sentence they introduce or are contained in and the preceding clause or sentence with which they form a cohesive relationship – *however, yet, on the other hand, nevertheless.*
- *Causal conjunctions* make a link of cause or consequence between two clauses or sentences – *therefore, as a result, hence, because.*
- *Temporal conjunctions* make a time link, usually of a sequential nature – *finally, next, subsequently, after that.*

REFLECTIVE TASK

To check your understanding of these types of conjunctions, try to classify the underlined words in each of the following sentences according to the type of conjunction they represent. Try to do this **before** looking at the answers below.

(a) *Furthermore, I think there is little chance we will be successful in this.*

(b) *I will try to answer your question next.*

(c) *He was delayed in traffic, hence missing the train.*

(d) *The solution, therefore, is to make sure you get there early.*

(e) *Besides, he cannot really have expected to win that game.*

(f) *Your ideas, on the other hand, I find very challenging.*

(g) *My only reservation, however, concerns my ability to do this on time.*

(h) *Finally, we come to the question of your payment.*

The answers are as follows:

(a) Furthermore	*additive*
(b) next	*temporal*
(c) hence	*causal*
(d) therefore	*causal*
(e) Besides	*additive*
(f) on the other hand	*adversative*
(g) however	*adversative*
(h) Finally	*temporal*

In speech, four basic conjunctions – 'and', 'but', 'so' and 'then' – tend to be more used than any other. However, in many types of written discourse, a much greater variety of conjunctions will be found, as writers use different styles to suit their audience and purpose.

Lexical cohesion

Lexical cohesion occurs when two words in a text are semantically related in some way – in other words, they are related in terms of their meaning. Halliday and Hasan (1976) identify two major categories of lexical cohesion: reiteration and collocation.

Reiteration may be of four kinds:

- The same word may be repeated in succeeding sentences.
  There was a large <u>tree</u> growing in the meadow. From the top of that <u>tree</u> you could see for miles.

- A synonym or near-synonym of a word may appear in a following sentence.
  I began my <u>ascent</u> of the hill. The <u>climb</u> was quite easy and I reached the top in less than two hours.

- A word may be replaced in a following sentence by another that is superordinate to it.
  William has bought himself a new <u>Jaguar</u>. He practically lives in the <u>car</u>.

- The word may be replaced in a following sentence by a word that describes a general class of objects.
  'What shall I do with all this <u>shopping</u>?'
  'Just leave the <u>stuff</u> there.'

There are a number of these general words that have a cohesive function in texts. Words such as 'people' and 'person' refer to humans, words such as 'creature' refer to non-human living things, and words such as 'thing' refer to inanimate objects.

Reiteration is extremely common in English texts in which there is little direct repetition of words, and often considerable variation from sentence to sentence. Such variation can add new dimensions and nuances to meaning, and serves to build up an increasingly complex context, since every new word, even if it is essentially repeating or paraphrasing earlier words, brings with it its own connotations and history. Reiteration does not occur by chance. Rather, writers and speakers make conscious choices whether to repeat, or find a synonym, or a superordinate.

Collocation refers to the cohesive relationship between pairs of words that commonly occur next to each other in some recognisable meaning relation:

  bread and butter
  fish and chips

There are many examples in English, and in other languages, of words that are statistically more likely to occur close to each other. Implicit knowledge of these likelihoods makes the reading of text a much less strenuous activity since words can often be predicted from their collocates in advance of their being actually seen.

It has been argued that lexical cohesion is the most important form of cohesion, accounting for approximately 40 per cent of the cohesive ties in a text. It also appears that the number of lexical relationships between the clauses or sentences of a text will be directly related to the cohesiveness of that text.

Why is understanding cohesion important?

The material so far in this chapter should have convinced you that, even in apparently simple texts, there is a depth of complexity in the ways in which ideas and meanings link together.

As a teacher of reading, you need to recognise the complexity of what you are teaching, that is, the ability, albeit implicit, to recognise and respond to the elements in a text that make it more than just a collection of unrelated short sentences. Any model of reading must take account of the processing of complete texts, since this is how the majority of reading is done.

RESEARCH SUMMARY RESEARCH SUMMARY **RESEARCH SUMMARY** RESEARCH SUMMARY

There is evidence that many children find aspects of cohesion difficult to grasp and that their difficulties with it affect negatively their understanding of their reading. Chapman (1987, p49) has summarised the evidence on these issues from research and suggests the following:

- The ability to perceive and process cohesive ties is associated with reading proficiency and comprehending.
- The perception of cohesive ties is subject to a developmental pattern.
- This developmental pattern relates to types of ties, so that a typical order of perception among young children progresses from reference, lexical cohesion, substitution/ellipsis to conjunction.
- The number and types of cohesive ties in a text affect recall after reading that text.
- There are gender differences in the abilities of children to handle cohesive ties efficiently.
- Ties are handled to different degrees of efficiency depending on the register of the text.
- The relationship of cohesion and register to text comprehension is affected by cultural knowledge, assumptions and beliefs.

Studies from outside the discipline of education have also found significant effects of text cohesion on reading speed and comprehension. Liu and Rawl (2012), for example, found a significant increase in the reading comprehension of cancer patients when the pamphlets they were asked to read were deliberately written to include high levels of text cohesion.

PEDAGOGICAL LINK PEDAGOGICAL LINK **PEDAGOGICAL LINK** PEDAGOGICAL LINK

Anderson (1992, p40), building on the work of Chapman, suggests a range of classroom strategies to enable children to focus on and develop their proficiency with cohesion in texts. These strategies include the following guidelines for readers faced with complex texts:

- Look carefully at the connectives, particularly those that link sentences. Are the relationships in meaning between the sentences clear?
- Sometimes the order in which the sentences are presented implies a relationship. Does this occur in this passage?
- If the vocabulary is unfamiliar, this may be because unfamiliar synonyms have been used. Use a thesaurus to check alternatives for some of these.
- When in doubt, resort to reading aloud. The intonation pattern may help to clarify the meaning.

Coherence

In this chapter, we have outlined the ways in which a text is a cohesive entity. Cohesion, however, does not necessarily mean **coherence**. Texts can be cohesive without being coherent and vice versa.

Read the following passage. Your study of this chapter should instantly convince you of its cohesion.

> *Eric bought a car. The car in which my Aunt Mary was riding along Downing Street yesterday was green. Green has an /i:/ sound. You sound weird today. Tomorrow I'm going to Paris. Paris loved Helen. Proper names have certain semantic functions. I can't make head nor tail of semantics. If you are born with a pig's tail, you're cursed!*

This passage has texture as Halliday and Hasan (1989) define it, that is, a range of cohesive relationships within and between the sentences. The passage comprises a set of sentences that constitute a text because of the following cohesive markers: a car–the car, green–Green, sound–sound, today–Tomorrow, etc. These connections, or cohesive 'ties', bind the text together and help us interpret every single sentence as a whole. But is cohesion sufficient to identify any one 'passage' as a text? Why is it that we have been unable to exact any coherent (that is, at the text level) meaning from reading this passage?

According to Halliday and Hasan, a passage must exhibit some of these cohesive relationships in order to qualify as a text; otherwise, it is reduced to a mere list of sentences. Nevertheless, they agree that it is the *meaning relationships that are constitutive of texture* (1989, p71). It is hard to perceive a coherent set of meaning relationships between these sentences, although we almost instinctively try. Cohesion is a necessary, but not sufficient, condition for 'textness'.

If cohesion does not automatically guarantee coherence, is the reverse relationship true? Are coherent texts always cohesive? Look at the following example:

> *Jill: The phone's ringing.*
> *Jack: I'm tired.*

In this case, there are no explicit cohesive markers to bind these two sentences together. It seems that Jack has totally disregarded, or failed to interpret, the meaning of Jill's utterance. Nevertheless, in our everyday lives, we often engage in this sort of conversational exchange with few, if any, difficulties.

As a reader, we naturally assume that these sequences of sentences do constitute a text and we interpret the second sentence in the light of the first sentence. We assume that there is a semantic relationship between the sentences. Perhaps Jack's reply indicates that he feels he always has to answer the phone and wants Jill to do it on this occasion. Or perhaps Jack knows who is on the other end of the phone line and does not want to talk to this person this late at night.

What has happened here is that these seemingly unconnected sentences have been made to form a coherent text, but only by the reader supplying 'real world knowledge'. Making sense of any text involves interpretation and depends to a great extent on what the reader brings to the text. The reader has to rebuild the world of the text, see into the mind of the writer, using their experience of that world. The reader has to activate their background knowledge, make inferences and constantly reinterpret as new information is provided. Look at the following two sentences:

> *John was on his way to school last Friday.*
> *He was really worried about the Maths lesson.*

Ask yourself: Who is John? What is he carrying?

Your answers will probably be that John is a schoolboy and he is carrying his schoolbag with his books in it. But read on:

Last week, he had been unable to control the class.

Now ask yourself the same questions: Who is John? What is he carrying? Your answers will be different as you will have adjusted your interpretation in the light of new information: John must be the Maths teacher and probably he has a briefcase with his lesson notes in it. But, read on:

It was unfair of the Maths teacher to leave him in charge.

You have to abandon your previous interpretation yet again, but now you are at a loss as to how to answer the question: Who is John? A teacher of another subject? Read on:

After all, it is not a normal part of a caretaker's duties.

Everything is clarified! When we read, we construct an interpretation by using more than is explicitly given in the text, and drawing on our background knowledge. This is **schema theory** – a theory of language processing, which suggests that discourse is interpreted with reference to the background knowledge of the reader or listener. The reader brings to the text their schemata; a set of knowledge structures which are activated by interaction with the text.

Although an appreciation of how cohesion works to produce texts is a vital factor in understanding what one reads, it is not, therefore, the only essential ingredient to this. Readers need also to bring to bear previous knowledge and experience. The teacher's job is to develop both these sources of knowledge for reading.

A SUMMARY OF **KEY POINTS**

➤ An understanding of cohesion is useful for teachers attempting to develop children's reading of connected prose.

➤ Written language is different from spoken language because the contexts in which it is used are very different and often much more formal and complex.

➤ In some texts, facts may not be included in chronological order, for example in newspaper reports.

➤ Cohesion operates within and across sentence boundaries, and texts consist of chains of cohesive links that identify meaning.

➤ There are four categories of cohesive ties: reference; substitution and ellipsis; conjunction; and lexical; each of which has two or more subdivisions.

➤ By itself, cohesion is not sufficient to ensure coherence, i.e. sense, in a text. Reading also involves making connections between the material of a text and one's own world experience.

M-LEVEL EXTENSION > > M-LEVEL EXTENSION > > M-LEVEL EXTENSION

Look again at the four types of cohesive tie, and at their subdivisions. Choose a year group of children and decide on a programme of texts that will help them to identify the different types of cohesion as they further their study of text structure and organisation. You may find it helpful to discuss this aspect with teacher colleagues and with an experienced subject leader for Literacy.

FURTHER READING FURTHER READING FURTHER READING FURTHER READING

Anderson, E. (1992) *Reading the Changes.* Buckingham: Open University Press. An overview of research and development in the literacy field with a good section on the implications of cohesion theory.

Chapman, J. (1987) *Reading From 5-11 Years.* Buckingham: Open University Press. A useful review of research into developing reading, with a substantial section on the implications of cohesion.

DfE (2013) *Teachers' Standards.* London: DfE. **(www.gov.uk/government/uploads/system/uploads/ attachment_data/file/208682/Teachers__Standards_2013.pdf)**

Halliday, M.A.K. and Hasan, R. (1989) *Language, Context and Text Aspects of Language in a social-semiotic perspective.* Oxford: Oxford University Press.

Liu, C. and Rawl, S. (2012) 'Effects of Text Cohesion on Comprehension and Retention of Colorectal Cancer Screening Information: A Preliminary Study'. *Journal of Health Communication: International Perspectives*, 17: sup. 3, 222–40.

10
The Qualities of Stories

Curriculum context

National Curriculum programmes of study

This knowledge is designed to underpin the teaching of the Key Stage 1 and Key Stage 2 programmes of study for English, which state, for example, that pupils should be taught

in reading to:

- develop pleasure in reading, motivation to read, vocabulary and understanding by:
  - listening to and discussing a wide range of stories at a level beyond that at which they can read independently Y1/2/3/4
  - continuing to read and discuss an increasingly wide range of fiction, poetry, plays, non-fiction and reference books or textbooks Y5/6
  - being encouraged to link what they read or hear to their own experiences Y1
  - becoming very familiar with key stories, fairy stories and traditional tales, retelling them and considering their particular characteristics Y1/2/3/4
  - increasing their familiarity with a wide range of books, including myths, legends and traditional stories, modern fiction, fiction from our literary heritage, and books from other cultures and traditions Y5/6
  - recommending books that they have read to their peers, giving reasons for their choices Y5/6

o identifying themes and conventions in a wide range of books Y3/4/5/6
o recognising simple recurring literary language in stories Y2

- participate in discussion about books that are read to them and those that they can read for themselves, taking turns and listening to what others say Y2
- participate in discussions about books that are read to them and those they can read for themselves, building on their own and others' ideas and challenging views courteously Y5/6
- explain and discuss their understanding of books, both those that they listen to and those that they read for themselves Y2/3/4/5/6.

Early Years Foundation Stage

The Early Learning Goals specify that, by the end of the Early Years Foundation Stage, children should:

- listen to stories, accurately anticipating key events and respond to what they hear with relevant comments, questions or actions.

Introduction

Trainee teachers need to know a lot about imaginative literature for children – especially stories. This is because stories provide ideas and models that relate not just to reading but also to speaking and listening and to writing.

Analysing different kinds of fiction requires knowledge of some literary critical procedures and understanding of some technical terms. Making judgements about different kinds of fiction is a highly subjective operation and takes us into the realms of opinion, taste and even prejudice. One person's great book is another's turkey! In order to make judgements some criteria are needed and this, too, presents problems. Any criteria depend entirely on the purpose for which the judgements are being made and a particular story might be excellent for supporting some aspects of required teaching but very poor at supporting others.

What is sure, however, is the value of fiction in children's cognitive learning and in their personal development. From the Early Learning Goals through to Key Stage 2 – and beyond – a wide experience of both reading and working with stories is advised. Why should this be? What is so important about stories? The answers to those questions open up many issues.

REFLECTIVE TASK

Read Andrew Davies' frank and funny account of his reactions to reading *Tom Sawyer* as a primary school child. It is to be found in *Children's Literature in Education*, March 1997, Vol. 28 (1): 3–10.

Now recall a book that was important to you during your primary school years and try to list some of the qualities that made it special for you. What implications do your memories have for you as a teacher selecting books for children?

Why are stories important?

Stories are important for teachers and children for many reasons – some pedagogic and some personal. Here are some of the reasons.

• To satisfy curiosity – we want to know what happens next.

It is a common technique in primary classrooms to provide children with the opening of a story and then ask them to continue it. The opening may come from anywhere – newspaper cuttings, TV programmes, fairytales, jokes, books, even – if all else fails – out of the teacher's own head. But the important thing about the opening, whatever its source, is that it should catch children's interest and make them want to carry the story on – to provide an account of what happens next.

That is probably the most important thing about reading stories as well as writing them. They catch our interests and imaginations and they make us want to know what happens next. We may be disappointed in the way that some stories develop; we may be puzzled; we may be surprised; we may be delighted; we may be entranced; but the underlying urge for reading stories is to find out what happens next. We get interested in the people and in the situations and we want to know who are the winners and who are the losers in their outcomes. That response to stories is one of the reasons why they are so important to teachers. They are natural arousers of interest and, as any teacher will agree, it is much easier to teach interested children than uninterested ones.

• To help us make sense of the world.

What made you want to become a teacher? What made you pick this book up? What are your plans for the future? The answers to all those questions are a series of causes and effects. They are stories. We all think in stories. We make sense of events in our lives by telling stories about them. We really know that the way we live is not neat and tidy with a convenient beginning and a middle and an end – except for birth and death. But within that universal beginning and end there is likely to be a very confused, and confusing, and a very individual middle. If your life is typical of most people's it is probably very messy indeed. Things overlap and get disorganised and messy.

Nonetheless, we insist on trying to impose some kind of order on the mess and the order we impose is the order of story. We spend much of our time with stories – exchanging tales and gossip, reading newspapers, watching the TV, dreaming and fantasising. We tell stories to ourselves and others about what has happened to us – and through stories we test out possibilities about what might have happened or what might happen in the future. Stories are the way we try to make sense of the vast range of amorphous, often unrelated experiences that we have. We organise it, shape it, give it a starting point and an ending point, and try to give it a coherent shape that real life events don't really have. We turn aspects of our lives into an enormous number of stories. In that sense, everybody is a story maker if not a story writer, and reading stories gives us, and children, valuable models, both structural and linguistic, for the creation of our own.

• To experience the world vicariously – by sharing and perhaps learning from the experiences of others.

When writers write their stories they often draw on their own experiences or on those of other people for raw material. They might need to make a few adjustments for particular narrative purposes or to avoid libel actions, but real experience generally is at the heart of stories. That's why many writers keep notebooks to jot down scraps of dialogue or to note interesting situations or aspects of behaviour. They want to use what they can from real life to make their books sound true. Even in fairy or fantasy stories there needs to be some sense of reality in what characters do and why they do it; of cause and effect. Readers have to believe that, in the world the story presents, the characters would behave in the way that the author tells us they do behave. One common reason for a reader abandoning a story is that it is too daft – it could never happen.

Stories, therefore, provide readers with access to a vast databank of other people's experiences from which they might learn in the living of their own lives. Indeed, some people find it easier to understand life better from the stories of other people than from their own personal experiences. By spending time in school with stories – helping children to become sophisticated readers and makers of stories – we are helping them to understand life as it is lived by others and perhaps making them wiser human beings.

- To put us in touch with a common culture.

Stories contribute to a literary culture that forms an important thread in any social fabric. They are one of the bonds that tie us together. Virtually every child born in Britain shares a vast story heritage. You will, for instance, have little trouble in immediately completing all of these titles and the list could probably be extended into hundreds: *Jack and the...? Harry Potter and the...? Alice...? Charlie and...?* The reason you can do that so easily is that the stories in question have been either listened to or read by you and all of your peers at some point in your lives. You share a great many narrative points of reference.

Stories also give us access to a world tradition – an international multicultural narrative culture. Stories, particularly folk and fairy stories that happen 'Once upon a time' and therefore out of the present, and in lands far away and therefore non-existent lands, give us a shared humanity. The same stories and characters – or very similar ones – crop up over and over again in widely disparate cultures. *Rumpelstiltskin,* first collected and written down by the Grimm brothers in Germany, is none other than our very own *Tom-Tit-Tot,* first collected and written down by Joseph Jacobs in Suffolk. *Anansi the Spider Man* – with his cheerful resilience and constant assertion of the power of the ingenuity and imagination of the little person over brute strength and stupidity – who began his life in Africa before being taken, as *Anancy,* to the Caribbean with the slave trade and then emigrating to Britain in the 1950s, is instantly recognisable as both *Aunt Nancy* and *Brer Rabbit* from the southern states of America.

Out of this similarity between characters comes a similarity of themes. Many fairy and folk tales from all cultures, for instance, are moral in purpose, underlining that children (especially little girls) should be aware of the many dangers around them. The sensible course of action for them is to do as sensible adults – particularly mothers and fathers (though not *step*mothers and *step*fathers!) – tell them to do. The woods, the forests and the jungles contain all sorts of nasty possibilities and if children don't do as they are told then they are likely to be imprisoned by witches, eaten by wolves or, as in an African story, swallowed by drums! There are all sorts of complex symbols at work in fairy and folk tales, which give them a meaning far deeper than their surface one. Such stories also provide lessons in what positive qualities to cultivate – qualities like kindness, generosity and compassion – particularly to humble people and to animals. The spider that you do not tread on could easily turn out to be the king of the spiders with remarkable powers to have on your side in an emergency; the toad you are nice to might just turn out to be a handsome prince under a spell; and the old lady you meet gathering sticks in the forest might be your fairy godmother. There is no doubt that stories like these give us a shared humanity, and as Britain becomes increasingly multicultural the range of stories that forms part of its culture constantly extends.

• To help to improve children's literacy.

Children should develop through the key stages not only in the range of stories that they are familiar with but also in their ability to read them, understand them and respond to them. Stories provide a great deal of the raw material for work at word, sentence and text level to enable children to develop their understanding of and skills in phonics, grammar, levels of meaning and the linguistic and structural conventions of a range of genres. Stories give children material with which to extend their ability to use a range of strategies for reading and responding.

Stories have long been regarded as a key element in developing children's literacy. Most preschool children have stories read to them, and hearing and responding to stories is one of the key elements of the Early Learning Goals. It is well known that many young children want to learn to read so that they can read stories for themselves and not rely on a willing adult. Unfortunately, many reading schemes contain custom written 'stories' that are not particularly interesting in their own right, but form part of the scheme because they use and reuse certain words in sentences of a preordained length. They have controlled vocabulary and grammatical structures. This obviously limits a writer's range and the result is that many reading scheme stories are very dull compared with the real stories that children read for themselves and have read to them.

RESEARCH SUMMARY RESEARCH SUMMARY **RESEARCH SUMMARY** RESEARCH SUMMARY

Gordon Wells' (1985) longitudinal project on children's language development at home and at school pointed out the role of stories in developing children's literacy skills and their abstract thought processes. Children most successful in literacy tests at ages 7 and 11 could all be positively identified as having had experience of stories told or read to them before beginning school. Wells argued that the process of understanding the world presented by stories obliges children to use decontextualised language by creating a world inside their heads.

He made even stronger claims for the importance of stories by arguing that they contribute very positively to children's wider learning. His research evidence supported the view that in order to understand a story a child has to pay particular attention to symbolic language. This requires high levels of cognitive thought. The child who listens to or reads stories regularly spends more time using these high levels of thought than the child who does not. In other words, stories make children smarter.

• To help children extend their knowledge and experience of language forms.

It is generally through stories that children get their introduction to written language. Like spoken language, written language is complex and has many forms, but it is often very different from spoken language. A writer is aware that all a reader has available to help them make meaning is the text itself – the words and the pictures on the page. There can be no help from intonation, repetition, emphasis, gesture or any of those other aids that spoken language often calls on. In written language, therefore, vocabulary is often much more precisely selected, structures are more formal and grammatical rules and conventions are more rigorously adhered to than in spoken language. This is not easy for children to learn, and stories provide interesting and satisfying models of one form of written language in action.

Stories also have their own narrative conventions which are peculiar to them and which must also be learned because children don't meet them in their other day-to-day language experience. Nobody actually says or even writes 'Once upon a time' or 'They all lived happily ever after', for example, in any context other than stories – unless they are deliberately referring to story conventions.

RESEARCH SUMMARY RESEARCH SUMMARY **RESEARCH SUMMARY** RESEARCH SUMMARY

In her detailed analytical study of the stories told by five children between the ages of four and five, Carol Fox (1993) demonstrated that the children had all acquired an understanding of the way that stories operate structurally and linguistically. She called this modus operandi a 'story grammar'. She argued that the children had made this acquisition so early and painlessly because they had all had a great many stories read to them in their preschool years.

- Because they have the propensity for giving children great pleasure.

This is a reason that teachers must not forget as they work hard to cover the curriculum. The pressure to raise literacy standards is intense and, unless teachers are careful, there is the possibility of seeing stories in school as little more than a means of reaching that particular end. However, for some of the reasons already given, that should not be the case. Stories have enormous potential for enriching people's lives and teachers must take care not to limit that potential by treating stories as just a vehicle for skills teaching.

A parent tells the tale of her six-year-old, a story lover, who was asked what story she would like at bedtime. She chose one, but then asked her mother, 'Please just read me the story, mummy. Don't make me talk about the cover.'

What are stories?

The answer to that question may seem self-evident. They are accounts of events – real or imaginary. Because they are accounts, they tend to be chronological – the order in which events happened is the order in which they are narrated. They involve people doing things in places. In other words, they have characters and actions and settings. The things that the people do and the way they relate to one another form the sequence of events in the stories and constitute the plot. The plots of good stories have a significance that goes beyond the simple 'what happened next?' They are about something. They have themes. Betsy Byars' books have splendid plots, characters and settings – the things that happen and the people to whom they happen are interesting and powerful and funny – but that is by no means all there is to them. The books do not stop at plot level. A book like *The Eighteenth Emergency* may relate the events that arise from the arresting circumstance of what happens when a sensitive, arty and very engaging boy labels a picture of a prehistoric man with the name of the school bully – unaware that the bully is behind him as he does so – but it also presents some ideas and some questions to the reader about the nature of fear and how it can be coped with and about friendship and social relationships. This exploration of ideas and the raising of questions together constitute the themes of the book, which are presented through the plot.

Stories tend to be told in the third person (he/she/they) by a narrator who knows everything about the events and the characters – including what they are thinking and feeling – and tells us in all the detail considered appropriate. Normally these narrators like to keep their heads down and simply tell the story. They are not generally part of it. However, some writers do like to get involved. If we take two immensely popular writers for children, we can see two quite different approaches to this issue. Enid Blyton never becomes part of a story. Hers is the narrative voice simply recounting what happened to Noddy or the Famous Five or the Old Saucepan Man. We never get to know much about Enid Blyton herself from the texts, beyond what is implicit in the kinds of things she chooses to describe, the kinds of language she chooses to describe them in and her presentation of the characters she chooses to create. Roald Dahl, on the other hand, can never remain in the background for long and he regularly shoulders his way into his stories he tells in order to speak to the reader directly and in his own voice. Such is the power of his presence that he almost becomes a character in the stories in his own right. The famous opening to *The Witches* is an example of this.

The last two paragraphs suggest what stories 'tend' to be. But creative writers (and some of our very best and most creative of writers use their talents to write for children) are constantly looking for unfamiliar and intriguing ways of telling stories. So the statements made in the paragraphs are by no means invariably true. Stories do *not have* to have a single plot line presented chronologically. There can be more than one plot line with a number of sub-plots being developed, or flashbacks to the past or visions of the future. Nor do they *have* to be told in the past tense by an omniscient narrator. Stories can, for example, be told in the first person (I or we) past tense with the narrative voice being that of one of the characters. In other words, the author is choosing to speak through one of the characters in the story. Of course, the author is still writing the story and is in control but considers that the story gains something by letting one of the characters appear to be doing the writing work for them – assuming the narrative voice. Anne Fine's *Goggle Eyes* is an example of this technique. In *Double Act,* Jacqueline Wilson (a constant experimenter with a variety of narrative voices) has two narrators, Ruby and Garnet. They are a pair of identical twins each with their own perspective on events in the story – and much of the story is told through direct addresses to the reader, conversation (in which the respective characters are differentiated by print font), notebook jottings and cartoons. Jacqueline Wilson's own narrative presence is minimal though, of course, she wrote everything, so her authorial presence is total. In Florence Parry Heide's and Judith Gilliland's *The Day of Ahmed's Secret* (brilliantly illustrated by Ted Lewin) there is an extreme rarity – a first person narrative but told in the present tense.

Passing the responsibility for telling the story to one of the characters in it certainly has some advantages. It helps the reader to understand the character of the storyteller more thoroughly; it makes for greater immediacy because the reader is brought much closer to the events of the plot by having the information provided by somebody who is apparently part of it; and, because of increased immediacy, it perhaps gives a greater sense of realism. But against that, a writer has to consider that authorial omniscience has been lost. Because characters and events in the story are only seen through one person's eyes, we can never know how another person truly sees events and thinks or feels about them. The storyteller/character has no means of knowing this. Only the author can know because they are making up the story, but the author has chosen to put the story into the mouth of somebody else and so has no individual voice. It is in stories told through one of the characters that we can most clearly see the difference, which exists in all stories no matter how they are told, between the voice and views of the author and the voices and views of the characters in the plot.

PRACTICAL TASK PRACTICAL TASK PRACTICAL TASK PRACTICAL TASK PRACTICAL TASK

Read at least three books by different 'significant children's authors' in which you consider different narrative techniques are being used and analyse those techniques. If your knowledge of stories for children is limited at this stage and you are stuck for inspiration you might try stories by Anne Fine, Philip Pullman and Jacqueline Wilson. Note particularly the verb person and tense of the story, the possessor of the narrative voice, and the extent of the author's involvement. Decide why you think the author has chosen to adopt the particular technique in the story, the advantages and disadvantages of the technique and which of the three books you prefer. If you are feeling particularly creative, take the opening of one of the three books and rewrite it from a different point of view by using a different narrative voice.

Story genres

Stories come at us in a variety of forms and a variety of types. As far as forms are concerned we can have, amongst others, picture books, pop-up books, make-your-own story books, books with holes through them, books with tabs to pull, buttons to push and flaps to lift, and straightforward, common or garden narrative books. As objects they can be short and fat, long and thin, multicoloured or plain, very small and, of course, big. Amongst the types there are fairy stories, fables, myths, mysteries, adventure stories, school stories, fantasy stories, science fiction stories, funny stories, tragic stories, historical stories, futuristic stories and many more. These types of story are all **genres** of story and have their own characteristic generic language and narrative styles.

Consider these two openings:

> *Once upon a time there was a little girl called Goldilocks. One day she was walking in the forest. She had been walking for a long time and was tired and hungry. To tell the truth, she was lost. Suddenly she came into a clearing. In the clearing there was a little house. Goldilocks walked up to the house to see if anybody was at home.*

> *We get back late on Tuesday and I have a reccy round the living room and kitchen. Something is wrong. I try to tell the others. 'Look/I say', 'somebody's been in here. You got eyes. Use them. Look at the evidence. That porridge! Tampered with. Yeah? That chair! Busted. Right? See them strands of yellow hair around the place. Look at us. Three brown bears. Anybody here got yellow hair? Speak up. I'm talking to you. Anybody? Nope. Nary a yellow hair between us. For all you bears know we got a serial killer sleeping upstairs on one of our beds. Somebody's been in here when they got no right and I mean to find out who.'*

They are, of course, both telling the story of *Goldilocks and the Three Bears* but they are telling it in different ways. The first is the more traditional of the versions with its instantly recognisable 'Once upon a time' opening, its omniscient narrator, its imprecise setting in place and time, its vague and rather suspect landscape of little girls walking alone and getting lost in dark woods, its very simple sentence structure and its past tense, chronological narrative.

The second is more like a detective story. It plunges us straight into the action but does not have an omniscient narrator. It is told by one of the characters and therefore has the advantages and disadvantages of first person narrative discussed earlier. The sentences are again short but this time not for simplicity but in order to give pace. The opening uses a lot of direct speech and the language is very informal with grammatical errors and slang words. It uses phrases that we generally associate with crime and criminals.

You may prefer one opening to the other but this is a matter of personal taste. They are generically different and the language and the structures and the narrative devices that are used help to define this generic difference.

PRACTICAL TASK PRACTICAL TASK PRACTICAL TASK PRACTICAL TASK PRACTICAL TASK

For this task, use the three stories that you read for the previous task. This time classify each story generically. Is it a love story, adventure story, fairy story, myth, legend – or what? Your response to this will almost certainly, and quite rightly, be to classify the story according to its content. But now go on to examine the stories for their language and their narrative styles and find words, phrases or narrative techniques that seem to you to be typical of the particular genre of the particular book.

Story structures

Whatever genres they are written in and whatever their linguistic differences, stories tend to have a similar overall structure. They have what is sometimes referred to as a **story grammar**. The shape, if not the detail, is consistent and they work in the same very general ways. Teachers are required to know these general ways in order to be able to talk with children about details of stories and in order to help them with their own story writing.

Aristotle famously wrote of the need for plays to have a beginning, a middle and an end – by which he meant that there should be a clear starting point, a coherent and comprehensible development, and a satisfying conclusion. Teachers often make the same requirement of children in their story writing – but that is not particularly helpful if the children are not well informed about the language of beginnings, about the ways of cohesively linking aspects of the story in a development or about the linguistic indicators of endings. Stories can help to provide young readers with this kind of knowledge through modelling it.

It may seem obvious to say that stories have to have an **opening**. But, obvious or not, they do. Readers need some indication very early on of when and where a story takes place and who is in it – of **time, setting** and **character**. If a writer withholds that information for very long then readers become exasperated.

The simplest kind of opening is undoubtedly the classic fairy tale one which often performs all three functions in one simple sentence and may go something like:

> *Once upon a time, in a far-off land, there lived a rich king.*

Everything is there in splendid economy. When? 'Once upon a time' – a marvellously evocative phrase that has no precise meaning but gives a mysterious sense of some time out of time. Where? 'in a far-off land' – a similarly imprecise phrase that gives the story an exotic feel and removes it safely from the boundaries of normality. In far-off lands anything can happen, and, in this story the reader hopes, will. Who? 'a rich king'. The adjective and the noun combine to tell us all that we need to know about this fellow. He has all the power that money and status can give, but our knowledge of stories tells us that money and power will not be enough to prevent some rum things happening to him as the story takes its course and he will probably find that money and power do not always make for an ordered and trouble-free existence. Such openings are brilliantly effective because they plunge the reader into the situation with maximum clarity and minimum fuss. Most modern writers choose to work in a more sophisticated way and concentrate on one of the issues – setting or character are the likeliest – and then they fill in other details as they become relevant or necessary.

The opening to a story goes under several pseudonyms depending on which genre theorists you want to trust. It is known in some places as the **'Orientation'** or the **'Exposition'**. Others, who regard the events of a story as a kind of hiccough in the normality of things, see this part of a story as **'The State of Equilibrium'**. This suggests that the situation at the beginning of a story is about to change – as, of course, it undoubtedly will. Otherwise there is no story.

The opening of a story is often the most difficult part of a story for children to read (and for writers to write) because it tends to contain the most information and the least action. The scene has to be set in some way and the situation and characters established. Most stories, as we have seen, are told in the third person and it is often in the opening that the authorial omniscient narrative voice is most clearly heard – before the events of the story kick in and the plot gets under way. The opening, therefore, establishes the relationship between writer and reader. It tells you what kind of a person the writer is and suggests what kind of person the writer thinks the reader is. It is important that they are going to get on together and the opening is the preliminary testing ground. It needs great care. Many books are thrown down, never to be picked up again, because the reader finds the opening to be dull and uninspiring.

After the opening, things start to happen and there is generally a moment when we realise this. It may be known as the **'Inciting Moment'** and it is signalled linguistically in phrases like 'One day', or 'now it happened that'. There are other names for this point in a story, like 'crisis' or 'problem'. It is the moment when the state of equilibrium is about to be threatened, when normality starts to become abnormality. It is the moment when the wolf springs from behind a tree to speak to Red Riding Hood on her way to her grandmother's house, the moment when Alice leaves the boring security of the river bank and her sister's side to follow the white rabbit, or when Charlie finds Mr Willy Wonka's last golden ticket. Bruner (1986), who sees the structure of story as essentially a trip away from the normal into the abnormal – and then back again – in fact refers to this moment as the **'breach'**. Others talk about **'complicating action'** or **'disruption'**. Call it what you will, it is an important moment in the structure of a plot because it is where events start to move and the story starts to get up a head of steam.

After the inciting moment, the action becomes more involved in a plot through the **'Development'** stage. There are further crises, problems, complications and disruptions, which interrelate in the narrative structure and which the writer has to present as clearly but as interestingly and vividly as possible. The development stage of more complex stories generally contains a number of events or episodes. Little Red Riding Hood has her various transactions with the wolf dressed up as her granny, Alice moves from wonder to wonder, each becoming 'curiouser and curiouser', and Charlie has his adventures with the assortment of terrible kids in Mr Wonka's chocolate factory. The development stage is almost always the largest section in a story.

When the development is complete and the whole plot is about to be rounded off, there is often a moment when something happens that makes the **ending** of the story possible. The wolf has his mouth open to eat up Little Red Riding Hood when the woodcutter leaps through the window with his axe poised; Alice, now up to her normal size, contemptuously sweeps aside the playing card courtiers; and Willy Wonka makes Charlie a present of his chocolate factory. These moments are moments of **'denouement'** when the reader can sense that the ending is coming up. An alternative term for this moment is **'resolution'**, and after this moment we generally are bundled helter skelter into the **'ending'**.

The 'ending' is precisely what Aristotle considered it should be – that part of the story where all complications are resolved and redressed, normality is restored and the events of the plot are concluded. Other terms for this point in the story are 'redress', 'reinstatement', 'conclusion' or 'coda'. The world at the end of the story is not quite the same as the world at the beginning. The wolf is dead, Alice is wiser and Charlie is richer, but the hiccough of abnormality is over and everybody can live happily ever after – a phrase, which, significantly, ends so many fairy tales. They probably won't, of course, because that is not the way of life but we, as readers, won't know because this particular story is finished. New but generally untold stories would certainly affect the characters if they had any existence at all outside a writer's imagination or a reader's head or if they had any substance at all beyond words and pictures on a page.

PRACTICAL TASK PRACTICAL TASK PRACTICAL TASK PRACTICAL TASK PRACTICAL TASK

Use one of the books that you read for the previous two tasks and examine the narrative structure carefully. Decide what the author is establishing in the opening (Time? Place? Setting? Character?) and determine where the 'Inciting Moment' is to be found. Decide whether the development presents a single strand plot or whether there are one or more sub-plots. How many episodes can you identify in the development stage? Determine the point of 'Denouement' in the story and how the writer re-establishes normality in the ending.

Evaluating and making judgements about stories

Here is where we hit tricky territory because literary judgement is ultimately a very personal matter. Even when the same evaluatory criteria are applied to a piece of text, different people's conclusions about its quality can vary enormously. If that were not the case and everybody thought the same, then the world would be a duller place, argument about books would disappear and literary critics would be out of a job! So all anybody can do is remember the criteria, apply them honestly and make their own judgements on the basis of their responses. It should be remembered that it is possible to appreciate the authorial qualities of writers without actually liking their work much. What is important is to keep an open mind and perhaps look again at the work of writers to whom others react differently from you.

Here is the opening of a book for Key Stage 2 primary children:

> *Jackson was thin, small and ugly, and stank like a drain. He got his living by running errands, holding horses, and doing a bit of scrubbing on the side. And when he had nothing better to do he always sat on the same doorstep at the back of Paddy's Goose, which was at the worst end of the worst street in the worst part of the town. He was called Jackson, because his father might have been a sailor, Jack being a fond name for a sailor in the streets around Paddy's Goose; but nobody knew for sure. He had no mother, either, so there was none who would have missed him if he'd fallen down a hole in the road. And nobody did miss him when he vanished one day and was never seen or heard of again.*
>
> *It happened when Christmas was coming on – about a week before. Dreadful weather, as hard and bitter as a quarrel. Dreadful weather, with snow flakes fighting in the wind and milk freezing in the pail.*
>
> *Jackson was out in it, sitting on his doorstep with his hands cupped together just above his knees. There was a whisker of steam coming up from his mouth and another from between his hands. It wasn't his soul going up to heaven, it was a hot pie from a shop round the corner where he'd been scrubbing the kitchen since before it was light.*

> *Fair's Fair by Leon Garfield (1981)*

This is a splendid opening for a number of reasons.

First, the setting, situation and character are established quickly and vividly enough to seize readers' interest and make them care what happens next. It involves them quickly. Who, where and when are clearly defined – though the reader is not told but has to deduce the Christmas of roughly which year the writer is referring to. There are enough clues in the text, though, to make this a comparatively simple job. An enormous amount of basic information is packed even into the first paragraph and readers will want to know more.

Second, the writing is vivid, direct, imaginative and original. There are similes and metaphors that are lively and new. The weather is conveyed in a very effective simile: 'as hard and bitter as a quarrel'. The snowflakes' movements are presented in the vivid metaphor 'fighting in the wind' and the steam from the pie becomes a metaphorical 'whisker'. There are no flat character stereotypes or puddingy writing in image-free simple sentences here. This is a writer who is taking language by the scruff of the neck and making it work for him spectacularly hard. Images are arresting and vivid. Sentences attack and grab the reader with their rhythm – 'the worst end of the worst street in the worst part of the town' – and their balance – 'It wasn't his soul going up to heaven, it was a hot pie from a shop round the corner'. This writing is being done by a real writer who is not remotely interested in how many words he's got in a sentence or making sure that the vocabulary he uses is phonically consistent. He simply wants to write what he wants to write as effectively as he possibly can in his own individual style.

Third, the story so far is likely to begin to stir some vague feelings in the reader. It's funny, but there is menace there too. Jackson is due for disappearance. How? When? Why? This opening tells us that the book is going to entertain but is probably going to raise some questions as well. We may never have met him but we trust the writer of these words to continue to interest and involve us. He sounds a very entertaining chap who is prepared to treat readers without patronisation and as intelligent human beings. We want to read on.

However, that very same opening may affect some readers quite differently and stun them into boredom. Ultimately the decision is always going to be subjective and depend on personal taste and experience. Readers are never all going to like exactly the same things. There is much debate amongst literary critics about precisely how texts carry meaning. A shared view in the debate is that meaning exists in the relationship between the words on the page and the life experiences and attitudes of the reader. The words are always the same. The reader is not. A country-born child almost certainly reacts differently to Dick King-Smith's stories of farm life than does a town-born child because the reactions are coming from different experiences and understandings. A town-born child might well think the notion of a pig acting as a sheep dog in *The Sheep Pig* both unlikely and ridiculous. A country-born child might not be so dismissive, knowing the intelligence of pigs, and be more interested in the particular breed of sheep that are being rounded up. In this sense if no other, reading is a very active process. There can never be complete agreement over the value of texts because readers are all different. However, it is very helpful if teachers can justify their own reactions to a book as a model for when children are required to do this, and there are some criteria you might start from. Remember, though, that different readers might well come to quite different conclusions in responding to the very same criteria.

Criteria for evaluating stories

Appropriateness

As children mature, their interests inevitably change. It is important that teachers are able to choose books that are appropriate in terms of subject matter and language to the children with whom they want to read the book. This is not always as easy as it sounds. Picture books, for example, are often thought of as the appropriate form for Key Stage 1 children and no higher. But a book like Raymond Briggs' *Fungus the Bogeyman* is clearly not appropriate for Key Stage 1 and not just because of the nature of some of the jokes. There is no problem with the snot and slime stuff – Key Stage 1 children are as at home with snot and slime as anybody else! There are other contextual, linguistic and practical reasons. Such reasons include the range of the references in the book, the difficulty of the language, the variety of fonts, the size of the print, the complexity of the layout and even the colour of the text and the pages. All of these combine to make it a very difficult book to read physically. It is often enjoyed for the first time by Key Stage 3 or 4 pupils or even adults. A book like Maurice Sendak's *Where the Wild Things Are* poses some difficulties of level and appropriateness because, though its word count is small, its sentences are short, its pictures are large and its central character is a child – appearing to make it an obvious Key Stage 1 text – the sophisticated relationship between the pictures and the words and the complexity of the themes being explored make it perhaps more appropriate for Key Stage 2. Many of Judy Blume's books, like *Are You There, God, It's*

Me, Margaret, use vocabulary and sentence structures that are very simple and apparently make them ideal texts for Key Stage 2 children, but the themes generally appeal to a rather older reading audience and some Key Stage 2 teachers are not always comfortable in working with the books with still immature children.

It is certainly important that stories do not patronise children in terms of language and content, but, on the other hand, they should not be over challenging or they will not be read or enjoyed. Nor should stories for children patronise them in terms of morality or sentiment. *Charlotte's Web* is a very tough book. From the outset, Wilbur the pig is threatened with slaughter because he is the runt of the litter. He is protected and saved by the unlikely combination of a little girl, a rat and a spider, but Charlotte the spider dies. The book pulls no punches about the harsh realities of daily existence and has remained immensely popular with children because of that (even though they often cry at moments in the book – as do their teachers!).

Social awareness

This phrase, together with its companion – 'political awareness' – is often used as a term of mild derision as though to attempt to present class, culture and gender in unbiased and unstereotypical ways was unworthy and absurd. However, it is important that books for children do reflect the world in which they live and not that in which some adults think they live and teachers need to consider this aspect of any books that they choose to work with.

Much literature for children written before 1950 is middle class in its values and attitudes, all white in its characters, and shows clear expectations of the way boys and girls should behave and the interests they should have. The world has moved on since Hurree Jamset Ram Singh at Greyfriars (Frank Richards in the Bunter stories might at least have checked out Hindu and Sikh names!), the Swallows and Amazons on the Norfolk Broads or the Cumbrian Lakes (though at least the girls in the Arthur Ransome books are forces to be reckoned with for the most part) and even the wonderful William Brown and his boy band of Outlaws in rural village England. This is not, of course, to say that all those stories now have no value. They are generally well crafted, splendidly vigorously written and thoroughly entertaining (especially the William stories), but they all portray a world that is no longer experienced by the vast majority of children. This can well be an issue to be considered by teachers should they wish to read those books with children.

More modern writers are generally at pains to be more accurate in their portrayals. Bernard Ashley, for instance, writes of working-class children in state primary and secondary schools as they really experience them, Anne Fine returns regularly and brilliantly to themes of gender roles and expectations, and children of different ethnic origins now assume their place quite naturally in the work of virtually every realistic writer for children. If they do not, then teachers need to question the usefulness of the story to their class.

Plot and themes

The plot of a story is what really holds the interest. It is mainly the plot that stimulates a reader's curiosity and the desire to read on in order to find out what happens next. Teachers need to make judgements about whether the plot of a particular story is appropriate to the children with whom they intend to read it. This certainly does not mean that a story has to reflect directly the lives that the children in question live. Stories are wonderful vehicles for extending and enriching children's experience vicariously. It does mean, though, that the events and relationships in a story need to be comprehensible to children given their age and stage of intellectual and emotional development, and that it is constructed and told in such a way that it not only entertains, excites and intrigues children but it says something that is worth saying. This is not always an easy judgement to make given the range of children in most primary school classes and the fact that some stories make different appeals at different ages. The events of Ted Hughes' *Iron Man,* for example, a story magnificently constructed and told, can be understood by children as young as five, but its true complexity is probably not grasped by children until they are at the top end of Key Stage 2.

RESEARCH SUMMARY RESEARCH SUMMARY **RESEARCH SUMMARY** RESEARCH SUMMARY

This is not strictly an academic research summary but refers you to a key article by a 'significant children's author' about his own view of his best known story. In *Children's Literature in Education,* (1970) Vol. 1 (1) pp55–70, Ted Hughes considers the meaning of *Iron Man.*

His book, he argues, is about the human need to come to terms with its own darker side and to put its energy to creative use, rather than try to destroy it. Iron Man himself – with his enormous power for destruction – is first befriended and understood by Hogarth, the child hero of the story, and subsequently makes his spectacular contribution to bringing the Space Bat Angel Dragon into harmony with humanity. This is not a set of ideas easily grasped by a Key Stage 1 class but does demonstrate that stories can make demands of their readers at deeper and deeper levels as underlying themes become relevant to them.

As we have seen, good stories go beyond mere plot and it is important that the themes they explore are also relevant and comprehensible to the children. This does not mean that they have to be simple or comfortable. *Charlotte's Web* is neither of those, nor is the best work of Philippa Pearce or Philip Pullman. Even 'fun' and funny and apparently very simple writer/illustrators like Pat Hutchins, Babette Cole or John Burningham produce extraordinarily theme-rich texts. Mere escapism in books that offer nothing beyond their plots is fine in moderation. It accounts for the continuing enormous popularity of Enid Blyton, but children are far more likely to read this for themselves at home and teachers need to supplement it in school with stories that go beyond mere escapism.

Characters

In a famous phrase, E.M. Forster wrote of 'flat' characters and 'round' characters in literature. By 'flat' characters he meant characters who remain exactly the same throughout a book. By 'round' characters he meant characters who change and grow as a story progresses. The best stories for children (as for adults) are largely peopled by round characters – characters who are described so carefully and who behave so convincingly that they live and breathe on the page and whom the reader actually gets to care about. This can happen at any level of book. With the sparrows, we implore Peter Rabbit to exert himself to escape from Mr McGregor's net because we like him and we don't want him to die, and at the end of the story he is a different, much chastened bunny from the one who paraded around and tempted fate in his new blue jacket at the beginning. We just know that he will never go stealing carrots from people's gardens, against his mother's express instructions, ever again. He has grown and changed. At the end of Mark Twain's story, Huckleberry Finn is a sadder and wiser figure than the one who, admittedly rather grumpily, agreed to play Tom Sawyer's childish games of adventure-story brigandry at the beginning. In both cases, the characters are so skilfully created and presented that children of appropriate age can easily identify with them and share their experiences.

Language

An author makes characters and events accessible to the reader and draws the reader into a story through language. Sometimes language can be effectively used and sometimes not. A most obvious requirement is that the language an author uses must be appropriate for and comprehensible by the child audience. Again, this does not mean that the children should not be challenged, but if the difficulty of the language means that the children cannot decode it, or have to go scurrying to the dictionary every two minutes to check for meaning, then the language is not appropriate. Sometimes, of course, the context of a word can make it comprehensible, and sometimes authors can explain a word's meaning by other means. When Beatrix Potter announces in the first sentence of one of her books that the effect of eating too much lettuce is said to be soporific, she quickly goes on to say that personally, she has never felt sleepy after lettuce. Sometimes the meaning of every word is not overwhelmingly important because the story itself is so intriguing that individual words do not matter all that much – as long as the general gist is clear.

However, in the best stories, the language is not only comprehensible; it is rich and inventive. Similes and metaphors are imaginative. The story writer tells the story and expresses the thoughts and feelings of the characters in vivid ways. When characters speak, they speak in ways that seem realistic, with something of the rhythms of real speech and using vocabulary, phrases, idioms and structures that seem appropriate to the speaker. Any of the stories meant for primary school readers by Philip Pullman give clear examples of this.

Illustrations

Illustrations can serve many purposes in stories. They can simply freeze a moment, show a character, enhance a mood, or help children to decode words by providing additional information and context. In the best picture books, however, the pictures add meaning by complementing the words or by relating in witty or ingenious ways with them. In Pat Hutchins' *Rosie's Walk,* for example, the pictures tell quite a different story from the words so that the reader gets two stories for the price of one. Anthony Browne's words are often very simple but the accompanying pictures present quite a different and surreal world and need to be lingered over to pick up all the visual jokes. In John Burningham's 'Shirley' books, the pictures on either side of the central gutter illustrate quite different but co-existing states of being. The important thing about illustrations is that they should have vitality, imagination and freshness. Again, these adjectives mean quite different things to different teachers, and their own judgement in relation to the children they are teaching becomes crucial.

The book as an object

No matter what the quality of the story, there are matters of presentation that are important to children – and to adults for that matter. Books need to be visually attractive, with an appropriate size of font and a reader-friendly layout. This is particularly important for primary school early readers because where pages are cluttered or the print too small with too many words to the line, a reader's interest and enthusiasm soon wane.

PEDAGOGICAL LINK PEDAGOGICAL LINK PEDAGOGICAL LINK PEDAGOGICAL LINK

Children pick up a book first because they are interested in it as an object. Publishers know this and ensure that the cover is bright, colourful and attractive. If books are displayed in classrooms or school libraries with the spine out, then the attractiveness of the cover is lost. Try to make sure that as many books as possible – and particularly the ones you are recommending at any particular time – are displayed so that the publisher's hard work can be put to use and the covers can be seen.

PRACTICAL TASK PRACTICAL TASK PRACTICAL TASK PRACTICAL TASK PRACTICAL TASK

New writers for children are constantly appearing. It is important that teachers keep up to date. There are a number of ways of doing this and a list of possibilities follows. Make sure you do at least one of them.

- Visit a bookshop regularly and browse in the children's section.
- Visit a library regularly. Browse and ask advice from the children's librarian.
- Read reviews of children's books: there are specialist journal publications, the *TES* and Sunday broadsheet newspapers have reviews, the bookseller Waterstone's produces a yearly *Guide to Children's Books* and Penguin publications has its own *The Good Book Guide to Children's Books.*
- Look regularly at the books that specialist book clubs or publishers are offering. Letterbox Library lists form a particularly up-to-date and multicultural source of information.
- Listen to children's views. Children introduced most teachers to Harry Potter!

Teacher interest

As well as ensuring that the stories you choose for your class meet all of the above criteria, remember that you will make it more interesting for children if you like the text yourself.

No teacher ever made a book interesting for children when she didn't like it herself.

A SUMMARY OF **KEY POINTS**

➤ Good stories are natural arousers of interest and curiosity.

➤ They provide a framework for organising experience and an opportunity for extending it.

➤ They provide access to a national and international cultural heritage.

➤ They contribute to the development of literacy and of the capacity to learn.

➤ They extend children's knowledge about language.

➤ They give pleasure and should never be seen just as vehicles for teaching skills.

➤ Stories are accounts of events that fall into several genres.

➤ They may be told in a variety of ways though their basic structure is similar.

➤ There are a number of criteria that can be used to evaluate stories. These criteria relate to plot, theme, characters, language, illustration and layout.

M-LEVEL EXTENSION > > M-LEVEL EXTENSION > > M-LEVEL EXTENSION

Any work with children and stories depends on a teacher's knowledge of texts. This does not just mean knowing about the language, structures and narrative devices of stories; it means knowing who are the good writers most likely to stimulate your class. That, in turn, means reading a lot of stories for children. This task is a long-term one. It is to read at least one book for children every month for the rest of your training and teaching career. This is a minimum requirement. It would be far better to read more stories more often, but other matters sometimes press. Start to build up your own lists of stories that you have evaluated following analysis of the key features, as described in this chapter, noting which age groups you feel they will be best with. Start with the three books you worked on in the Practical Tasks and add to the list as often as you can.

FURTHER READING   FURTHER READING   FURTHER READING   FURTHER READING

Applebee, A.N. (1978) *The Child's Concept of Story.* Chicago, IL: Chicago University Press. This is a book which is a modified version of a PhD thesis and is therefore both technical and academic. It provides illuminating insights, via case studies, into the way that primary children develop in their acquisition of story grammar, although, leaning heavily on the work of Vygotsky, it does tend to go into rather more complex analytical detail than most teachers really need.

Bettelheim, B. (1989) *The Uses of Enchantment.* New York: Random House. Here Bettelheim examines some of the meanings and interpretations of a range of folk and fairy tales as well as the contribution that they make to children's cognitive, emotional and social development.

Davies, A. (1997) 'Tom Sawyer'. *Children's Literature in Education,* 28(1): 3–10. An amusing account of the author's reactions to reading the book as a primary child.

DfE (2013) *Teachers' Standards*. London: DfE. **(www.gov.uk/government/uploads/system/uploads/attachment_data/file/208682/Teachers__Standards_2013.pdf)**

Hughes, T. (1970) 'Myth and Education'. *Children's Literature in Education,* 1 (1): 55–70. A key article by a significant children's author giving his own views about the meaning of his story *The Iron Man.*

Sanger, K. (1998) *The Language of Fiction.* London: Routledge. Sanger explores a great many issues about the relationship between a writer, a text and a reader. He is particularly good on the way characters are constructed and interpreted with a special consideration given to uses of description and dialogue.

11
The qualities of poetry

Curriculum context

National Curriculum programmes of study

This knowledge is designed to underpin the teaching of the Key Stage 1 and Key Stage 2 programmes of study for English, which state, for example, that pupils should be taught

in reading to:

- develop pleasure in reading, motivation to read, vocabulary and understanding by:

  - listening to and discussing a wide range of poems Y1/2/3/4/5/6
  - learning to appreciate rhymes and poems, and to recite some by heart Y1/2
  - learning a wider range of poetry by heart Y5/6
  - preparing poems to read aloud and to perform, showing understanding through intonation, tone, volume and action Y3/4/5/6
  - recognising some different forms of poetry [for example, free verse, narrative poetry] Y3/4

- participate in discussion about poems that are read to them and those that they can read for themselves, taking turns and listening to what others say Y2
- explain and discuss their understanding of poems, both those that they listen to and those that they read for themselves Y2.

and in writing to:

- develop positive attitudes towards and stamina for writing by:

  ○ writing poetry Y2.

Early Years Foundation Stage

The Early Learning Goals specify that, by the end of the Early Years Foundation Stage, children should:

- listen attentively in a range of situations.

Introduction

Trainee teachers need to know as much about poetry as they do about stories. The word 'poetry', though, is used to cover a whole range of rhythmical and rhyming texts and it is as well to establish a few definitions from the start.

At home, preschool children are likely to hear, learn and recite lots of nursery rhymes. These are generally bizarre, often surreal, and always packed with symbolism of one kind or another. In their early years at school children continue to hear, learn and recite a lot of verses and rhymes and they add to their stock with the verses that form part of what Iona and Peter Opie (2001) call 'The Lore and Language of Schoolchildren' – their own childhood culture. These additions might include clapping rhymes, skipping rhymes, rhymes for ball games, and subversive rhymes about teachers and school dinners, as well as the range of rude, often bodily function and underwear-related rhymes that most children delight in for no other reason than that they are rude. Adults can be quite shocked by some of these. For instance, two very well brought-up eight-year-old Asian girls startled their teacher when they sang and clapped to *When Susie was a Baby* and celebrated Susie's adolescent years with:

> *Ooh, ah, lost my bra,*
> *Left my knickers in my boyfriend's car.*

Though these rhymes are a lot of fun and certainly have a major significance in children's cognitive, emotional and social development, they should not really be categorised as 'poetry'. They belong more to an imaginative oral tradition that uses rhythm and rhyme very effectively but which lacks the linguistic complexity and emotional richness of more deliberately written 'poems'. The boundaries between rhymes, verses and poetry are hazy and hard to define but nonetheless poetry is different from the other two. However, in this chapter, for the sake of simplicity, the term 'poetry' will be used to cover all three generic forms, though unless it is made clear otherwise the main emphasis will be on the more complex literary manifestation of poetry rather than the orally inspired rhymes and verses.

PRACTICAL TASK PRACTICAL TASK PRACTICAL TASK PRACTICAL TASK PRACTICAL TASK

Make a list of as many nursery rhymes as you can recite from start to finish. Choose three of them and try to work out what they are about. This does not just mean restating the obvious meaning of, say, Little Miss Muffet sitting on a tuffet, but means thinking about implicit meanings. That particular rhyme is a pretty scary one and seems to be about the dangers that confront little girls when they are out and about alone. Does any pattern emerge from the rhymes you best remember?

In some respects, the knowledge about poetry is more demanding than that required for stories. This is because poetry is not a form that all adults find particularly accessible or pleasurable whereas story, on the whole, is. Children, on the other hand, like the rhythm and the rhyme of poems a great deal – particularly if they are delivered with enthusiasm and verve. The reason for the unease that some adults, including many teachers, feel is probably something to do with the fact that poetry is a much more concentrated, contrived (poets would say 'crafted') and artificial medium than prose. The language of poetry is further removed from the language of everyday speech than the language of stories. We don't naturally speak in poetry and sometimes feel uneasy when confronted with unfamiliar language used in unfamiliar forms that do not necessarily offer up meaning at first try. Perhaps because their language development is still in its early stages, children seem to feel less anxious about these things and can simply give themselves over to the rhythm, the rhyme and the general feel of a poem with far less nervousness.

Whilst it is true that the language, forms and structures of poetry make it obviously different from prose, this should not be seen as a problem. Because poems generally have fewer words to work with than stories, the words simply have to be made to work harder in order to supply the same depth of meaning. The meaning of a poem is conveyed as much in its rhythms and sounds, and the **associations** and **figurative use of its language** as in the strict lexical meanings of the words used.

It is valuable to a teacher to know some of the technical terms relating to these aspects of poetic analysis and be able to apply them, but this must not become the be-all and end-all of working with poems with children. Like stories, poetry has the potential for giving children enormous emotional and spiritual stimulation as well as classroom pleasure and fun. If teachers ignore this then they are not working with poems particularly well or delivering what children need.

Like stories too, poems are an important resource for *all* aspects of Literacy because they provide language, structural models and ideas that relate to all of them. In reading, the words, rhythms and repetitions of poetry help to develop children's phonological awareness and prediction abilities, which are important in the early stages of learning to read. The themes, language and structures of poems for Key Stage 2 children enable them to scrutinise texts carefully in order to understand implicit meanings. In writing the forms, themes and language of poems can be imitated by the children before they go on to develop their own work. In speaking and listening, ideas contained in poems and the way that those ideas are expressed give opportunities for discussion and part of the particular pleasure of a good poem lies in saying it aloud. Analysing poems can be done with a similar battery of straightforward literary critical procedures and technical terms, but evaluating different kinds of poetry is just as subjective and hedged around with just as many (some would say more) provisos.

Why are poems important?

Poems are important to children for many of the same reasons that stories are important. Like stories, they have the capacity for stimulating imagination, interest and enjoyment. They help children to understand the thoughts and feelings of others, to enter their world, see things through fresh eyes in situations sometimes similar and sometimes different from their own. They provide a similar cultural heritage and bond (what British adult cannot recite *Jack and Jill* or has never read or heard Wordsworth's *Daffodils!*). In doing all this, they help to improve children's literacy. This last point needs further comment.

Make sure that poetry books are properly represented in any classroom book collection, and in your 'emergency' collection of books to read to classes. It is unlikely that children will read poems unless they are easily available to them.

One important strategy in children's acquisition and development of reading is phonic knowledge – the ability to match the sounds of the language to the way they are represented on the page, i.e. to match phonemes to graphemes. It is well understood that English is a phonically highly inconsistent language and that this searchlight alone can only provide partial illumination but it is also well understood that a child with a knowledge and understanding of phonics is in a stronger position to do battle with unfamiliar words than a child without. In order to develop phonic knowledge and understanding, a child must be able to hear and to distinguish between the sounds of the language – to have 'phonological awareness'. Much research has demonstrated that substantial early experience of rhythm and rhyme is highly effective in developing children's phonological awareness and in positively influencing their future literacy achievement.

Peter Bryant was involved in several projects aimed at clarifying the relationship between children's early experience of nursery rhymes and their subsequent phonological awareness and phonemic understanding. In one, Maclean, Bryant and Bradley (1987) worked with 66 preschool children over a year. The children were selected to represent a balanced gender, social and IQ group, and with parents with a wide spread of educational achievement. The result of the work demonstrated that children's early knowledge of nursery rhymes was very strongly linked to the development of a wider set of phonological skills and was a highly effective predictor of and contributor to later literacy skills. Interestingly, it was not linked at all with achievement in other school curriculum areas.

In another project, Bryant and Bradley (1985) worked with 400 non-readers between the ages of four and five who were tested initially on their ability to hear rhyme and alliteration. When 368 of the children were followed up four or five years afterwards, it was found that those children who had scored highly on these initial tests were progressing well in their reading. When similar tests were also given to a group of what Bryant and Bradley call 'backward readers', the children scored very poorly.

It is extremely important that children have experience of as much rhyme and rhythm in their preschool and in their Key Stage 1 primary classrooms as possible. This is not only because the rhyme and rhythm have long-term functions in relation to children's overall literacy development, but also because they introduce children to ways of structuring language poetically into lines and verses, to vivid, sometimes even bizarre or surreal, language use (think about the contents of contrary Mary's garden, for instance, or the medical treatment for Jack's broken crown) and, most importantly, because they help to liberate children's imaginations and are fun. All of these benefits are not only to be found in nursery rhymes. There are similar imaginative, linguistic and structural rewards in finger rhymes, action rhymes, songs, chants, playground games and even advertising jingles. All of them are grist to the phonemic mill as well as providing rich opportunity for shared play and enjoyment.

At Key Stage 2, poetry has further potential. Inevitably, it will still make its contribution to children's imaginative development and their language and literacy skills because it will need to be analysed, discussed and tried. In that process children will learn much about the ways in which language can most effectively be manipulated to produce particular effects. Getting properly to grips with a poem demands and develops high level comprehension skills because words work harder than they do in prose where the demands of meeting a tight form are not so intense. But in dealing with such cognitive matters, teachers must not lose sight of the fact that poetry has the power to enrich children's imaginative and emotional lives. It is not easy to make this kind of point without making the whole area sound 'wimpy' – and it has suffered too long with that kind of reputation. Wimpiness is one of the reasons why boys in particular lose interest in poetry as they approach adolescence and why comparatively few adults read poetry for pleasure after they leave school, but poetry is not wimpy. Most good writers for children can produce poems that are realistic and very tough. When Kit Wright in *Useful Person* writes about a Down's syndrome child in a crowded grumpy railway waiting room or Charles Causley in *Timothy Winters* about an abused child in morning assembly, they are writing tough poems for primary school children. What these poems do is to touch on areas of deep personal feeling in very intense ways. It is the compression and resonances of language that only poetry offers that allow the feelings of such poems to be so powerfully expressed and which in turn give so much to children's personal and imaginative lives.

PEDAGOGICAL LINK PEDAGOGICAL LINK **PEDAGOGICAL LINK** PEDAGOGICAL LINK

Poetry book covers are just as attractive and stimulating as storybook covers. Make sure that at least some poetry books are displayed in the classroom so that the covers can be seen in all their enticing glory.

What is poetry?

Once, the story goes, Duke Ellington was asked, 'What is swing?' The great jazz composer gazed at the questioner through his wonderful baggy eyes and considered lengthily and deeply. Finally he uttered, 'Man, if you have to ask, you ain't got it.'

That evasive answer doubtless did not satisfy the questioner and Ellington could certainly have defined swing technically perfectly well. If he had, his answer would probably have involved the consideration of aspects of rhythm, emphasised offbeats in 4/4 time, syncopated and slurred sounds, musical dynamics and a host of arcane aspects of musicology. But any definition would not have clarified the appeal of swing, which is as much physical and emotional as intellectual. In the end, a musician and listener understand swing in music by feeling it. If you have to ask, you ain't got it.

The same is true of poetry. Dorothy L. Sayers (1946) makes the point vividly when she argues that each word in Shakespeare's great line about honey bees in *Henry V*:

The singing masons building roofs of gold

can be analysed and explained perfectly well and might actually be questioned for its scientific accuracy by pedantic readers. Bees, after all, do not sing; they buzz. What the bees are creating are not roofs – they are more like walls, which the bees are filling, not building, and beeswax is actually white in its pure form. But that analysis and explanation would not explain the emotional impact of the line, what Dorothy Sayers describes, deliberately pedantically, as the *effect on blood and tissue known as 'making one's heart leap'* or the *reaction from the tear-glands, resulting in a measurable quantity of brackish water* that the line can produce.

Poetry cannot be responded to entirely through its content, forms, rhythms and language. In the end it is creativity of spirit, freshness of vision and intensity of feeling that lie at the heart of poetry and these cannot be defined; they have to be felt. Also, as with swing, that feeling is best nurtured and developed by experiencing it – in the case of jazz by listening to it and in the case of poetry by reading and listening and tuning in to get the feel of it.

This is not to say that a knowledge of technical terms and the ability to apply them to poems is not useful. It does give children and teachers some tools with which to analyse poetry – to enable them to talk about aspects of language, rhythm or form. But the main problem with poetry is that it is so compressed that any crude attempt to decompress it can easily result in the whole thing imploding. In over-analysing poems, there is a danger of destroying them. Though teachers are expected to understand and to be able to handle some of those tools, they should be used carefully and sensitively.

Here are four definitions of poetry provided by four different writers:

> *Nature to advantage dress'd*
> *What oft was thought but ne'er so well expressed.*
>
> (Alexander Pope)

> *The spontaneous overflow of powerful feelings: it takes its origin from emotion recollected in tranquillity.*
>
> (William Wordsworth)

> *The best words in the best order.*
>
> (Samuel Coleridge)

> *The sort of stuff that doesn't reach the edge of the page when you write it down.*
> (Michael Rosen)

That last was an off-the-cuff response to a student questioner at a lecture. There is probably just a touch of Ellington mischief about it!

All of these definitions are interesting, and, even though they are very different, they are all good ones. Their differences simply reflect the attitudes of the particular periods in which they were written or spoken. Pope, writing in the early eighteenth century, was clearly concerned with the intellectual content at the centre of any poem and its relationship with form and language. Wordsworth, writing in the late eighteenth century, was much more interested in the surge of emotion that poetry can express. Coleridge, in the early nineteenth century, was commenting on the language and structures of poetry, while Michael Rosen, in the late twentieth century, found layout of particular interest. The simple fact is that poetry is diverse – there are so many different kinds of poetry about so many different things written in so many different ways that any one definition, unless it is long and complicated, cannot cover everything. However, what is true is that all of them, intellectual content, form, language, emotion, structure and layout, have a contribution to make to the 'meaning' of any poem. Sometimes some are more important than others, but all are important.

Poetic devices

It is easier to deal with these through examples.

John Agard (1990), a poet born in Guyana, offers a very dynamic view of what poetry is in *Poetry Jump Up* and in doing so demonstrates some ways of achieving effects through skilful use of poetic devices. A 'jump up', by the way, is a dance performed behind the costumed floats and characters by children at carnival time in the Caribbean. This is a brief extract from the poem:

> *Words jumpin off de page*
> *tell me if Ah seeing right*
> *words like birds*
> *jumpin out a cage*
> *take a look down de street*
> *words shakin dey waist*
> *words shakin dey bum*
> *words wit black skin*
> *words wit white skin*
> *words wit brown skin*
> *words wit no skin at all*
> *words hug gin up words*
> *an saying I want to be a poem today*
> *rhyme or no rhyme*
> *I is a poem today*
> *I mean to have a good time.*

Here, a poem is seen as a joyous dance performed by language. The words are vivacious and exuberant and active – jumping, shaking, hugging – and are seen as people intent on enjoying themselves. As Agard shows it, they put on their best dresses, make themselves as attractive as they possibly can, and then get out and dance. They have a good time. They show off. They snuggle up to one another, try to surprise one another, excite one another, intrigue one another, tempt one another, and make interesting and sometimes surprising relationships with one another. The poem is a celebration of the excitement that poetry might offer. All that can be felt in the poem without any knowledge of poetic devices, but there are technical terms that can help to explain how the joyous effects are achieved, because they are certainly not accidental.

To begin with, the whole poem is a **metaphor**. A poem is compared with a dance. It jumps with the **rhythm** of a Caribbean jump up, helped along by its repetitions, its short fairly staccato lines, its occasional rhymes both at the ends of lines (page/cage, rhyme/time) and inside lines as internal rhymes (words/birds) and it is given directness by its use of non-standard words and structures. The spelling of 'jumpin' and 'shakin' and 'huggin', perhaps the use of the slightly suspect 'bum' and certainly the spelling and use of 'Ah' for 'I'm' and 'dey' for 'they' when really the standard form should be 'their' and the pronoun/verb mismatch in 'I is a poem today' all contribute to the lively and colloquial tone of the poem. The poet is amazed by what he is seeing in his imagination and speaks directly and conversationally to the reader. The extract is little more than a series of quick impressions of activity. The sections in which Agard describes the words strutting their stuff are rapid phrases rather than sentences because the participles 'jumpin', 'shakin' and 'huggin' are not finite verbs. If I were one of Dorothy L. Sayers' pedants I would have to say that the grammar is technically wrong! However, I'm not and the fact is that the non-standard forms actually work to the poem's advantage, not only because they give a sense of immediacy and vitality, but also because they provide a dynamic additional syllable to each verb, which the grammatically correct 'jumps', 'hugs' and 'shakes' would not give. There is one telling **simile** that gives us the idea of words in poems fluttering and flying like liberated birds, and a series of metaphors. There is **personification** as the words in the poetic dance shake their booty and hug and speak and flash their various coloured skins.

On the page, the poem looks long and straggly, and is carried along by the natural rhythm of Caribbean speech rather than by any imposed form. Lines are of inconsistent length and the rhythm continually shifts in its emphasis. It may not be stretching things too far to suggest that the poem has the loose, flowing structure and the look of an improvised dance and that the lack of a tight form is actually part of the meaning of the poem.

That kind of analysis demonstrates clearly the dangers of too much emphasis on poetic devices. In treating Agard's joyful celebration in this detailed way we are in danger of chilling it and even killing it. Understanding how the effects are achieved does not necessarily increase the pleasure that the poem will give if it is simply responded to. Even that small extract sparkles. The writer has certainly made the language work hard to get the best out of the words to make them jump up off the page to best effect. As John Agard says later in the *poem, A little inspiration – plenty perspiration.* Part of the craftsmanship of the poet, though, is in disguising the perspiration and by analysing the poem in this way we are drawing attention to it. It is important that children do understand how the language is being made to work by the writer, but teachers still need to tread with great care, and it is important too that once having understood some of the craftsmanship at work in the poem, children are given the opportunity for testing it out for themselves in their own imaginative writing. John Agard would certainly be seen as a writer of good quality modern poetry for children and his work is, as ever, redolent of a non-white culture.

Here are the first and third verses of John Masefield's well-known classic poem *Cargoes* (1979, first published in 1903):

> *Quinquireme of Nineveh from distant Ophir*
> *Rowing home to haven in sunny Palestine,*
> *With a cargo of ivory.*
> *And apes and peacocks.*
> *Sandalwood, cedarwood and sweet white wine.*
>
> *Dirty British coaster with a salt-caked smoke stack*
> *Butting through the Channel in the mad March days.*
> *With a cargo of Tyne coal.*
> *Road-rails, pig-lead.*
> *Firewood, iron-ware, and cheap tin trays.*

This is obviously a very different kind of poem from John Agard's. To begin with, it is shorter and is much more formally organised into **stanzas**, each with precisely the same rhyming pattern and a very similar rhythmical pattern too. However, within that similarity of formal structure Masefield has created quite different effects. The first verse is exotic, elegant, flowing and sensuous while the third is grimy, ugly, grimly practical and even brutal. He has managed to make the two verses so different with a string of clever linguistic and technical devices.

To begin with, each verse is dedicated to one ship and the names and natures of the two ships is important. One is a quinquireme, the other a coaster. The very sounds of the words establish a mood. We may not know what a quinquireme is but it certainly sounds a lot more romantic than a coaster. It is actually a Middle Eastern ship propelled by five banks of oars (hence the prefix 'quin') so it may not have seemed quite so romantic if you had happened to be sitting in the middle of the bottom bank, having been rowing for a month or so with the Palestinian sun hammering down! However, Masefield does not give us the opportunity to consider this because first of all he personifies the ship to make it do the rowing itself – that would save the rowers a good deal of effort! – and second the language of the verse diverts us and points us in other directions.

Why should a 'quinquireme' sound a more attractive seagoing proposition than a coaster? It is because the word is more languorous and slides off the tongue more easily – given that it is tri-syllabic with two of the syllables beginning with the comparatively unfamiliar (at least in English) 'qu' sound. Coaster is a more mundane bi-syllabic word with the second being the most familiar, workaday and commonplace vowel phoneme in English – 'uh'.

If we were in any doubt about what Masefield intends by these names, he helps us out by further language-juggling in the first lines of each verse. There are no adjectives to describe the quinquireme – he lets that single noun carry all the overtones for him – but we are told that it is travelling from Nineveh to distant Ophir. The 'distant' is, of course, significant. Not many readers, certainly not many British child readers, could confidently point out Nineveh and Ophir on a map. They are simply faraway places with strange sounding names. Nineveh again is a tri-syllabic with a very foreign looking 'veh' ending and Ophir has the soft 'ph' at its heart and a similarly remote 'ir' ending. The two lines of the verse flow smoothly and without vocal effort from the reader, helped by the fact that 'distant' is next to Ophir' so its final consonant merges effortlessly into Ophir's' opening vowel, by the softly aspirated **alliteration** of 'home' and 'haven' (rather like a gentle breeze), by the temperate warmth of 'sunny' and by the tri-syllabic exotic welcome of 'Palestine'.

The lines also have a prevailing set of vowel sounds, which contribute to their effect. In the first line the prevailing sound is a thin T and in the second line this is supplemented by a string of open vowels – of 'o's and 'a's. This **assonance**, too, helps to give the lines a lightness and delicacy of tone.

The cargo that the quinquireme carries is equally attractive. It exudes Middle Eastern luxury and indulgence for use by opulent Palestinian hedonists. Every item on the bill of lading has overtones and associations of wealth and pampered ease, but not only that; there is a similar smoothness of construction and careful selection of sounds as in the first two lines that helps to give the stanza its particular musicality and tone. There is, in particular, a syllable slipped into line four that is missing from line four of the third stanza. The additional syllable is 'and', which is a connective serving to make the line flow more elegantly. This elegance is emphasised by the soft alliterative sibilants of the last line, the aromatic and pampering **associations** of 'sandalwood' and 'cedarwood', and the seductive assonance and alliteration of 'sweet white wine'.

In short, the effects of the first stanza have been deliberately created by a writer who is far more interested in what poetry can offer beyond rhythm and rhyme. There is very tight control and where structural patterns are broken they are done so quite deliberately in order to create specific effects. The same is, of course, true of the third stanza. Here, the details of the sailing conditions are rather different. If matters were set fair in the sunny Mediterranean, they are a lot wilder and windier in the grey English Channel. The difference of effort in the movement of the ships is conveyed in the participle that opens each second line. The quinquireme may row itself smoothly and gracefully home; the British coaster has to fight every inch of the way. The metaphorical and **onomatopoeic** 'butting' hits the reader like a Glasgow kiss!

The whole stanza has a far jerkier feel to it. The rhythm of the two stanzas is, actually, much the same, with four strong stresses in the first, second and fifth lines and two in the third and fourth. It is easy to recognise these by simply saying the stanza aloud and clapping where the strong beats come. However, the feel is totally different. The effect is achieved by a deliberate selection of words that it is comparatively difficult to get the tongue round – the first line in particular, with its string of monosyllables, with each one demanding a preceding pause in order to reshape the mouth for its initial consonant, almost reads like a tongue twister – by a deliberate use of hard alliteration and by control of associations. The soft and lingering alliterative sibilants of Palestine have been replaced by harsh consonants. Even where Masefield does use sibilants for alliteration (as in line 1) the c's have their hard form.

The overtones of the language are different too. The final syllable of Palestine is 'tine', which is pronounced exactly the same as Tyne. Yet somehow 'tine' in 'Palestine' creates a quite different mental association from 'Tyne' in 'Tyne coal'. All the items of cargo are different in quality too. Gone is the luxury. It is replaced by harsh practicality and tawdry cheapness – a practicality and tawdriness emphasised by the associations of 'pig' and 'tin'.

In overall terms, the poem, like Agard's *Poetry Jump Up,* is highly impressionistic and direct. Masefield does not write in sentences. There is no finite verb in any of the stanzas. The poem is given greater immediacy and colour because of this. In breaking the grammatical rule that teachers work so hard to teach children – that every sentence must contain at least one finite verb – the poet has written a better poem.

REFLECTIVE TASK

Choose either a poem by a significant modern children's author or a classic poem and examine it carefully for poetic devices. Do not be content simply to identify them, but try to determine why the poet has chosen to use them and what contribution they make to the overall meaning of the poem.

PRACTICAL TASK PRACTICAL TASK PRACTICAL TASK PRACTICAL TASK PRACTICAL TASK

Use Masefield's *Cargoes* as a model for writing two additional verses about motor cars. Why not try a Bentley and an old banger? Try to use as many of the poetic devices that Masefield uses as you possibly can and then add some others, just for you.

Rhythm

The word 'rhythm' has recurred regularly through this chapter and it needs some clarification. It means much the same in poetry as it does in music and most people have little problem in understanding it as a concept. Poetry, like music, falls almost naturally into small units. In music the unit is a musical bar, in poetry it is a metrical foot. In music, a bar is generally of a regular length with one or more regular strong beats and the same is generally true of a metrical foot in poetry. The position of the strong beat or beats in both cases is variable. In popular music, the commonest form is a bar of four beats with the second and fourth being emphasised. In poetry, the commonest form is a metrical foot of two beats with the second being emphasised. This pattern of stresses is then repeated to give a recurrent and regular pulse, which is rhythm. This is a massive simplification, however, and there are numerous other patterns that both music and poetry can follow. In the hands of the most sophisticated composers and poets rhythm can become extremely complicated. Whether complex or simple, though, rhythm is always very important in the overall 'meaning' of any musical work or any poem.

Rhythm contributes a great deal to the tone of a poem and poets know that a bad choice of rhythmical form can have dire consequences in creating a mismatch between tone and meaning. For example, in this extract from *The Song of the Low* Ernest Jones laments the Victorian working man's lot, doomed forever to poverty and hunger whilst at the same time serving the wealthy. This would appear to give it all the makings of a deeply depressing poem – which is certainly what Jones intended. Unfortunately, he chooses to voice the lament largely in a cheery di-di-dum rhythm and with this one stroke manages to turn tragedy into something approaching an after-hours raucous drinking song:

> We are low, we are low, we are very very low,
> As low as low can be;
> The rich are high for we make them so
> And a miserable lot are we, are we,
> A miserable lot are we.

Sadly, the rhythm doesn't support the claim! On the other hand, rhythm can be used to support meaning as Robert Louis Stevenson demonstrates in the 'classic' *From a Railway Carriage:*

> Faster than fairies, faster than witches.
> Bridges and houses, hedges and ditches:
> And charging along like troops in a battle.
> All through the meadows the horses and cattle;
> All of the sights of the hill and the plain
> Fly as thick as driving rain;
> And ever again, in the wink of an eye.
> Painted stations whistle by.

It is not just the choice of words with their associations, the figurative language, or the rhymes that give this poem its appeal. They have a significant part to play but they are supported by the control of rhythm, which makes the poem actually sound like a rushing train. The lines brilliantly meet Alexander Pope's demanding requirement for poetic lines:

> 'Tis enough no harshness gives offence
> The Sound must seem an echo to the sense.

PRACTICAL TASK ~~PRACTICAL TASK~~ PRACTICAL TASK ~~PRACTICAL TASK~~ PRACTICAL TASK

Find any poetry collection directed at primary school children, skim through it and select two poems that appeal to you. Look particularly at the rhythm of the poems and decide whether it contributes anything at all to the poem or whether it is simply there as an organisational tool to give the poem shape. If it does make a greater contribution than this, what is it? If you do not know where to start on this task, use one of Kit Wright's collections. If you can't feel the variety of rhythms in the range of poems there, 'Man, you ain't got it!'

Poetry forms

Poetry, as we have seen, can take many forms. Some of them are not particularly demanding in terms of rhythm and rhyme; others are. Children need to become familiar with a number of these forms over their primary years. Many are familiar and need no clarification but others are less so and these are considered here.

You are referred to examples of the forms to check up on for yourself rather than having them quoted in full, which means that you have to pick up some poetry books and skim through them to find appropriate pages. Who knows what other treasures and pleasures you might stumble across in that process!

Riddles can be of any length, take many forms, have a variety of rhythms and rhymes – or none at all – and exist in every culture. They are ancient and they are modern. Some are easy to solve, some are difficult and some are downright impossible. They occur, sometimes in prose and sometimes in poetry, in numerous folk tales and legends.

Children will know many riddles of their own because wordplay is an important stage in the development of their language and sense of humour. More literary supplements for this store of knowledge can be found for Year 2 in *The Orchard Book of Funny Poems* (Cope, 1993), for Year 3 in *Who's Been Sleeping in My Porridge?* (McNaughton, 1994) and *The Kingfisher Book of Children's Poetry* (Rosen, 1985) and for Year 6 in *A World of Poetry* (Rosen, 1991), *O Frabjous Day* (Brownjohn, 1994), *Catching a Spider* (Mole, 1990) and *Wordspells* (Nicholls, 1993).

Shape poems are poems in which the appearance of the poem on the page reflects the theme of the poem. Sometimes the shape can be drawn first and the poem arranged inside it, but more ambitious versions do away with the drawing and simply let the words themselves make the required shape.

Examples by John Agard are in *We Animals Would Like a Word With You* (1996), and by Wes Magee in *Madtail, Miniwhale and Other Shape Poems* (1991). Further examples by other writers can be found in *The Kingfisher Book of Comic Verse* (McGough, 1991) and in *Word Whirls and Other Shape Poems* (Foster, 1992).

Performance poems are poems that are written especially for or benefit from being acted out or otherwise performed – perhaps by a dramatic reading with sound effects. Performance of one kind or another, as simple or as complex as you want, is a splendid way of focusing children on aspects of tone, language, rhythm and rhyme in poetry. There is no special shape or structure to a performance poem. The only requirement is that it should sound well – and a strong rhythm and rhyme does help in that respect.

Good examples can be found in *Gio's Pizzas* (Boon, 1998), *Mango Spice* (Connolly, 1981), *Heard it In the Playground* (Ahlberg, 1989), *Classic Poems to Read Aloud* (Berry, 1997) and *Talking Turkeys* (Zephaniah, 1995).

Cautionary tales are narrative poems that give examples of boys and girls behaving badly. The individuals concerned generally come to a very nasty end and the moral of the story is always perfectly clear even if it is not always stated. It is invariably the case that if boys and girls do not conform to social and parental rules then the consequences are likely to be extreme.

The acknowledged master of the form is Hilaire Belloc and all of his cautionary tales are collected in *Cautionary Verses* (Belloc, 1940).

Nonsense verse can take a number of forms. The two most common ones are:

- those in which a realistic story is told but many of the words used to tell it are made up;
- those in which normal words are used but the events of the poem are surreal and far detached from normal experience.

These two can be, and often are, combined.

That definition is a grotesquely pompous attempt to define the undefinable. Nonsense verse at its best is a joyous romp through sound, rhythm, surrealism and all the bizarre possibilities that life and language can offer – generally, with a bit added on for effect! At its worst it is just silly. The best known writers of nonsense verse are Lewis Carroll, Edward Lear and Spike Milligan but playground rhymes are a rich source too. Numerous examples of these can be found in *The Sausage is a Cunning Bird* (Curry and Curry, 1983) and *The Beaver Book of School Verse* (Curry, 1981) while more 'literary' models are in *The Kingfisher Book of Children's Poetry* (Rosen, 1985) and *Michael Rosen's Book of Nonsense* (Rosen, 1997).

Calligrams are poems in which the look of the poem – the size and shape of the letters, the fonts used, their boldness and effects – support the poem's meaning. Examples by John Hegley (*I Need Contact Lenses*) and Doug Macleod (*O's*) are in *The Kingfisher Book of Comic Verse* (McGough, 1991) and many other examples can be found in *Picture a Poem* (Douthwaite, 1994) and in *Word Whirls and Other Shape Poems* (Foster, 1992).

Haiku is a Japanese verse form that is based on a syllable count and not on patterns of stress. A haiku contains 17 syllables in all and they are distributed over three lines. The distribution is normally five syllables in the first line, seven in the second and five in the third. The first two lines often set a scene and the third comments on it. The build-up of syllables in the second line almost inevitably gives the final line a dying fall. Examples by Kit Wright *(Irish Haiku* and *Acorn Haiku)* can be found in *Cat Among the Pigeons* (Wright, 1987) and by Sandy Brownjohn *(A Norfolk Haiku Bestiary)* in *Both Sides of the Catflap* (Brownjohn, 1996).

Cinquain is a form that originated in America and is said to have been invented by the splendidly named Adelaide Crapsey. Again, it is syllabic. It has 22 syllables in five lines, which are usually divided 2, 4, 6, 8, 2. This distribution not only means that the last line generally comes with a bump but also that the poem has a pleasingly symmetrical appearance on the page. The content of the lines normally is the subject of the poem in the first line, a description of the subject in the second, an action involving the subject in the third, a feeling aroused by the action in the fourth and a final comment in the fifth. Original Crapsey cinquains, *The Warning* and *November Night,* can be found in *O Frabjous Day* (Brownjohn, 1994). There are also examples by children in *Does It Have to Rhyme?* (Brownjohn, 1980).

Couplets are simply two consecutive lines of poetry that are linked by rhythm and rhyme. Couplets are almost always bits of a poem rather than poems in their own right. All of the poems in Roald Dahl's *Revolting Rhymes* (1982) are written in couplets.

Thin poems are exactly what they ought to be. They are poems in which the lines are very short syllabically (there is no rule but the fewer the better!) so that on the page they look skinny and straggly. There is no rule about rhyming either, though if the lines do have a regular rhyme the poem sounds longer and thinner. There are examples by David Orme (*Horribly Thin Poems*) in *The Second Poetry Kit* (Andrew and Orme, 1990) and Brian Patten (*Growing Pains*) in *Thawing Frozen Frogs* (Patten, 1990) and in *Long Tales, Short Tales and Tall Tales* (West, 1995).

Conversation poems simply record the conversation between two or more voices. They are often, but not always, funny and they make good reading aloud or performance material. The structure is often very loose with no strong rhythms or rhymes. The effect and meaning of such poems is to emphasise the quirkiness of human behaviour and relationships and they often suggest a moral, social or political authorial point of view. There are examples by Eric Finney *(Whoppers),* Jerome Fletcher *(Dialogue of the Deaf)* and Judith Nicholls *(Camping Out)* in the Oxford Primary English Unit, *Whoppers!,* by Kit Wright *(Dialogue Between My Cat Bridget and Me)* in *Cat Among the Pigeons* (Wright, 1987) and by Lesley Miranda *(Don't Hit Your Sister)* in *Poetry Jump Up* (Nichols, 1988).

Free verse is the loosest of all poetic forms because it is simply spilled onto the page with no regard for rhythm or rhyme. Much adolescent verse falls into this category, but better examples are in *Let's Celebrate* (Foster, 1989) and *This Poem Doesn't Rhyme* (Benson, 1990).

Concrete poems are related to calligrams and shape poems in that all of them link language and visual appearance. The meaning of such poems is given additional emphasis by the way it looks on the page. Concrete poems are more complex than the other two, though, because they often look like sculptures in which individual words or groups of words are used as material from which to construct the sculpture. Examples of concrete poems by Robert Froman *(Quiet Secret),* Pamela Gillilan *(Invasion)* and Judith Nicholls *(Ars Mathematica)* are in *A Fifth Poetry Book* (Foster, 1983) whilst *Picture a Poem* (Douthwaite, 1994) and *Madtail, Miniwhale and Other Shape Poems* (Magee, 1991) are collections dedicated to poems that use layout as a key element in their meaning.

Ballads are poems that tell a dramatic story – often bloody, or ghostly. Traditional ballads, which were often sung and were sometimes used as means of circulating news, tend to follow, however vaguely, a regular structure of metre and rhyme that is known as ballad form. This form is a four-line verse (or *quatrain),* rhyming abcb, with lines one and three having eight syllables and lines two and four six. Many modern narrative poems are also written in ballad form. Examples of ballads, both traditional and modern, are in *The Oxford Book of Story Poems* and *The Oxford Treasury of Classic Poems* (Harrison and Stuart-Clark, 1990, 1996).

Narrative poetry is a poetic genre that has no requirement of form or structure. It simply tells a story. Some narrative poems, particularly traditional ones, do follow ballad structure, but there are as many different poetic ways of telling a story as there are prose ways. There are examples everywhere but some of the best known 'classic' ones can be found in *The Oxford Book of Story Poems* (Harrison and Stuart-Clark, 1990) and *The Rime of the Ancient Mariner and Other Classic Stories in Verse* (Waterfield, 1996). A particularly popular narrative poem with Year 5 and Year 6 children is Alfred Noyes' *The Highwayman*.

Sonnet is one of the most demanding of all verse forms in English because it is of specific length, requires tight rhythmical control and has a rigorous rhyme scheme. It is often regarded as the most English of forms, not only because it was Shakespeare's favourite form but also because virtually every significant poet writing in English has had a go at writing a sonnet – not always very successfully. In fact, the form originated in Italy and was brought to England in the fifteenth century. The sonnet is a 14-line form with ten regularly stressed syllables to the line. The regular stress normally goes 'di-dum'. Early sonnets, modelled on the Italian form, rhymed abbabccbcdecde. This caused the sonnet to fall into two sections – the first of eight lines (the octet) and the second of six lines (the sestet) though the carry over of rhymes still emphasised the unity of the two sections. Poets attempting this strict form in English found it difficult to stick to because the limited number of rhymes available in English (as opposed to Italian where there are plenty) made the whole thing sound very artificial. Shakespeare changed the form slightly to give it a rhyme scheme of ababcdcdefefgg. This represented three quatrains and a concluding couplet. It also meant that the octet/sestet divide, though still available if required, was not a natural one and poets could think in slightly looser structural terms. The Shakespearean form is the one that most poets now use when they write sonnets.

Sonnets abound in English, though not many of them are written for children. The best bet for Year 5 children is to read one or two of the more famous ones for adults – Shakespeare's Sonnet 18, *Shall I Compare Thee to a Summer's Day?* or Wordsworth's *Composed Upon Westminster Bridge* and supplement these with sonnets by children to be found in *Does It Have to Rhyme?* (Brownjohn, 1980).

Rap is probably more familiar to chidlren than adults because the form is such a common one in pop music. What now passes for rap, however, has very little in common with its origins. Rap emerged around 1976 and was the term given to a musical style associated with urban American black and hispanic groups. Its form was loose – but it was highly rhythmical, used rhyme when it suited and not when it didn't and was oral. Often rap was improvised, went very fast and used a great deal of slang and obscenity. Its main themes were highly political, involving black experience of urban deprivation, drugs, violence and sex. Rap has, over the years, become greatly watered down and has largely lost its political impetus. It now means little more than a rhythmical chant that is easy to dance to. Lyrics of original rap records can be found in *Rap: The Lyrics* (Stanley, 1992), but these, for obvious reasons, should be used highly selectively. More specifically Year 5 targeted examples of the rap genre are in *Royal Raps* (Mitton, 1997) and in *Rap with Rosen* (Rosen, 1995).

Choral poetry is related to performance poetry in that it is poetry that is suitable for reading aloud in groups. However, where performance poetry contains potential for actions to gain effects, choral poetry relies entirely on the voice. The poems may be scored for choral speaking, using solo voices, groups of voices in various combinations or contrapuntal effects, but it is the voice that does the work. Poems are not generally written simply for choral purposes but many do lend themselves to such treatment.

The sources recommended for performance poems will provide many examples of poems that are suitable for being spoken chorally.

Kennings are two-word phrases used in Anglo-Saxon and Ancient-Scandinavian poems. They name something without actually using the common noun. A Viking spear and a modern dentist might both have the kenning 'pain giver'. My own literary favourite is the kenning used to describe Flashman by the Native American Indians in George MacDonald Fraser's *Flashman and the Redskins.* Flashman, they think, rides so fast that his speed breaks the wind. Consequently, they always refer to him as 'wind breaker'. More proper examples can be found by Sandy Brownjohn *(Kennings Cat)* in *Both Sides of the Catflap* (Brownjohn, 1996), by John Agard *(Don't Call Alligator Long-Mouth Till You Cross River)* in *Poetry Jump Up* (Nichols, 1988) and by a number of children in *The Ability to Name Cats* (Brownjohn, 1989).

Limerick is a verse form reputedly from Ireland, first developed rather dully by Edward Lear but then exploited **gleefully**, and often very rudely, by any number of authors – only some of whom were prepared to put their names to their efforts! In technical terms, the limerick is a five-line regularly rhythmical form. The basic rhythm is di-dum-di though slight variations on this are common. The first, second and fifth lines each contain three of these di-dum-di's while the third and fourth have two. The rhyme scheme is aabba. The trick is in the fifth line. Edward Lear simply used it as a minor variation on the first line. This will not do nowadays! A modern limerick really does have to clinch the poem in a wittier way with a pun or a joke of some kind.

Year 6 children will almost certainly know a number of limericks. You ask them to repeat them at your peril! It is much safer to start from the examples by Edward Lear in *The Puffin Book of Nonsense Verse* (Blake, 1996), and then work through the examples in *Poems of A. Nonny. Mouse* (Prelutsky, 1992) and *A World of Poetry* (Rosen, 1991).

Tanka is a Japanese syllabic poem related to the haiku. The form is 31 syllables altogether, divided into five lines of 5, 7, 5, 7 and 7 syllables each. Those who have been reading carefully will immediately see that the tanka is really a haiku with an additional two lines tacked on the end. This is, in fact, exactly how the form originated. In Shogun Japan, when a courtier wrote a haiku, for whatever reason, and sent it to another, Japanese courtesy required the recipient to return it with two lines added. There are several examples of tanka written by children in *Does It Have to Rhyme?* (Brownjohn, 1980).

PEDAGOGICAL LINK PEDAGOGICAL LINK **PEDAGOGICAL LINK** PEDAGOGICAL LINK

Make sure that whenever you read a poem to or with children, that poem is available for the children to read for themselves at another time. Alternatively, you can put some readings of poems (you don't just have to use your own voice for these – rope in friends) onto a tape for the children to listen to.

Evaluating and making judgements about poems

Once again, we approach difficult ground because responses to poems, just as to stories, depend on taste. A reader may have a great deal of knowledge about poetic forms and structures and about poetic devices and figurative language that will help to analyse a poem, but in the end an evaluation or a conclusion on its worth is personal. There are criteria that might help in an evaluation, and these are very similar to those for evaluating stories; but readers' responses to the same poem are likely to be different simply because their life experiences, sensitivity to language and personal taste are different, even if the same criteria are being considered. As with stories, all a teacher can do is apply the criteria honestly and then trust their judgement.

Appropriateness

The questions that should be asked about appropriateness are probably:

- Is the theme appropriate to the children in the class?
- Is the language used in the poem on the whole within their experience or understanding?
- If the poem is to be part of the programme of work for literacy, does it fit reasonably well with current curriculum requirements?

Theme

Considering appropriateness of theme is as tricky for poems as it is for stories, and for much the same reasons. A teacher must try to assess whether the theme of a poem is one that is within the probable grasp of the children in the class, but that judgement is a difficult one to make. Poems can communicate before they are understood and there is no reason to suppose that a class of Year 4 children doing their work on poems based on common themes and using animal poems as a resource would not respond as well to extracts from W. B. Yeats' *Minalouche* or Christopher Smart's *My Cat Jeoffrey*, which are both clearly written with an assumed adult audience, as they would to Eleanor Farjeon's *Cats Sleep Anywhere* or Kit Wright's *Applause,* which are more clearly directed at children. They might need a little more help with aspects of the language but certainly any child who has a cat as a pet would recognise the aspects of cat behaviour that are at the heart of all four poems. There can be no hard-and-fast rules here. It is simply a matter of judgement.

Language

Poets are notoriously cavalier in their use of language – as they should be because it is in poetry that language is generally used most innovatively, impressively and entertainingly – and part of the joy of reading a good poem is to feel, if not fully understand, the words working on us. When Walter de la Mare writes in *The Listeners,*

> *The silence surged softly backwards*

we might be hard pressed to explain exactly what the line means. Some children might well not know the meaning of 'surged' or pick up on the personification and alliteration in the line or grasp the implications of the metaphor being used. It is probable that the line produces different images even for different adult readers. Is the comparison with waves, for example, or a crowd of people, or maybe animals? However, the inability to specify detail and technicality does not mean that that wonderful line cannot produce a response; it can and it does. It is simply not necessary for children (or adults) to understand the meaning, both literal and figurative, of every word. It is often through poetry that children's feeling for imaginative use of language can be extended.

Tone

Poems, as we have seen, can be written in many forms and for many purposes. However they are written, though, and for whatever purposes, they must address the reader as an intelligent human being and they must tell the truth. They must not patronise by speaking down and they must not embarrass by pretending to convey feelings or ideas that are obviously false. A good poem does not posture – it reflects a writer's experiences, thoughts and feelings honestly. It is easy enough to recognise falseness – it can be seen in self-consciously 'poetic' language, in forced rhymes and rhythms and in cliché-ridden thought and feeling.

Michael Rosen is an immensely popular writer for children who seems to have a hotline into his own childhood. He writes regularly about his long-suffering mother, his rude and irascible father, his conspiratorial brother and his numerous school friends. He draws on personal private experiences, on family experiences and on school experiences. His output is massive and he could well be excused the occasional lapse, but at no time does he ever do anything other than write honestly and directly to his child audience, recalling and recording his experiences in a direct, uncluttered and generally very funny way. This is what makes him such a popular writer. Children recognise themselves in much of what he writes – any experience, no matter how apparently trivial, can be shared, can be written about and can be made important. Some people claim that Rosen's work is better spoken than read (especially when he speaks it himself) because of the directness and unfigurative nature of the language, but he remains an excellent example of a writer who never patronises or embarrasses his audience by underestimating it.

Language

Poems, as we have seen, represent the most compressed form of language use because, in a good poem, every aspect of a word or group of words can contribute to the poem's total meaning. In evaluating a poem a teacher has to decide whether the cold dictionary definitions of the words are supported by their sounds, their associations, their rhymes and their rhythms. In the best poems there is vigour and imagination in the language use. It is impossible to help in the definition of those abstract nouns – what do we mean by 'vigour' and 'imagination' in the use of language? You simply have to feel it. We are driven back to Duke Ellington. 'If you have to ask, you ain't got it!' If you didn't have it before, your reading of this chapter should at least have set you on the way to getting it.

In *We Animals Would Like a Word With You* (1996) I feel John Agard demonstrating this vigour and imagination over and over again and he allies it to a sly and very witty view of the world of human beings. I particularly like the two poems in which Mr Hippo writes a love letter to his wife and Mrs Hippo responds. Not only are they a joyous celebration of the sounds, associations, rhythms and textures of language in poetry, they are also remarkably tender for such galumphy, tubby stuff. Here is Mr Hippo's letter poem:

> *Oh my beautiful fat wife*
> *Larger to me than life*
> *Smile broader than the river Nile*
> *My winsome waddlesome*
> *You do me proud in the shallow of morning*
> *You do me proud in the deep of night*
> *Oh, my bodysome mud-basking companion.*

PRACTICAL TASK PRACTICAL TASK PRACTICAL TASK PRACTICAL TASK PRACTICAL TASK

Read John Agard's poem aloud. If you can find a copy of *We Animals Would Like a Word With You* (Agard, 1996), read Mrs Hippo's response aloud too. Listen carefully to the sounds of the words. The poems are beautifully plump, muddy and wobbly. Decide for yourself precisely how (and why) John Agard has achieved this effect.

Now use the structure of either of the poems to write an imitation. The Hippo poems are about short and fat animals, so try one about a long thin one – maybe a giraffe. Choose your language with care to get long thin effects.

Imagery

The best poets try to convey experiences, thoughts and emotions as honestly and as clearly as they can. This is not easy – particularly if they are very personal experiences, thoughts and emotions. Consequently, in order to make the unfamiliar more accessible to readers, poets often work through comparisons – through **imagery** – usually similes and metaphors. Vernacular English is rich in imagery. We often use similes and metaphors in everyday speech without even thinking that that is what we are doing – as cool as a cucumber, as flat as a pancake, as thick as two short planks, blankets of fog, riots of colour and light pouring into the room. These are such familiar comparisons that they have long since lost any effect they may once have had and have become clichés. In order for a comparison to be effective, it needs to be original, innovative, and perhaps even startling or outrageous. When evaluating a poem, one consideration must be where the imagery stands on the scale that stretches from 'weary, stale, flat and unprofitable' to fresh, energising and helping us to look at the world through new eyes.

In a little and unexpectedly very serious poem called *New Members Welcome,* Spike Milligan writes:

> Pull the blinds on your emotions
> Switch off your face.
> Put your love into neutral.
> This way to the human race.

The poem is simply three startling metaphors, with a final, rather gloomy line that has just a hint of metaphor about it itself. In the poem, human emotions are seen as a curtained house, the human face is seen as an electrically-lit room, human love is seen as a motor car, and the human race is seen as a signposted destination which, because of the build-up of images in the first three lines, is dark, unenergised and lacklustre. The images, though depressing, are fresh and surprising and without them it would not have been possible to convey the same thought and feeling with such economy.

Rhythm

Poems depend on their rhythm. Not only does rhythm help to give poems form and shape, it can also make a contribution to the meaning. Any evaluation of a poem needs to take some account of how well a poet makes their rhythms work.

When Vachel Lindsay tells us in *The Daniel Jazz,* for example, that:

> *Daniel was the chief hired man of the land*
> *He stirred up the jazz in the palace band*
> *He whitewashed the cellar. He shovelled in the coal.*
> *And Daniel kept a-praying: - 'Lord save my soul.'*
> *Daniel kept a-praying: - 'Lord save my soul.'*
> *Daniel kept a-praying: - 'Lord save my soul.'*

not only is he drawing on the themes, language, rhymes and repetitions of black American spiritual music, he is drawing on its rhythm too and making the poem swing in a way appropriate to the subject matter. Duke Ellington would certainly approve of that!

He would probably have approved too when Jack Ousbey's grandma answers the question of whether she can rap or not enthusiastically in the rhythmical affirmative:

> *I'm the best rapping Gran this world's ever seen*
> *I'm a –*
> *tip-top, slip-slap,*
> *nip-nap, yip-yap,*
> *hip-hop, trip-trap,*
> *touch yer cap*
> *take a nap,*
> *happy, happy, happy, happy,*
> *rap – rap – queen.*

PRACTICAL TASK PRACTICAL TASK PRACTICAL TASK PRACTICAL TASK PRACTICAL TASK

Any poetry work with children depends on a teacher's knowledge of texts. This does not just mean knowing about the forms, language and technical aspects of poems, it means knowing who are the good writers most likely to stimulate your class. That, in turn, means reading a lot of poems for children. This task is a long-term one. It is to read at least one poetry book for children every month for the rest of your training and teaching career. This is a minimum requirement. It would be far better to read more poems more often, but other matters sometimes press!

Breaking the rules

Poems are ideal vehicles for teaching the kinds of technicalities for word/sentence level matters which are required by the Primary Framework for Literacy and which have been considered in this chapter. There is a danger, though, if teachers do too much of that sort of thing with poems or, even worse, only that then their power to free the imagination and to give delight will be lost. So by all means with your class discuss the rhymes betimes and think up new lines, clap out rhythms, articulate the antics of alliteration and bang on about onomatopoeia. Seek out the similes like one panning for gold and put as many metaphorical eggs as you think appropriate into the basket of poetry. But remember that good poems are a lot more than just a heap of tricks with words and that poets are concerned with stretching language and do not always stick to the conventional rules.

In *According to My Mood,* Benjamin Zephaniah (1995) delights in the freedom from linguistic and grammatical constraints that a poet has when he has passed the test for his poetic licence. Remember it when you are thinking about using a poem to teach some matters of grammar or technical English.

I have *poetic* licence, i WriTe thE way i waNt.

i *drop* my full stops where i like …
MY CAPITAL LeteRs go where I liKE,
i order from MY PeN, I verse the way I like
(i do *my spelling write*)
According to My *MO*od.

I HAve Poetic licence,

I put my commers where i like,,((0))-

IIImy brackets *are* write ((
I REPEAT WHen I likE.
i can't go rong.
I *look* and i.c.
It's rite.
iI REPEAT WHen I likE. i have
poetic licence!
don't question me????

A SUMMARY OF **KEY POINTS**

➤ Poetry for children exists in many forms – some of them are more crafted than others.

➤ Poetry contributes to children's emotional, cultural and spiritual development as well as to their linguistic and literacy development.

➤ There is no agreement about what actually constitutes poetry. It has meant different things at different times – and still does.

➤ In poems, words are made to work harder than they do in prose and poets use a number of different linguistic and structural devices to squeeze as much labour from them as they can.

➤ Knowledge of these devices can help in the analysis of poetry but should not be overused.

➤ Poems can be written in many different forms and children should experience a wide range.

➤ Evaluating poems is difficult because much depends on personal taste. However, there are some approaches that can help. These include such aspects as appropriateness, tone, language, imagery, rhythm and the extent of teacher interest.

➤ Poets do not always stick to conventional linguistic, grammatical and structural rules.

M-LEVEL EXTENSION > > M-LEVEL EXTENSION > > M-LEVEL EXTENSION

As you undertake the poetry reading challenge detailed in the final practical task of this chapter, start to develop your own anthology of poetry that you want to use with children over your career. Divide it into the various forms described in the chapter, and record for each poem particular devices used and examples of appropriate use of rhythm, tone, language and imagery. Note which age groups you feel that each poem is suitable for and which topics/themes they could support.

FURTHER READING FURTHER READING FURTHER READING FURTHER READING

Balaam, J. and Merrick, B. (1987) *Exploring Poetry 5–8.* Exeter: NATE. This book is very practical in its concern with imaginative ways of getting Key Stage 1 children to respond to poems. In putting forward stimulating classroom ideas it also clarifies the importance of poetry in a range of forms to young children and conveys notions of the particular nature of those forms.

Brownjohn, S. (1990) *To Rhyme or Not to Rhyme?* London: Hodder & Stoughton. The book is largely about the imaginative responses to poetry required by the NC but the more technical aspects of the PFL are certainly not ignored. Indeed the book will both help you to understand better some of these matters and also help to equip you to teach them to children.

Carter, D. (1998) *Teaching Poetry in the Primary School.* London: David Fulton. This inspirational book explores ways of linking poetry with other expressive media (like art, music, dance and drama) and, though it does give guidance on the technicalities, it helps the reader to understand the special qualities of poetry which lie beyond them.

DfE (2013) *Teachers' Standards*. London: DfE. (**www.gov.uk/government/uploads/system/uploads/attachment_data/file/208682/Teachers__Standards_2013.pdf**)

Merrick, B. (1991) *Exploring Poetry 8–13.* Exeter: NATE. This is a companion book to *Exploring Poetry 5–8,* aimed at Key Stage 2, and it has similar qualities. The choice of high quality poems is impressive and the classroom ideas are both practical and appropriate. Reading this book will help you to better understand the things that make poetry poetry and equip you to help children reach a similar understanding.

Opie, P. and Opie, I. (2001) (new edn) *The Lore and Language of Schoolchildren.* New York: NYRB Classics.

12
The qualities of drama

Curriculum context

National Curriculum programmes of study

This knowledge is designed to underpin the teaching of the Key Stage 1 and Key Stage 2 programmes of study for English, which state, for example, that pupils should be taught

in spoken language to:

- participate in discussions, presentations, performances, role play/improvisations and debates

in reading to:

- develop positive attitudes to reading, and an understanding of what they read, by:
   - listening to and discussing a wide range of plays Y3/4/5/6
   - preparing play scripts to read aloud and to perform, showing understanding through intonation, tone, volume and action Y3/4/5/6.

Early Years Foundation Stage

The Early Learning Goals specify that, by the end of the Early Years Foundation Stage, children should:

- listen attentively in a range of situations
- express themselves effectively, showing awareness of listeners' needs.

Introduction

The place of drama in the primary school is usually seen as within the Spoken Language Programme of Study in the National Curriculum at Key Stages 1 and 2, although it also appears, through a focus on plays and play scripts in the Reading Programme of Study. This suggests a strong place for drama, but it would be a mistake to consider drama only as literature study. Techniques such as role play, hot seating and flashbacks can be used to explore other aspects of the curriculum such as history, science or PSHE. In this sense, drama is a vehicle for learning as well as a subject for study, and is cross-curricular in its application.

REFLECTIVE TASK

Drama in schools can have a number of meanings and different people interpret it in different ways. Before you read our discussion about the nature of drama in primary schools, it would be useful for you to think about this question for yourself.

- What examples of drama have you seen, led or taken part in in schools?
- Why were these examples being taught? In other words, what particular skills, attitudes or knowledge did the teacher hope to foster through them?
- Does drama only take place in drama lessons? What other contexts might there be for it?

Drama in primary schools

This chapter is concerned with required subject knowledge. It will, therefore, have little to say about the classroom techniques associated with drama as pedagogy that are not part of this required subject knowledge. They are more fully explored in the companion volume to this book. In this chapter, the focus will be on the analysis and evaluation of drama texts and a consideration of some of the technical language involved.

Analysing play texts can be done with a similar battery of straightforward literary critical procedures and technical terms to those used in the analysis of story and poetry, but evaluating different kinds of drama is just as subjective and hedged around with just as many provisos. Before any kind of analysis can be made, however, we need to consider why it is that drama games and performances and the reading and writing of drama texts are important in primary school classrooms.

Why is drama important?

It is difficult to be precise in a consideration of drama because it can be seen in at least three lights – as a teaching methodology, as a performance art, and as a literacy-directed activity. What these aspects share, however, is the notion that drama is associated with role play – of acting out a story. Children either make the story up for themselves (generally, but not necessarily, centring their improvisations on personal experience or an already known story), act out other people's stories, or study the methods writers have used and the opportunities they have provided in drama texts for acting out a story. When seen in any of these ways, drama is another version of fiction. Even where the story told is a factual one, it is fictionalised by the dramatising process. A creator of drama, child or adult writer, selects and orders incidents for maximum effect and makes up the things that people say to give the chosen story momentum. Most functions or versions of drama in primary classrooms are important, therefore, for many of the same reasons that stories are important. We will begin then to consider why drama is important with a brief recap of those.

Drama as story

Like stories, drama has the potential to give great pleasure. It can do this by creating and satisfying the very basic human desire when confronted with narrative, which is to know what happens next. Like stories too, by encouraging children to organise their own and others' experience into narrative form, drama helps them to make sense of the world. It can also enable children to experience the world vicariously. Active role play, perhaps more than the reading of stories, places children firmly into the situations of others and almost obliges them to see the world from different points of view. By being placed in this position, children discover aspects of human motivation and behaviour – what makes people act as they do – and this learning can often stimulate moral questions.

It is sometimes argued that the experience of drama and the study of drama texts puts children in touch with a common cultural heritage – much as the reading and study of stories does. This is not altogether true. It is the case, as Suzi Clipson-Boyles (1998) passionately argues, that *drama is a universal cultural phenomenon, crossing geographical boundaries as it emerges in many forms around the world* and that *the power of story, the transmission* of knowledge, the shaping of ideas and emotions into an art form which is alive, dynamic and interactive all make connections with human response which resonates with life itself.

The experiential and performance aspects of drama work, therefore, almost certainly do help children to understand and respond to that cultural heritage. There are crucial quantitative and qualitative differences between stories to be read by children and plays to be read by children. In less pompous words – there are a lot more stories than plays written for children to read and they are a lot better. The sheer body of outstandingly well-written stories for children, which are such a rich resource in primary classrooms, does not exist for drama. This is not to say that many plays have not been written by 'classic' and 'significant modern authors' for children. Writers like J. M. Barrie, David Wood, Brian Patten and Ken Campbell have all written plays for children; some for the theatre, some for television. However, these are plays written for performance generally by adults for a child audience rather than for children to read and perform themselves. The outstanding writers of drama for reading and performance by primary school children in their classrooms and school halls have yet to emerge. It is interesting to note that there are numerous awards for writers of stories for children, some for writers of poetry for children, a few for writers of information books for children, but none at all for writers of drama for children.

Drama as an aid to learning

There is a great deal of anecdotal evidence – though, it must be admitted, little objective research – to support the view that the acting out in role of issues arising from such things as historical events or incidents in poems or stories is both a popular and effective learning strategy. Some drama specialists go so far as to claim that there is nothing in the entire primary curriculum, including such unlikely areas as numeracy and science, that drama techniques cannot support and enhance. In a Year 2 classroom, for example, one of us had the pleasure of watching a group of English as a second language learners, wearing appropriate masks to represent the planets, spinning and revolving around a splendidly fiery sun!

Most young children enjoy performance and many children's games have an acting content. From the moment that they line up dolls and stuffed toys to represent the class while they rant and rave and apply sound teachers' tellings-off to recalcitrant teddies, or wrap up and nurture poorly dolls because they are ill, children engage in role play. Such role play games have an educational and a socialising function. Even at this preschool level, role play enables children to see matters from different perspectives. Where the observation and information to support such role play comes from it is hard to know – particularly in the representation of teachers. If real teachers went in for the corporal punishment, personal humiliation and downright sadism of their child imitators – many of whom will have never seen a real teacher at the age at which they are beating the stuffing out of their soft toy comforters – they would be whistled up before the beak before they could say Children Act. Mr Punch and *The Beano* have much to answer for!

The drama activities are encouraged, of course, through the early years in school with home corners and varieties of pretend environments from shops to ships and castles to coffee shops. Many action rhymes and songs from which children learn aspects of language and number have a role play element. When children's fingers become *Incey Wincey Spider* climbing up the spout or the tops of children's heads become the icing on *Five Little Buns in the Baker's Shop,* the children are not just having a nice time taking part in drama activities. They are also learning both socially and cognitively.

PRACTICAL TASK PRACTICAL TASK PRACTICAL TASK PRACTICAL TASK PRACTICAL TASK

Make a list of as many children's games as you can, using as much of your own experience as possible. How many of them involve some kind of role play? It is often said that children's games are very important in children's educational and social development. What sort of contribution might those that you have marked as role play games make to either or both of these? Be as specific as you can.

Drama can be more formally harnessed to support learning through the later years of Key Stage 1 and through Key Stage 2. Key moments in RE or history, for example, can spring to life through improvised or scripted drama. The flight of the Israelites from Egyptian bondage via the parting of the Red Sea for a whole school assembly is as nothing to an imaginative Year 1 teacher. What took Cecil B. De Mille a cast of thousands and millions of dollars can be managed perfectly well with two blue saris, a few dressing gowns and a willing suspension of disbelief. In the version we saw, however, after the Israelites had made good their escape between the saris held aloft and flapped energetically by a number of blue-clad sea sprites, the pursuing Egyptians were not keen on being engulfed by the returning waters. Much to the entertainment of the rest of the school audience, they put up a brave if ultimately unsuccessful fight. A re-enactment of a Viking funeral with Year 4 gives greater immediacy, involvement and potential for learning than any information book can give – though experience forces us to warn against any re-enactment of any battles, and you should steer well clear of the storming of the Bastille!

Drama as a resource for moral education

It can be argued that, even at this early developmental stage, such dramatic representation is a means of dealing with some tricky issues of social and moral education. We have already seen that stories for children, particularly fairy tales and legends, have a very strong moral purpose. By dramatising them, it becomes possible for children to experience the moral dilemmas for themselves and to consider aspects of human motivation and behaviour and of personal relationships that would be much more difficult to deal with in any other way. *Goldilocks and the Three Bears,* for instance, does not just enable children to produce different voices and give different characters to those involved in the story or to understand a plot that is strong on events – particularly the chronology of events – and of cause and effect. It also enables them to consider and discuss some matters concerning Goldilocks' pretty unsocial behaviour (breaking and entering, theft, malicious damage and squatting) which, given the affection that children have for the story and the fact that their sympathy is nearly always with Goldilocks, might well go unnoticed. As the stories become more complex through the two key stages, so do the moral ideas that they embody. Dramatic representation can help children to understand that people and situations are not always good or bad. There are always complexities.

RESEARCH SUMMARY RESEARCH SUMMARY **RESEARCH SUMMARY** RESEARCH SUMMARY

The moral educational aspects of drama with primary school children are the ones that have most interested drama writers and researchers. The most articulate arguments are produced by Joe Winston in a series of articles and books – of which the most useful to trainee teachers is probably *Drama, Literacy and Moral Education 5–11* (Winston, 2000). Here, Winston argues vigorously that dramatic enactment of stories and situations inevitably leads to moral questions that are important in children's personal and social development. The book is particularly useful because it is rich in clear examples – and helpful plans!

PRACTICAL TASK PRACTICAL TASK **PRACTICAL TASK** PRACTICAL TASK **PRACTICAL TASK**

Choose any well-known fairy tale (apart from *Goldilocks and the Three Bears*) and imagine that you are going to dramatise it with a primary class year of your choice. Draw up a cast list. Now choose any one of the characters and write no more than a side of A4 describing the character and outlining the motivation for their behaviour in the story. Dig deep. You can make up incidents in the character's past to explain or justify their actions if you like. Was the big bad wolf really brought up by his grandmother and physically abused as a cub? You tell me. It would explain a lot!

What are the moral issues contained in the story that dramatisation is likely to bring out?

You may be interested to know that this technique was used a great deal by Stanislavsky – the founder of the method school of acting!

Drama as an aid to language and literacy development

Drama activities with stories and poems in English or with situations and materials drawn from across the primary curriculum make a strong contribution to children's literacy and language development.

For spoken language, they provide opportunities to engage actively with language issues in unfamiliar contexts, they provide new purposes for language and they often involve new audiences – or a familiar enough audience in a new role. Children both demonstrate and further their knowledge about such matters as language register by pretending not only to behave but also to speak like somebody else in a particular situation.

The re-enactment of rhymes and stories, for example in the Reception Year and the first two terms of Year 1, sharpens children's awareness of the way that different kinds of people actually speak, of the importance of body language in the conveyance of meaning, and of the conventions of conversation – taking turns and listening, or at least appearing to listen. This improvised linguistic role play will later, at Key Stage 2 and beyond, be developed into considerations of the nature and functions of dialogue as a narrative device and as a means of revealing character.

Here are just a few of the possibilities of the drama activities that can make a contribution to children's language range and experience:

- **Improvisation** – the children assume roles and improvise dialogue to suit the role that they are playing in a given situation. Such improvisation can easily lead on to presenting the outcome as a drama script and so make a very laudable link with literacy work.
- **Simulation** – a bit more preplanned and researched than an improvisation, in which children assume roles in an open-ended situation and dramatise the events. The teacher might well be in role here too. An example might be the teacher as a local government official at a public meeting to consider the selling off of the school's grassy playing field for commercial development and the children as supporters, opponents or don't knows.
- **Tableaux and thought tracking** – the children assume roles and freeze a moment in a narrative. While the moment is frozen, each character takes it in turn to speak aloud the thoughts of the character they are representing at the moment that they have chosen to freeze. Afterwards they can explain, again in role, the significance of the moment for their own character.
- **Hot seating** – children assume roles and are placed in the hot seat, where they have to withstand some rigorous questioning by the rest of the class about their motives and behaviour in the narrative.
- **Puppets** – children make puppets and then use them to perform an improvised or scripted story. The puppets can be as simple (finger puppets, paper bag puppets, sock puppets) or as complicated (jointed cardboard marionettes) as you like. Similar use can be made of masks that the children make.

The National Curriculum for English assumes that the reading of play scripts makes a contribution towards the development of children's literacy. There *is* evidence to support the view that the wider the children's experience of reading different kinds of texts, the better readers they become. As Margaret Meek says, *children learn to read by reading* and reading and working with drama texts obviously helps children to become familiar with a generic structure and layout quite different from any other kind of text. We will explore this generic structure and layout later.

Apart from this, however, the most significant value of the drama techniques described above lie in their text-level application – they help children's literal and inferential comprehension of texts.

Role play activities with stories and poems enable children to clarify stories and get a firmer grasp on such issues as chronology of events, notions of cause and effect and the contributions of particular characters to the story, and therefore prepare the ground for more formal considerations of these matters in text-level work with written play scripts themselves. It is to such texts that we must now turn.

Analysing drama texts

Play scripts are similar to stories in some ways but different in others. They are similar in that they present a narrative that has a plot that is normally developed chronologically, and which involves characters doing things in a setting. The main and very important difference is that a story is meant to be read and only achieves its proper meaning in the relationship between writer and reader via the text. Plays, on the other hand, are meant to be acted and only achieve their full meaning in the relationship between writer and watcher via the text, the director, the actors, the designer, the lighting engineer, the sound engineer, the ticket sellers, the programme sellers and so on and so on. Play scripts are not intended simply to be read – there would be no point in writing them for that purpose. A dramatist might just as well write the story as a novel if that were the only intention. The relationship between a dramatist and an audience is far less intimate than the relationship between a story writer and an audience because it depends on many more intervening figures. A brilliant script can appear rubbish when it is incompetently directed or acted.

Much of what a dramatist writes in a script, therefore, is intended for a variety of audiences. It provides the words to be said by the actors, but it also implies the way that they should be said, the general tone of a scene, the way that that tone might be enhanced by sound or lighting effects and so on. These are buried messages that a story writer does not need to consider. Nonetheless, the play's the thing, and the comparison with stories in the way that they are structured is a close one – even if the way of expressing the story is different.

The structure of play scripts

The notion of plays needing a beginning, a middle and an end derives from Part 2, Section 4 of Aristotle's *Poetics* and is a familiar one in talking about any kind of composition. It implies that a story, however it is told, is a self-contained free-standing unit. As Aristotle puts it:

> A beginning is that which does not necessarily suppose anything before it, but which requires something to follow it. An end ...is that which requires something to precede it ... but which nothing is required to follow. A middle is that which both supposes something to precede and requires something to follow.

As we have seen in the earlier analysis of story structures, contemporary genre theorists have accepted Aristotle's broad definitions but have looked in rather more detail at the individual components. They may use different labels, but the ideas themselves are consistent enough. A beginning, for example, may consist of the 'Orientation', the 'Exposition' or the 'State of Equilibrium'. This is a difficult enough section for story writers to write and it is perhaps even more difficult for dramatists. The reasons for this are all to do with the relationship between the author, the text and the audience.

Here is the opening of a well-known story – the orientation section, if you like:

> *Alice was beginning to get very tired of sitting by her sister on the bank, and of having nothing to do: once or twice she had peeped into the book her sister was reading, but it had no pictures or conversations in it, 'and what is the use of a book,' thought Alice, 'without pictures or conversation?'*
>
> *So she was considering in her own mind (as well as she could, for the hot day made her feel very sleepy and stupid) whether the pleasure of making a daisy-chain would be worth the trouble of getting up and picking the daisies, when suddenly...*

And then something happens that takes us out of the orientation section and into the 'Inciting moment', the 'Crisis', the 'Problem', the 'Breach', the 'Complicating action' or the 'Disruption' – the start, if you like, of Aristotle's 'middle'. If you don't know what that something is, then you had better read *Alice's Adventures in Wonderland* immediately to find out! In fact ...

PRACTICAL TASK PRACTICAL TASK PRACTICAL TASK PRACTICAL TASK PRACTICAL TASK

If you have never read Lewis Carroll's *Alice's Adventures in Wonderland you* should seriously consider doing so if you can make time to do this before reading any further in this chapter!

If you have already read our earlier chapter on stories, you will immediately recognise that Lewis Carroll's authorial voice is that of an omniscient, third-person narrator. He knows everything about the characters and events – even to the extent of what characters are thinking and feeling. In fact, this orientation is all about thoughts and feelings – there is no action at all. A dramatist, however, cannot step in in this way to tell the audience about the inner trials and tribulations of a character's mind or soul. For a dramatist, virtually every-thing has to be done through the **dialogue.**

There are a few devices that may help – **asides, voice-overs, soliloquies** – but these are more appropriate for film and television. If they are overused by a dramatist they soon pall – unless the dramatist happens to be Shakespeare.

Of course a dramatist can make clear to actors and to a production team precisely how they want words to be said through the use of **stage directions** – but these stage directions in the script are not seen by an audience when a play is eventually presented.

There are other non-verbal means of conveying the way that characters are thinking and feeling. Sound effects – particularly music – and lighting effects can help. Again, however, these are particularly used in film and television drama, but are also valuable in theatrical performance.

However, even with these limited tools and devices available, it remains almost entirely through the dialogue that a dramatist tells a story and explores dramatic themes.

PRACTICAL TASK PRACTICAL TASK PRACTICAL TASK PRACTICAL TASK PRACTICAL TASK

Turn the opening two paragraphs of *Alice's Adventures in Wonderland* quoted above into the beginning of a play script. You will have to solve the problem of conveying Alice's thoughts to an audience in some way. Use stage directions and any other devices that you like – ancient or post-modern – to do this.

Now briefly note the problems that you met as a would-be dramatist and how you solved them. Are there any implications for the way that children might need to be helped in their reading of play scripts?

As in prose stories, after the inciting moment, the action becomes more involved in a plot through the 'Development' stage. The plots of plays – particularly those for primary school children – tend to be a good deal simpler than the plots of stories, with not so many narrative threads being woven together. This is true even in plays for adults. However, in the development of what is normally a single plot line, there are further crises, problems, complications and disruptions that the dramatist has to present as clearly but as interestingly and vividly as possible. Again, dialogue is almost the only medium available to the dramatist and they are in no position to step in to explain just why certain characters have behaved in the way that they have. If the dialogue does not make the events and the characters clear, then it has to remain unclear. There can be no other authorial presence.

The development, of course, as in stories, normally constitutes the bulk of the play – the largest component of the plot. It is in watching the twists and turns of story that is contained in the episodes of the development stage that much of the pleasure of a play exists. There are other pleasures, of course: the overall concept of the play, which is the work of the director, the individual performances of the actors, and so on, but these are not to be found in the text itself and are normally entirely outside a writer's control. Again, like stories, when this stage is done with and the play is about to reach its conclusion, there are often moments when something happens to make this conclusion possible. These are moments of 'Denouement' or 'Resolution' when the watcher or reader can sense that the end is nigh, and after these moments, a play reaches its 'Ending'.

The 'Ending', sometimes called 'Redress', 'Reinstatement', 'Conclusion' or 'Coda', is that part of the play's plot line where all complications are resolved and redressed, order is restored and the events of the plot are concluded. Aristotle, you may remember, defined an ending as *that which requires something to precede it but which nothing is required to follow.* A small representation of some aspect of life is over and we can take from it what messages we will. The writer has nothing else to say on the subject. As Shakespeare put it in *Hamlet, the rest is silence.*

PRACTICAL TASK PRACTICAL TASK PRACTICAL TASK PRACTICAL TASK PRACTICAL TASK

Choose a play script aimed at primary school children and examine the dramatic structure carefully. Try to isolate the 'Inciting Moment'. Decide whether the Development presents a single strand plot or whether there are one or more sub-plots. How many episodes can you identify in the Development stage? Determine the point of 'Denouement' in the story and how the playwright re-establishes normality.

The organisation of play scripts

Plays are organised in a different way from stories. Story writers for primary school children, especially picture book writers and illustrators, often think page by page. Of course, pages are linked together into a developing story and theme, or by some trickery with the book (holes through pages, lift-up flaps and so on) but it is important that small sections of text can be taken in as a self-contained chunk. Have a look at *Rosie's Walk, The Very Hungry Caterpillar,* or *Come Away from the Water, Shirley,* for clear examples of this. More extended continuous prose writers for primary school children organise stories into chapters. These can be as numerous and as long or as short as a writer wishes – though teachers quite like books that have chapter lengths that are either appropriate for an end of the day story session or for 15 minutes of shared reading in a literacy session. Writers ignore these requirements at their peril! A chapter, too, is self-contained and tends to represent a single episode in the plot. The best chapters end on a very tense note (writers call it a hook), which leaves a reader just dying to know what happens next and rushing to read on. However, the thing about both of these organisational methods is that a story can be put down at any point and returned to, or not, whenever a reader decides.

Plays are not like that. If they are to be received as the author intended – that is, performed and watched rather than just read – they have to be received at a sitting – though an interval or two is probably acceptable if a play is a long one. This is not normally the case with play scripts for primary children, but playwrights do not have the same freedom with structure that story writers have. They organise their work into large sections called acts, and within these large sections there are shorter sections called scenes. Sometimes, these scenes are labelled as such by the writer – sometimes they are not. In that case a play's director decides where one scene ends and another begins. Shakespeare's plays are written in five acts with any number of named scenes inside each act. Modern full-length plays are normally written in two or three acts with individual scenes unidentified in the text. Plays for primary school children rarely have more than one act, though there may be any number of scenes, which an author sometimes identifies. Writers tend to try to maintain an audience's interest by ensuring that individual scenes end on an exciting note.

The layout of play scripts

A drama script looks different from a story and children often have problems in reading it appropriately. Here is the first page of *Love Me Tender,* a play script by Alison Chaplin for upper Key Stage 2 children. It is a version of the first half of *Romeo and Juliet* and might well be appropriate for use in Year 5, before studying a Shakespeare play in Year 6.

SCENE 1: In a street in Verona

---

*MONTAGUE SERVANTS 1 & 2 are standing around chatting together
when CAPULET SERVANTS 1 & 2 enter:*

MONTAGUE SERVANT 1:	(*Noticing the CAPULETS*) Well, look who it is!
MONTAGUE SERVANT 2:	Capulets! (*Nastily*) Ugly lot, aren't they?
MONTAGUE SERVANT 1:	Very: Shouldn't be allowed to walk the streets with mugs like that.
MONTAGUE SERVANT 2:	Yeah. Scaring children, frightening old ladies, should be made to stay inside.

CAPULET SERVANT 1:	(*To MONTAGUE SERVANT 2*) Well, YOU'RE allowed out so what's the problem?
CAPULET SERVANT 2:	(*To CAPULET SERVANT 1*) Yeah, wouldn't win any prizes for beauty contests would they?
CAPULET SERVANT 1:	(*Agreeing*) Nope. Never seen a more unpleasant bunch, have you?
CAPULET SERVANT 2:	And look at their clothes. (*To MONTAGUE SERVANT 1*) Who got you dressed this morning?
MONTAGUE SERVANT 1:	(*Angrily*) You what?
CAPULET SERVANT 2:	(*To CAPULET SERVANT 1*) Oh, stupid as well!

The text here contains a lot of information intended for different people and presented in different ways. The font and typography differentiates to some extent between the intended different recipients of the different messages, but the fact that a variety of audiences is implied can cause confusion in inexperienced readers. Of course, this text is not meant for reading – it is meant for performing, and in the performance a good deal of the information on the page becomes irrelevant.

The text begins by locating the **setting** as 'a street in Verona'. This is not principally a message to the actors, though it certainly has implications for them. It is really a message to the set designer, the prop-maker and costumier – and the message is simple. Make sure that the setting, costume, make up and general demeanour of the actors looks like Verona. The fact that it is Verona where all of this takes place is actually very important in terms of the play itself because, well, they're all Italians you know! Passionate, hot-blooded, dashing and romantic characters, the lot of them – loving, laughing, hating and fighting with equal enthusiasm! Obviously, the children will need to have done quite a lot of work on aspects of the location and historical period in which the play is set before they get round to this text (Alison Chaplin makes a great many valuable suggestions in the book containing the script about the nature of such work) but, even in that short introductory locating sentence, the limitations of a playwright to influence the story are clear. They cannot go into detailed descriptions and explanations. They can simply give a few indications of what they would like in an ideal world, then everything is passed into the hands of someone else.

A **stage direction** follows. This is again not really a message to the actors but to the director. It is isolated from the main text by lines and by the fact that it is set in italics. The names of **characters** are set in capitals both in stage directions and in the indications of which character says what in the dialogue sections. There is no universal convention for doing things in precisely this way. This is a pity because layout and typography vary from author to author and publisher to publisher and this inconsistency can present problems for inexperienced readers of play texts who are unused to their generic characteristics. In a story, every bit of text is required to be read. In a play, only bits of it are. The problems lie in knowing which bits! Here, Alison Chaplin and her publishers, Scholastic, have made a clear and very laudable effort to differentiate on the page between those sections of text that are to be read, learned and subsequently spoken aloud by actors as part of the play and those parts which are not. Unfortunately, there are instances (for example one on page 180) where bits of dialogue are also set in capitals and those bits do need to be spoken aloud.

In the **dialogue** sections themselves, there are also italicised sections that do not need to be read or spoken by performers because they indicate the ways in which the author wants the lines to be spoken and sometimes to whom the particular lines are to be directed to make sense of the story. These are clearly messages to the reader/performer, though the director might well be interested in these as well.

The point of all this is that there is quite a different relationship between a playwright, a play script and a reader from that of an author, a story and a reader. A playwright has far fewer descriptive tools at their disposal and a reader has to select very carefully from a text to decide what needs to be spoken and what does not, while at the same time picking up relevant messages in the text outside the dialogue. There is a real need for teaching and learning relating to these sorts of practicalities in the reading of the texts to take place during both the shared and any guided reading sections of a play script targeted literacy session for Key Stage 2.

Shakespearean drama at Key Stage 2

One of the recurring recommendations throughout the development of the National Curriculum for English has been for the study of a Shakespeare play towards the end of the primary years. Shakespeare wrote or had a hand in writing well over 30 plays, of which very few, because of their themes, are actually appropriate for ten-year-old children. Even those few are not appropriate in their entirety. A teacher needs to be careful in the selection of Shakespearean material for primary children and in practice many have found it far more sensible to work with extracts from texts rather than with complete plays. There are available numerous versions of Shakespeare's plays written as stories and these can form very good starting points for the study of extracts from the plays themselves. As far as your own knowledge as trainee teachers is concerned, you will obviously need to know a little about Shakespeare's plays and that means reading some or, far better, going to see some performed.

Shakespeare's theatre

Shakespeare's plays were written around 400 years ago at a time when the theatre and the conventions of play writing were very different from what they are today. The theatres were open air – if it rained, most of the audience got wet – and the stages protruded into the audience, which meant that entrances and exits were largely from the back of the stage rather than the sides. There was a gallery on which scenes could be played, and a trap-doored under-stage area that could also be used at appropriate moments. There was minimal scenery, and no artificial lighting. Props, too, were fairly basic. This meant that all of the scene creation had to be done in the audience's imaginations and these had to be stimulated by Shakespeare's powers of language. Have a look at the speeches by Chorus at the beginning of each act of *Henry V to* see the clearest examples of this.

The structure and forms of Shakespeare's plays

The plays are now all divided into acts and scenes, though in the earliest printed versions of many of them this was not the case. In those versions, the plays were continuous with no demarcations at all. Subsequent editions, though, have all the plays divided into five acts with any number of scenes in each act. Individual scenes are located in a single place and when that place changes, so does the scene.

They are written in a mixture of prose and verse. In many cases, Shakespeare makes his lower-class characters speak in prose while the upper classes use poetry – though this is not invariably the case. The poetry that Shakespeare uses varies. The most consistent rhythmical form divided each line into five metrical sections, each with two beats. The second beat is stressed. Another famous opening provides an example:

> *Now is the winter of our discontent*
> *Made glorious summer by this sun of York.*

The mechanical way to read this is to read each line as five di-dums. In English prosody, a di-dum rhythmical pattern is called an iamb. The adjective from iamb is iambic. There are five iambic metrical beats to the line. The Greek prefix (and when talking about poetry, most of the technical terms originate in Greek) is pent. Each line is a pentameter and because it is composed of iambs it is an **iambic pentameter**. Shakespeare's plays are written very largely in iambic pentameters. He does occasionally throw in a few songs in a different rhythm, but iambic pentameter is largely the form for the verse passages. Of course, the lines are not actually spoken with the mechanical di-dum stresses of iambic pentameter. That would make them very monotonous and very dull, and pretty well strip them of meaning. A good actor superimposes the iambic form with the stresses of everyday language. Nonetheless, the pulse of the iambic pentameter beats fairly insistently underneath the speeches.

Most of Shakespeare's verse passages do not rhyme. He used rhyme sometimes for particular effects – when he wanted to give an especially romantic feel to a section of dialogue, for instance, or for magical effects between fairies or spirits – and he often used a rhyming couplet to signify the end of a scene. For the most part, however, the verse is unrhymed.

The dialogue is not naturalistic. Nobody spoke in iambic pentameter all the time in Shakespeare's England and certainly nobody used the same range and invention of figurative language – of similes, metaphors, personifications and the whole gamut of rhetorical devices that are available in the English language – as richly and brilliantly as Shakespeare's characters use them in the plays.

Nonetheless, Shakespeare's dialogue is brilliant in conveying character. It is often said that even the smallest walk-on role in Shakespeare presents a fully rounded character to the audience. We only see the drunken porter once in *Macbeth,* but in 40 lines of that one short scene (Act 2, scene iii) Shakespeare has created, using dialogue alone, a complete human being. There are some difficulties with the language, though. Shakespeare's characters use the lexis and the language styles of Tudor England at the end of the sixteenth century. Twenty-first-century primary school children inevitably find this a challenge. So, sometimes, do twenty-first-century adults. This is particularly true of comic scenes. Just as any dramatist writing nowadays would, Shakespeare gives such scenes lots of topical references, lots of currently popular songs, and lots of trendy jokes that no doubt had people falling about in Pudding Lane in the 1600s but somehow fail to hack it today. We have to accept that on the page many of those scenes are not particularly funny nowadays. However, as has been frequently emphasised in this chapter, plays are not intended to be responded to 'on the page' but 'on the stage'. In performance and with inventive direction and some judicial cutting, even the most dated of Shakespeare's comic scenes can spring to life and to laughs.

PEDAGOGICAL LINK PEDAGOGICAL LINK PEDAGOGICAL LINK PEDAGOGICAL LINK

Make sure that drama books are properly represented in any classroom book collection. It is unlikely that children will read plays unless they are available to them. In Year 6, collections of tales from Shakespeare – of which there are a generous abundance – should form a conspicuous part of the classroom book corner and be well represented in the school library.

Evaluating drama texts

It has been stressed in the chapters on story and poetry that literary judgement on them is ultimately a very personal matter. The same is true for drama. The value that any individual places on any text in any genre is, in the end, a matter of taste. There are certain aspects of the text that may provide the basis for an evaluation – certain criteria – but when two people make judgements about precisely the same aspects of the text using precisely the same criteria they are quite likely to come to different conclusions because their tastes are different.

Before we come to those criteria, though, it has to be re-emphasised that drama texts for reading and performance by primary school children are a comparatively recent phenomenon. The availability of primary targeted play scripts is steadily increasing – though this does not necessarily mean that the quality of the texts themselves is improving. The texts have been written often simply to fill a hole in pedagogical resources and to make a publisher's profit – not necessarily because the writers have a burning, artistic need to write them. I do not think that writers of drama for reading and performance by primary children will be offended by the judgement that the equivalents amongst them of story writers of the quality of such as Philippa Pearce, Betsy Byars, Anne Fine or Philip Pullman, or of poets such as Kit Wright, Michael Rosen or John Agard, have yet to emerge.

PRACTICAL TASK PRACTICAL TASK PRACTICAL TASK PRACTICAL TASK PRACTICAL TASK

Read at least one play from at least three of the following series of drama scripts for primary school children:

- *Oxford Reading Tree Play Scripts (OUP)*
- *Performance Plays (Scholastic)*
- *Plays for Infants: Traditional Tales (Ginn)*
- *Reading 2000 Play scripts (Longman)*
- *Sunshine Plays (Heinemann)*
- *Whodunnits (Collins)*

Now why not try writing one of your own? You will probably learn more about technicalities from that activity than from reading a book about them!

In overall terms, the criteria for evaluating the quality of play scripts are very similar to those for evaluating stories. There are a few adjustments to be made to emphasis, however, since plays reveal their plots in a different way from stories – namely, through the dialogue. Nonetheless, dramatists do have a similar range of approaches at their disposal. They can, as Polonius puts it in *Hamlet,* write *Tragedy, Comedy, History, Pastoral, Pastoral-Comical, Historical-Pastoral, Tragical-Historical, Tragical-Comical-Historical-Pastoral.* There are many others! On the whole, though, we assume that most dramatists try to make their plays naturalistic – that is, they try to represent the world as it really is, to make characters speak and behave in as realistic a way as possible and to make stories develop as they might be expected to in the real world outside the play script. However, there is no reason why this should be so. Drama for children can be as fantastic, as anthropomorphic, as whimsical, as metaphorical and as symbolic as stories can be and provide just as effective a launch pad for children's imaginations. They can also use conventions that are not open to story writers – like mime, song, visual jokes and tricks or choruses.

Appropriateness

Like stories, the content and the language of plays need to be appropriate to the children with whom you plan to use them. Since children mature at different rates and develop their range of language skills at different rates, this is not always an easy judgement to make. Actually, the danger with some drama for children is not that it is too difficult in content and language but that it is too simple. There is often more than a mere whiff of patronisation – of writing down, but this is a judgement that teachers can only make given the age, language skills and ability range of the children in front of them. It is also important to choose texts that you find interesting – your enthusiasm can be infectious to the children.

Plot and themes

The plot of a play is what really holds the interest. It is mainly the plot that stimulates a watcher's or reader's curiosity and the desire to keep on watching or reading to find out what happens next. Adults in the theatre have been known to walk out very noisily when they are bored or disappointed by the quality of a play. Children are not generally in a position to do that or to throw a play script down in disgust – particularly if it is being used as a literacy resource. It is important, therefore, to make sure beforehand that the plot of a play is likely to be interesting to the children and to hold their attention – to make them actually care about what happens to the characters in the play and about how the plot will turn out.

As with stories, the plots of good plays do more than just develop a storyline and tell us what happens to the people involved. They raise issues for an audience or a reader – they explore and develop themes. In evaluating the worth of a play script, therefore, teachers need to make a judgement first of all about whether the plot is appropriate to the children with whom they intend to read it and act it out. This does not mean that a play has to reflect directly the lives that the children live. It may do that, but it may also extend and enrich children's experience by placing them into the roles, giving them the thoughts, feelings, language and characteristics of others. What is necessary in either case, however, is that the events and relationships in a story need to be comprehensible to children given their age and stage of intellectual and emotional development. A teacher needs to judge whether a play is likely to entertain, excite, interest and intrigue children and whether it says something that is worth saying. Good plays take an audience or a reader beyond mere plot and it is important that the themes they explore are also relevant and comprehensible to the children.

Characters

Characters in plays are often delineated in much less detail than they are in stories. This is because a playwright does not have the same resources as an author to delineate them. Characters in plays are established entirely through what they say and do or by what other characters say about them and this last is not always trustworthy. Much, therefore, has to be made of an actor's or reader's interpretative and performance skills. In plays for children, because they are short, characters are generally only very broadly sketched. All a teacher can do is be convinced that the characters are solidly enough presented to be credible and that the children will care about what happens to them.

Dialogue

Since it is mainly through dialogue that characters are conveyed and that the story is told, it is important that the writing is strong and convincing enough to do both. If the writing is poor then plays lose momentum and become turgid. If the writing is good then dialogue sparkles and delights. This is a section from a very surreal little play called *Hoff the Cat Dealer* by Andrew Davies (1986). Hoff has got the sack from his job at the car factory and has come home to tell his wife the bad news – he's got the sack – and the good news – he's got a cat:

MRS HOFF:	*You call that good news? We're starving, and Hoff gets a cat!*
HOFF:	*Wait till you see him. He's almost human. He followed me all the way home. Come in boy.*
CAT:	*(Coming in) Haywow.*
HOFF:	*Haywow. Say haywow to the cat. He's saying haywow to you.*
MRS HOFF:	*(sarcastically) Haywow!*
HOFF:	*Would you like some milk, cat?*
CAT:	*Now?*
HOFF:	*Yes.*
CAT:	*Wow!*
HOFF:	*You see? How could anyone be depressed with a cat like this?*
CAT:	*Cheroot?*
HOFF:	*No thanks. I don't smoke.*
MRS HOFF:	*I can't stand this. Hoff, you're going crackers. We cannot afford a cat. You'll have to get rid of him! She storms off.*
HOFF:	*Wow.*
CAT:	*Meek. Meek.*
HOFF:	*Meek meek? What does that mean?*
CAT:	*Well, not very much really. Just yes indeed, see what you mean, mate.*
HOFF:	*You can talk!*
CAT:	*Naturally. If you're kind enough to invite me in, give me milk, and talk my language, it's only polite to talk yours as well.*
HOFF:	*Meek. Meek. Wow.*

The ear for dialogue here is brilliant. To begin with, the characters speak in ways appropriate to their very broadly drawn characters – Hoff, long-suffering but basically kind, Mrs Hoff, ambitious, long-suffering in her marriage to Hoff, sharp and short-tempered, and the cat, as unforecastable and eccentric as most cats are and with a wide range of vocabulary and phraseology in fluent Catese. Beyond that, the dialogue has the vocabulary and the rhythms of everyday speech that children will recognise and associate with. It is easy to say and comes in rapid interchanges. There are no moments when a character makes a long speech while the others stand around listening and admiring. Even though the plot is unlikely, the dialogue isn't. This is far from easy to achieve and in some plays for both children and adults the vocabulary and rhythms are so far removed from normal speech patterns that lines become virtually unsayable. As a matter of interest, in this particular play, there are opportunities for children to bring and use their own experience and knowledge of the Cat language, but in order to find out how you will have to read the play!

Language

As with stories, the most obvious requirement of the language in a play script is that it must be appropriate and comprehensible to the child audience. Children should certainly be stretched linguistically in the texts that they read, but if the level of difficulty of the language means that they cannot decode it, or have to go scurrying to the dictionary every two minutes to check for meaning, then the language and the text itself is not appropriate. It is largely this criterion that causes a controversy over the inclusion of Shakespeare in Year 6.

Shakespeare, though, is a special case. Obviously, teachers will need to work very hard to make some of the language accessible to Year 6 children and obviously the story of any chosen extract needs to be clarified before any work on the text itself can take place. Once the story is clear, however, the difficult aspects of the language generally become less difficult and the children can often be astonished at the wonderful opportunities that Shakespeare's rich and inventive language provided for application outside the literacy session. Certainly Sir Toby Belch's 'Sneck up' and 'Shog off' have stood me in good stead over the years, and I have heard children wince with a mixture of horror, pleasure and astonishment when they have understood the imagery and vocabulary of the Captain's praise of Macbeth in Act 1, scene i *he unseam'd him from the nave to the chaps.* Reading Shakespeare has the potential to wake children up to the enormous richness of spoken language – as well, of course, as beginning a process of familiarisation with the work of arguably the greatest poetic user of the English language that the world has ever known.

In the primary years, however, the dialogue of plays tends to reflect the ordinary speech patterns of everyday life as it is lived by the children. They can generally make such language sound much more convincing than any other kind. Consequently, there is less opportunity for a writer of plays to go in for fancy figurative language to the same extent as story writers or poets. Similes, metaphors and rhetorical devices are a lot less common in plays than they are in other genres of imaginative language work. When evaluating a play, therefore, we need to ask whether the language and the dialogue are clear, authentic and with a sense of the rhythms of everyday speech.

The play script as an object

All of the things that have already been said about story and poetry books apply equally well to drama books. Presentation is just as important for play scripts as for anything else. This does not simply mean that the various facets of the text (characters, stage directions and dialogue) should all be indicated clearly in font and typographical differences but that the book should encourage a child to pick it up and read it independently or with friends. Individual and collections of play scripts need to be visually attractive, with an appropriately sized font and a reader-friendly layout and intelligent and appropriate use of illustrations.

PEDAGOGICAL LINK PEDAGOGICAL LINK PEDAGOGICAL LINK PEDAGOGICAL LINK

Children pick up a book first because they are interested in it as an object. Publishers know this and ensure that the cover is bright, colourful and attractive. Play scripts, because of the special requirements that they have of their readers, are the least likely of all the primary school textual genres to be picked up and read independently by children. If plays are displayed in classrooms or school libraries with the spine out, then the attractiveness of the cover is lost. Try to make sure that as many playbooks as possible – and particularly the ones you are using at any particular time – are displayed so that the publisher's hard work can be put to use and the covers can be seen.

PRACTICAL TASK PRACTICAL TASK PRACTICAL TASK PRACTICAL TASK PRACTICAL TASK

Any drama work with children depends on a teacher's knowledge of the play texts available. This does not just mean knowing about the language, plots and structures of plays; it means knowing who are the good writers most likely to stimulate your class. That, in turn, means reading a lot of plays for children. This task is a long-term one. It is to read at least one collection of plays for children every month for the rest of your training and teaching career.

PRACTICAL TASK PRACTICAL TASK PRACTICAL TASK PRACTICAL TASK PRACTICAL TASK

New writers for children are constantly appearing. It is important that teachers keep up to date. There are a number of ways of doing this and a list of possibilities follows. Make sure you do at least one of them.

- Visit a bookshop regularly and browse in the children's section.
- Visit a library regularly. Browse and ask advice from the children's librarian.
- Read reviews of children's books. There are specialist journal publications, the *TES* and Sunday broadsheet newspapers have reviews, the bookseller Waterstone's produces a yearly *Guide to Children's Books* and Penguin publications has its own *The Good Book Guide to Children's Books*.
- Look regularly at the books that specialist book clubs or publishers are offering.
- Listen to children to hear what they are reading and for ideas of what is popular on film and television – these could be useful stimuli for children writing their own play scripts.

A SUMMARY OF **KEY POINTS**

➢ The term 'drama' has a number of possible interpretations.

➢ Drama strategies and scripts can be used for a number of different purposes in primary class-rooms. They provide a framework for organising experience and an opportunity for extending it.

➢ Drama shares many of the qualities and uses of story, though there is not an equivalent canon of outstanding work available to teachers and therefore not the same sense of a common culture. It can, however, provide similar support for learning across the curriculum, similar support for moral education and similar support for language and literacy development.

➢ The plots of plays can be analysed in exactly the same way that the plots of stories are analysed.

➢ There are significant differences between stories and play scripts in their presentation because play scripts are written for a variety of audiences looking at the text for different purposes rather than a solitary reader.

➢ Where Shakespeare is taught in Year 6, it must be remembered that his plays are very much of their time in matters of structure and language.

➢ There are a number of criteria that relate to the evaluation of play scripts for primary children. These include appropriateness, plot and themes, characters, dialogue, language, and overall presentation.

M-LEVEL EXTENSION > > M-LEVEL EXTENSION > > M-LEVEL EXTENSION

As good quality play scripts for primary children are not as readily available as stories and poems, work collaboratively with colleagues (fellow trainee teachers as well as the teachers and subject leaders with whom you work) to compile a list of favourite play texts that children of different ages have enjoyed. Include notes of any cross-curricular links and aspects of children's development that each support.

FURTHER READING   FURTHER READING   **FURTHER READING**   FURTHER READING

DfE (2013) *Teachers' Standards*. London: DfE. (**www.gov.uk/government/uploads/system/uploads/attachment_data/file/208682/Teachers__Standards_2013.pdf**)

Somers, J. (1994) *Drama in the Curriculum.* London: Cassell. This is a detailed examination of most aspects of drama work in primary schools. It is very strong indeed, however, on issues of role play and of theatricality and Somers writes about these from both theoretical and practical viewpoints.

Winston, J. (2000) *Drama, Literacy and Moral Education 5–11.* London: David Fulton. This is rich in practical ideas for using stories as starting points for drama work which is designed to develop both literacy skills and moral education.

Woolland, B. (2010) *Teaching Primary Drama.* London: Longman. This is another book which is full of practical ideas for using drama techniques in a variety of ways, including suggestions for using drama as a strategy for teaching poetry and story.

13
Looking at information books

Curriculum context

National Curriculum programmes of study

This knowledge is designed to underpin the teaching of the Key Stage 1 and Key Stage 2 programmes of study for English, which state, for example, that pupils should be taught

in spoken language to:

- give well-structured descriptions, explanations and narratives for different purposes

in reading to:

- develop pleasure in reading, motivation to read, vocabulary and understanding by:

  o listening to and discussing a wide range of poems, stories and non-fiction at a level beyond that at which they can read independently Y1/2
  o listening to and discussing a wide range of non-fiction and reference books or textbooks Y3/4/5/6
  o reading books that are structured in different ways and reading for a range of purposes Y3/4/5/6
  o discussing the sequence of events in books and how items of information are related Y2
  o being encouraged to link what they read or hear to their own experiences Y1

- distinguish between statements of fact and opinion Y5/6
- retrieve, record and present information from non-fiction Y5/6

and in writing to:

- develop positive attitudes towards and stamina for writing by:

  o writing about real events Y2
  o writing for different purposes Y2

- plan their writing by:

  o identifying the audience for and purpose of the writing, selecting the appropriate form and using other similar writing as models for their own Y5/6
  o noting and developing initial ideas, drawing on reading and research where necessary Y5/6

- draft and write by:

  o in non-narrative material, using simple organisational devices [for example, headings and sub-headings] Y3/4
  o using further organisational and presentational devices to structure text and to guide the reader [for example, headings, bullet points, underlining] Y5/6.

Early Years Foundation Stage

The Early Learning Goals specify that, by the end of the Early Years Foundation Stage, children should:

- demonstrate understanding when talking with others about what they have read.

Introduction

Children's early reading experiences have traditionally been in the area of fiction. Research has shown that over 80 per cent of reading time between ages 4 and 7, including reading instruction, has been spent on reading fiction. In the past, it was assumed that children would only be able to read non-fiction texts once they were proficient readers of fiction.

However, children's reading experience outside school is rich with information print. Some of the first books ever given to children in the home (such as baby board books or picture alphabet books) are often simple catalogues of labelled items. These are information books. Even the youngest of children can often read and recognise packaging, adverts and shop signs. Most teachers recognise this environmental print as valuable reading experience, but may still neglect non-fiction books in the classroom as an early route to literacy.

Children may spend their early years immersed in poems, traditional tales, stories and reading scheme 'readers'. They start to learn about the conventions of character and plot. They learn that every story starts on page one, reads from top left down the page, and has a beginning, middle and end. By the time children are aged about 7, their reading diet suddenly changes. Almost overnight, it seems, they are expected to read and understand non-fiction books, textbooks, and specialist information books about science, geography or history.

It is now recognised that non-fiction books should be read and discussed by children from the earliest stages of reading:

- Their highly visual presentation can make them easier for the very young reader to access than fiction.
- They are ideal for shared or guided reading since they contain images from the child's real experience, which are very suitable for discussion.
- They offer a better route to literacy for some readers (often boys) who prefer the real-world content.
- The range of topics available provides a greater choice for readers of all abilities and interests.

The benefits of teaching young children early non-fiction skills from school entry are considerable. It can provide a foundation for the skills that they will need throughout their school life, and for their adult lives (most of the reading we do as adults is information reading). It will unlock other subject areas like science, history and geography, which rely on the use of non-fiction books and the interpretation of such things as charts and graphs, timelines, diagrams and maps. It is also the case that children's reading experiences directly influence their ability to write. Experience of different types of non-fiction in primary school can assist children's ability to write for different audiences in an appropriate style later on.

Overuse of stories as the major reading experience in the primary years can make it hard to 'wean' children off these fiction-based strategies later on. They may mistakenly try to apply these 'fiction rules' to non-fiction:

- They will find it hard to use contents pages and 'skim through', preferring to start at the beginning of a non-fiction book.
- Their unfamiliarity with non-fiction will hold them back when they move up the school and are required to read textbooks, history books, maps, etc.
- They will also find it hard to write in a non-fiction style, like writing a report, and will lapse into more familiar story-style writing.
- They will find it hard to find the books they need for research.
- They will have a tendency to simply copy out verbatim from books rather than put things in their own words.

A broad range of fiction and non-fiction books is essential for teaching children how to read, from the moment they enter school; but not just any books. In the same way as we need to be selective about the kinds of fiction that we make available for children, we need to be able to apply critical criteria to our selection of non-fiction texts.

Looking critically at information books

Non-fiction materials come in many different formats. Not only are there books and magazines, but newspapers, newsletters, almanacs, atlases, encyclopaedias, and documents that present factual information. There are a number of criteria by which we can judge the quality of non-fiction materials: they tend to be full of facts; they are accurate; they are written in concise form; they provide illustrative material; very often they contain specialised vocabulary and they are organised in particular ways. We will look more closely at each of these criteria.

Facts

Non-fiction, by definition, deals with – all kinds of facts – facts about today, facts about yesterday, and even facts about tomorrow. Books and materials vary immensely, of course, both in their selection and their treatment of these facts. Some non-fiction books, for example, especially those aimed at younger readers, choose to include very few facts. Some include facts which, it might be expected, young children already know. Compare, for example, the text on the first pages of two information books:

Book 1

> *Wood comes from trees. Trees grow all over the world. They grow in hot, damp lands of Africa, Asia and South America.*

Book 2

> **The storm chaser**
>
> *My name is Robert Davies-Jones. I work for the National Severe Storms Laboratory (NSSL) in the United States of America. I am a scientist. My job is to find out about storms so we can warn people about them. I am very interested in storms that cause tornadoes.*
>
> *On Thursday 8th June 1995, I set out to chase a storm. This is what happened.*
>
> **Fact Box**
>
> *Tornadoes are huge windstorms. They can tear up trees, knock down houses, and kill people and animals. The United States of America is hit by more tornadoes than any other country in the world.*

The first example contains very few facts that children of the target age (6/7 year olds) would not know, apart from the fact that trees grow in 'hot, damp lands'. This statement itself is a little misleading as, without reading on to the next page of this book, a reader could end up thinking that trees *only* grow in such places.

The second example, however, is much more fact-dense and sets out to engage its target readers (again 6/7 year olds) with the information it includes.

One of the criteria that you would want to apply to selecting information books for children is the degree to which the text gives sufficient facts to engage the reader's interest. Books can go too far, however, and if the information they provide is *too* dense, they risk overloading and putting off their potential readers.

Accuracy

High-quality non-fiction material should be accurate. How can you tell that you can rely on the facts provided? Publishers of non-fiction materials want to assure readers that they can depend on these publications, so they tend to supply information about the author's expertise and experience on the covers of books, in the introductory pages, in the preface, or throughout the materials.

Generally, you are much more likely to be able to trust the accuracy of non-fiction materials when:

- information is given about the author's and illustrator's expertise and experience;
- information is provided about the experts, if any, who were consulted during the writing of the materials;
- major references are cited in the text and in the bibliography;
- materials are up to date.

Even when such tests are passed, however, there is still a possible problem with accuracy in non-fiction books and this is connected with the issue of **bias**. The fact is that most of what we read, even those texts that deal with 'facts', may actually be propaganda. This is simply because all texts are written by someone and that person is certain to be the member of a particular political, social, religious or racial group and therefore have to some extent that political, social, religious or racial world view. Therefore, what they write is not completely objective. This does not mean that such a writer is deliberately intending to mislead readers. We have to distinguish between deliberate and involuntary bias. Authors may simply not recognise the perspective from which their writing comes because they are too close to it.

Bias in texts is, therefore, virtually universal. One of the aims of teachers should be to enable children to get beneath the surface of a text and become aware of the perspective from which it is written. To do this, teachers need to be critical readers themselves and to recognise the features in texts that indicate partiality. What are these features?

REFLECTIVE TASK

Examine these two passages, each of which describes the Battle of the Little Big Horn. As you read, make notes about what you know of the point of view of the authors of each passage. How are these points of view communicated?

Passage 1

It rapidly became clear that General Custer had been out-manoeuvred by a superior tactician. As the horses surged around his dwindling group of men, he must finally have realised he was not invincible after all. Sitting Bull had lured him into a trap in the same way that countless bands of native Americans had been lured in the past by white bounty hunters. And revenge was about to be exacted.

One by one the cavalrymen were brought down. Although outnumbered, their weapons were superior and an increasing number of horses began to speed away riderless from the battle. Many a family would grieve that night when those horses returned to their teepees. But the odds gradually began to tell. When Custer himself fell, beyond the protection of his hard-pressed men at last, it was only a matter of time.

Passage 2

Massacre at the Little Big Horn

No one can recall the countless deeds of heroism done that day: men dying to try to save their doomed comrades from the ravening hordes surrounding them. Custer himself was saved twice from arrows to his back by brave men who put themselves in the way.

Yet all this selflessness was to come eventually to naught. There were simply too many howling red attackers to resist. The Sioux had been waiting and building their strength and were now extracting their blood-thirsty revenge on the white men. Nobody would survive that day and the name of George Armstrong Custer would enter the annals of heroes who died defending their countries and their men.

The two extracts differ in their implied stories of how Custer and his men came to be involved in this battle. In one text, they have apparently been lured into a trap by a superior general; in the second, they are 'defending their country', a much more noble explanation of their involvement. The extracts also differ in their accounts of who was being killed in the battle. In the second text, there is no mention at all of Sioux casualties, whereas in the first this is dwelt on in an almost lyrical way. It seems clear that the first text was written by a writer sympathising with the Sioux viewpoint of this battle, whereas the second text takes the viewpoint of Custer and his men.

These perspectives are indicated in several ways:

- *details included or omitted* – e.g. white bounty hunters and grieving Sioux families versus Custer being saved from arrows to his back. The superior weapons of Custer's men are mentioned only in the first extract.
- *quality of description* – e.g. in the first extract, Custer is 'out-manoeuvred', his men are 'brought down', Sioux horses 'speed away riderless'; in the second, Custer's men perform 'countless deeds of heroism' and are selfless, whereas the Sioux are 'ravening hordes' and 'blood-thirsty'.

These two features of selection of events and vocabulary choice are those in which bias in texts is most commonly seen.

Conciseness

Individual facts are units of information. Their power rests not only in their content but also in their clear, generally brief form. It is such concise writing that grips the reader's mind and imagination. Readers need models of succinct composition in order to develop skill in expository writing. Fiction can help them to write narration; non-fiction can help them write exposition.

Specialised vocabulary

Non-fiction often requires a special vocabulary. To appreciate any topic fully, terms must be understood. Special terms are defined in non-fiction materials in different ways. They may be defined:

- as they are introduced – in some books, for instance, new terms are printed in italics and defined as soon as they are introduced;
- as part of captions or as additions to labels outside the main narrative;
- in a special glossary at the back of the book.

No matter how they are presented, new terms need to be defined and made clear to readers. This sometimes means that they need to be clarified by visual representation.

Illustration

When text is not enough to present information clearly, drawings, photographs, headings, highlighting, colour, and even paper engineering (foldouts, tabs and flaps) may be used.

Non-fiction materials provide opportunities to teach readers how to 'read' illustrative materials in order to glean all of the information that they offer. Sometimes, it is the strong appeal of remarkable illustrations that invite children to sit and stare and think about the books in their hands.

David Lewis, in his study of the breadth of reading in three Key Stage 2 classes (Lewis, 1992), found that collaborative reading, that is children sharing books with their friends, was only found when the text was non-fiction. It appeared to be the illustrations in a book that particularly prompted such sharing.

Organisation

It is fairly obvious that non-fiction books are organised differently from fiction books. Index pages, for example, make it possible for a reader to quickly find particular items in a non-fiction book, rather than adopting the typical fiction reading strategy of starting at the beginning and working through to the end.

What has really only been considered comparatively recently is the fact that non-fiction books themselves differ in terms of their organisation. A key concept here is that of text 'genre'. This term can be used in several ways, which can make it rather confusing, and the term 'text types' is often preferred. The thinking behind the way in which these terms are used to refer to non-fiction books is as follows:

- Non-fiction books and texts are written for a range of different purposes. Some are written to retell a sequence of events. Biographies are one familiar example of this. Others are written to give instructions, such as in recipe books. We have identified seven major purposes of non-fiction texts and books (see below).
- Depending on its purpose, a non-fiction book will be written in a distinctive form. Biographies and recipe books are structured very differently because they have different purposes.
- Non-fiction books are generally distinguished in form by:

  1. **Their structure** – A biography, for example, will generally take the form of a series of chapters, each containing descriptions of a series of events, usually in chronological order. A recipe book, on the other hand, will usually be divided into much shorter sections, each of which contains a heading (e.g. Rich chocolate cake), a list of ingredients and a series of steps to guide the reader in making the dish.
  2. **Their vocabulary and grammar** – A biography will refer to particular people and will be written in the past tense. A recipe book does not refer to people (other than perhaps a general 'you') and uses the imperative present tense (prepare the bowl, mix the ingredients).
  3. **Their connectives** – Both biographies and recipe books generally use connectives related to time (After that he; Next get), whereas other types of texts use more logical connectives (because, on account of, in spite of).

The seven major information book genres are:

1. Recounts
2. Records
3. Reference texts
4. Persuasive texts
5. Discussions
6. Reports
7. Instructions

Each genre has particular structural and language features and these are described below under the three headings of purpose, structure and language features. Under each genre, we indicate a typical type of book that exemplifies that genre.

Recounts

The purpose of a recount is to retell, in narrative form, a sequence of events with the purpose of either informing or entertaining an audience (or with both purposes).

A recount usually consists of:

- a 'scene setting' opening (orientation);
- a recount of the events as they occurred (events);
- a closing statement (reorientation).

Recounts are usually written:

- in the past tense;
- in chronological order, using connectives of time;
- focusing on individual or group participants;
- using 'doing/action' verbs.

Examples of recounts are biographies, autobiographies and newspaper reports. (Please note that the term 'report' is used rather differently later.)

Records

The purpose of a record is to record events, and the writer's feelings about those events, as they occur.

Records usually contain:

- accounts of a sequence of events;
- events ordered according to a clearly signalled system (usually dates);
- some commentary on each event as it is described (optional).

Records are usually written:

- in the past tense (with present tense for commentaries);
- in chronological order, using temporal connectives;
- focusing on an individual participant (the writer);
- using 'doing/action' verbs (with thinking/feeling verbs for commentaries).

Examples of records are diaries and log-books.

Reference texts

The purpose of a reference text is to present information in an ordered, easily retrievable way.

Reference texts usually contain:

- a number of short pieces of information about a large number of things, events or people;
- a clear system of organisation, e.g. alphabetical order or progressive questions leading to information location.

Reference texts are usually written:

- in the present tense;
- with logical connectives predominating;
- focusing on generic participants (dinosaurs rather than a particular dinosaur).

Examples of reference texts are encyclopaedias and identification guides.

Persuasive texts

The purpose of a persuasive text is to put forward an argument in favour of a particular point of view.

A piece of persuasive writing usually consists of:

- an opening statement/thesis (often in the form of position/preview);
- the arguments (often in the form of point + elaboration);
- a summary and restatement of the opening position (reiteration).

Persuasive text is usually written:

- in the simple present tense;
- focusing mainly on generic human participants;
- using mostly logical rather than temporal connectives.

Examples of persuasive texts are pamphlets and leaflets supporting a particular viewpoint.

Discussions

The purpose of a discussion is to present arguments and information from differing viewpoints before reaching a conclusion based on the evidence.

A discussion usually consists of:

- a statement of the issue + a preview of the main arguments;
- arguments for + supporting evidence;
- arguments against + supporting evidence;
- a recommendation given as a summary and conclusion.

(The arguments for and against can be presented in a variety of orders.)

Discussions are usually written:

- in the simple present tense;
- using generic human (or non-human) participants rather than personal pronouns (except in the thesis/ conclusion);
- using logical connectives.

Examples of discussion are issue books.

Reports

The purpose of a report is to describe and/or explain particular phenomena.

A report usually consists of:

- an opening, general classification;

- a more technical classification (optional);
- a description of the phenomena, which includes some or all of its qualities, parts and their functions, habits/ behaviour or uses;
- a series of logical steps to explain phenomena.

Reports are usually written:

- in the present tense;
- using non-chronological connectives;
- focusing on groups of things (generic participants);
- using 'being' and 'having' verbs, with some action verbs.

Examples of reports are explanations, scientific accounts and descriptions. Because these are ordered non-chronologically, they are often referred to as 'non-chronological reports', to distinguish them from newspaper reports, which are in fact recounts.

Instructions

The purpose of a set of instructions is to guide the carrying out of a set of actions.

An instructional book will normally consist of a series of instruction texts, each of which usually contains:

- a statement of what is to be achieved;
- a list of materials/equipment needed to achieve the goal;
- a series of sequenced steps to achieve the goal;
- often there is a diagram or illustration.

Instructions are usually written:

- in the simple present tense or imperative tense;
- in chronological order;
- focusing on generalised human agents rather than individuals;
- using mainly doing/action clauses.

Examples of instructions are recipe books and the instruction leaflets that come with games.

There are some important caveats to make when presenting the above descriptions. These relate to book genres; that is, particular types of books. This overlaps largely with the concept of text genres that teachers have become familiar with, but there are some important differences:

- Books, of whatever main genre, will almost always contain some sections of text of a different genre. Thus, in an autobiography, which we classify overall as recount genre, the author may well include some elements of report, explanation or even persuasion. In a book about volcanoes which, because its purpose is largely to give information about these natural phenomena, will probably be report genre, the author may also include some explanation genre text telling *how* a volcano is formed.
- Books therefore hardly ever contain text exclusively of one genre. Most books are, in fact, hybrids in terms of the text genres they contain.
- One important text genre often targeted for teaching is explanation. It is rare, in fact, to find books that contain exclusively explanation, so this is not listed in the seven book genres above. Explanation text is perhaps most often found in report books.

A SUMMARY OF **KEY POINTS**

➢ In the past, it was assumed that children would only be able to read non-fiction texts once they were proficient in reading fiction.

➢ It is now recognised that children should read and discuss non-fiction books from the earliest stages of reading.

➢ The criteria for looking critically at information books include evaluating their use of facts, accuracy, conciseness, how they present specialised vocabulary, their use of illustration, and how they are organised.

➢ There are seven major information book genres/text types: recounts, records, reference texts, persuasive texts, discussions, reports and instructions.

M-LEVEL EXTENSION > > M-LEVEL EXTENSION > > M-LEVEL EXTENSION

Information books will, of course, be used by teachers and children in many areas of the primary curriculum. It would be useful for you to make a comparison of the types of texts characteristically used in the major curriculum areas. Begin with one area, say history, and examine some of the information books you have available in that area. Can you spot examples of the seven main non-fiction text types as described above? (You should easily find examples of most of these text types, but might struggle to find examples of instructions.)

Now repeat this process with another area, say science. Are the characteristic text types the same? (Here you would expect to find some examples of instructions, but maybe not as much persuasive writing.)

What are some of the implications of this diversity of range for your teaching about text structures?

If, as seems likely, this teaching needs to be carried out across the curriculum, where the texts occur naturally, what implications does this have for how you organise your literacy teaching?

FURTHER READING FURTHER READING FURTHER READING FURTHER READING

DfE (2013) *Teachers' Standards*. London: DfE. (**www.gov.uk/government/uploads/system/uploads/attachment_data/file/208682/Teachers__Standards_2013.pdf**)

Lewis, M. and Wray, D. (1995) *Developing Children's Non-Fiction Writing.* Leamington Spa: Scholastic. As well as a thorough explanation of non-fiction text types, this book contains a rationale for an approach to teaching the writing of these.

Littlefair, A. (1991) *Reading All Types of Writing.* Buckingham: Open University Press. An early, but still useful, description of text genre and register.

14
Electronic texts

Curriculum context

National Curriculum programmes of study

This knowledge is designed to underpin the teaching of the Key Stage 1 and Key Stage 2 programmes of study for English, which state, for example, that pupils should be taught

in spoken language to:

*   ask relevant questions to extend their understanding and knowledge
*   consider and evaluate different viewpoints, attending to and building on the contributions of others

in reading to:

*   participate in discussion about other works that are read to them and those that they can read for themselves, taking turns and listening to what others say Y2
*   explain and discuss their understanding of other material, both those that they listen to and those that they read for themselves Y2
*   retrieve and record information from non-fiction Y3/4/5/6.

Early Years Foundation Stage

The Early Learning Goals specify that, by the end of the Early Years Foundation Stage, children should:

- demonstrate understanding when talking with others about what they have read.

Introduction

Traditionally, literacy has been simply defined as the condition of being able to read and write, and for most people this definition is adequate. However, it is becoming increasingly apparent that we need to expand our definition of literacy to include the reading and writing not only of printed texts but of electronic texts. Until recently, teachers could safely confine reading and writing activities to printed materials. Increasingly, however, reading and writing can be done electronically with the aid of a computer. Computers are being used to create and revise texts, to send and receive mail electronically, to present texts of all kinds onscreen instead of in printed books, and to access large databases of texts for research purposes. Electronic texts are becoming more prevalent as computers become an integral part of everyday experiences such as working, shopping, travelling and studying.

You need to include electronic forms of reading and writing in the literacy experiences that you offer your pupils. This raises the major question for your knowledge about texts of exactly how electronic texts are different from printed texts. What is distinctive about electronic texts? What do children need to know about such texts in order to use them effectively, and what do you need to know in order to develop their knowledge?

The characteristics of electronic texts

In this chapter, we will discuss three fundamental differences between printed and electronic texts. We will try to go beyond the merely surface differences between the two media. A screen looks different to a page but that in itself need not imply a different way of reading the text in this medium. Writing an electronic text will obviously be different to writing a paper-based text, in that the physical actions needed to create these texts are different. Yet the differences between these two activities can amount to a great deal more than just the difference between writing with a pen and typing at a keyboard.

REFLECTIVE TASK

It would be useful at this point for you to think about the differences between reading and writing paper-based texts and screen-based texts. Start by thinking of some recent occasions when you have read and written electronically.

You might have done any or all of the following:

- read a web page;
- read a document from the internet in PDF format;

- read a text on your mobile phone;
- written an assignment on a word processor;
- written an email;
- written during an instant messaging conversation with a friend;
- written a text and sent it.

Focus on one of these experiences and try to imagine a parallel literacy experience using pen and paper. If you chose reading a web page, for example, a parallel would be reading an information book. For writing an email, a parallel would be writing a letter. In what ways was the electronic experience different from how the paper experience would have been? Which of these differences was caused by the nature of the text you were reading/writing?

There are, of course, many electronic texts that are simply print texts put onto a screen, and these may not challenge their writers or readers any more than do print texts. Your word processed assignment may, in essence, look no different, and have demanded no more skill or effort, than producing such an assignment on a typewriter (although it will almost certainly have been easier to produce, unless you are one of these people who always write everything correctly the first time!). More and more, however, electronic texts are being created that do more than just duplicate print, and it is on the characteristics of these, more adventurous, texts that we will focus here.

Electronic texts are interactive

Reading is often described as an interaction between a reader and a text. However, readers and printed texts cannot literally interact. A printed text cannot respond to a reader, nor do printed texts invite modification by a reader. To describe reading as an interaction simply reflects the fact that the outcomes of reading are the result of factors associated with the text and factors associated with the reader. What we understand from a text is not exactly what the author put there, nor exactly what we already knew about this topic. Rather, our understanding is a transaction between these two things. When I read a text about, say, Australia, I will probably take something different away from it than an Australian would. For both of us, our previous knowledge (or lack of it) interferes with what we understand from the text.

Because reading is interactive in this sense, a successful reader must be mentally active during reading. Readers vary in their knowledge and their cognitive capabilities and because of this a basic part of understanding the process of reading has come to be seen as understanding the reader. Features of printed texts, such as the use of illustrations, have not been entirely ignored, but it is true to say that the role of the printed text in the reading process has not generally been emphasised in discussion about the reading process. One reason for this greater interest in readers than in texts is that texts are static and inert once they are printed. When a writer's intended meaning is viewed as frozen in a printed form, it is only logical to focus on a reader's efforts to construct meaning from this print.

Successful readers of printed texts know that it is their responsibility to derive meaning from those texts, and they approach the task of reading accordingly. A printed text cannot clarify itself if the reader is having difficulty understanding it. Readers may consciously interact with a text by applying their own knowledge to it, but they cannot literally carry on a dialogue with a printed text.

Electronic texts, on the other hand, can involve a literal interaction between texts and readers (Daniel and Reinking, 1987). Using the capabilities of the computer, reading electronic texts can become a dialogue. Electronic texts can be programmed to adapt to an individual reader's needs and interests during reading, which may in turn affect the strategies that readers use to read and comprehend texts.

RESEARCH SUMMARY RESEARCH SUMMARY **RESEARCH SUMMARY** RESEARCH SUMMARY

Reinking and Rickman (1990) explored the use of interactive electronic texts, which provided readers, on request, with definitions of difficult words as they were reading. The effects of reading such texts were compared to the reading of printed texts accompanied by conventional resources such as dictionaries and glossaries. It was found that 9 to 13 year olds reading the interactive computer texts investigated more word meanings, remembered the meanings of more words and understood more of the experimental text.

Other research (Reinking and Schreiner, 1985) has suggested that readers' comprehension of texts increases when they read electronic texts providing a variety of support options, such as definitions of difficult words, illustrations of processes described (sometimes animated) or maps of a text's structure.

In the future it will be possible to design electronic texts so that they respond to certain characteristics of the reader. Imagine a screen-based text that changes its format, content and speed of presentation depending on the rate at which a reader reads it. Texts are already available which, at some point on each screen, invite the reader to select another text to read. Most web pages function like this, as the reader navigates through the network of texts making up a website by clicking on 'links'. Interactive texts like these provide many potential texts. It is possible to read such a website several times without reading exactly the same text in the same order twice.

For screen texts to have such potential interactivity, of course, they have to be created this way. The structure of such texts makes the job of writing them a completely different experience from writing a single-dimensional paper-based text. Writing web texts like this sounds like a job for the expert, but the Framework for Literacy suggested that Year 5 children should 'Create multi-layered texts, including use of hyperlinks and linked web pages'.

Electronic texts have different structures

The idea that textual information might be structured differently if it is stored electronically is not new. In 1945, Vannevar Bush, a US presidential adviser, proposed that researchers develop electronic means for linking related information in a large database of microfilm documents. In 1960, Ted Nelson introduced the term *hypertext* in referring to electronic documents structured as non-linear, non-sequential texts (see Lunin and Rada, 1989). Hypertexts have three attributes that separate them from conventionally structured printed texts:

- a database consisting of distinct units of text (which may consist of words, pictures, sounds, or moving images);
- a network connecting the textual units (the textual units are referred to as 'nodes' in the network);
- electronic tools for moving flexibly through the network.

The technology available when the concept of hypertext was first proposed did not allow easy and widespread implementation of the idea but rapid developments in computing power over the past few years have made hypertext not only possible but virtually inescapable. Web pages are coded in hypertext markup language – HTML.

PRACTICAL TASK PRACTICAL TASK PRACTICAL TASK PRACTICAL TASK PRACTICAL TASK

Find an example of a web page in which many features of hypertext have been implemented and that contains a mixture of textual and graphic elements. Explore the page to see if you can find examples of the following features. In each case, what is the function of this feature within the web page?

Feature	What is the function of this?
Hot spot	
Link to other web pages	
Multimedia link	
Search box	
Navigation bar	

The fact that electronic texts are structured in different ways to printed texts brings the difficulties inherent in electronic literacy into sharp focus. Becoming literate for electronic reading will require that readers become familiar with the non-linear, non-sequential text structures that are the natural form of electronic texts. They will also need to develop appropriate strategies for reading such texts. Reading web pages like this is not straightforward and many otherwise skilful readers readily admit to getting lost quite easily within such material. Such text structures also place new demands on the writers of the texts, who must try to anticipate the way that readers will perceive their texts and make sensible navigation possible. Remember that older primary children can be taught to write in this reader-centred way.

Electronic texts employ special symbols

An important part of being literate is being good at using all of the symbols that are available for communicating meaning in a written language. Readers and writers must know the conventions for using these symbols and understand how they convey meaning in a written language. Such awareness includes being able to use and interpret symbols beyond words themselves, such as graphic aids (e.g. illustrations and tables), organisational units (e.g. chapters), and typographical marks (e.g. underlining or italics).

Electronic texts incorporate more symbols than those used in printed texts. For example, symbols used with electronic texts but not with printed texts include: flashing, animated or moving visual displays, sound effects and video. These elements create new possibilities for communicating meaning and they create the need for new conventions for using them in conjunction with traditional print.

The availability of more symbols is problematic in the development of electronic literacy, partly because agreed conventions for using the various symbols have not necessarily been established. Part of the problem is that the symbols available for use in electronic texts continue to expand rapidly, and the conventions for using them can change with each advance in computer technology and as newer versions of software packages become available. Think too of the rapidly increasing number of downloadable mobile phone applications.

A very simple example of how these complexities can affect the use of electronic texts that you have probably come across is when you have written a file on your own computer but then transfer it and try to open the document on another system and you experience problems because the software may have been set up differently and a different set of symbols used.

PRACTICAL TASK PRACTICAL TASK PRACTICAL TASK PRACTICAL TASK PRACTICAL TASK

Explore the use of special symbols used in electronic texts by looking at some computer working environments with which you are currently unfamiliar. You could use the internet to trawl for examples or browse the range of materials available via your local authority's virtual learning environment (VLE) if you have access to this. Jot down a note of any new symbols or changes in the use of older symbols that you come across.

REFLECTIVE TASK

Thinking about all of the characteristics of electronic texts that we have discussed (their interactivity, use of different structures and utilisation of a widening range of symbols), consider how technological changes have affected your own learning. At what age were you when you got your first mobile phone, PC or laptop? What features did these have?

Compare your responses with the experiences of the children you are currently working with. They may well have access to advanced mobile phones and Kindle technology at a very early age. Their digital literacy may be equal to or in advance of yours. How will you ensure that you keep up to date with the development of electronic texts and ensure that you can use them effectively in your teaching?

A SUMMARY OF **KEY POINTS**

➢ **Electronic texts make fresh demands on both readers and writers.**

➢ **Although some electronic texts comprise simply of print texts put on-screen, many have distinct characteristics that make them into much more adventurous texts.**

> ➤ Many electronic texts are interactive, allowing readers to navigate through a network of links, access illustrations or definitions and search for additional information.

> ➤ They have different structures and features from paper-based texts.

> ➤ They employ special symbols and an ever-changing range of conventions.

> ➤ As well as the demands that these characteristics place on readers, they have implications for teaching children to be successful writers of electronic texts.

M-LEVEL EXTENSION > > M-LEVEL EXTENSION > > M-LEVEL EXTENSION

The multi-modal dimensions of digital texts have challenged the notion of literacy as being principally about words, sentences and paragraphs. These represent only part of what is being communicated in digital texts. There is often a tension between the act of making meaning with written words, and the meaning-making that comes from layout and from other aspects of digital texts (e.g. hyperlinks). When we think about the forms and functions of writing on-screen and the texts and contexts in which digital literacy is situated, there are some large shifts of emphasis. Some of these shifts are listed below, and you might want to think about the implications of these for your teaching of literacy:

1. The move from the fixed to the fluid: text is no longer contained just between the covers of a book or by the limits of the page.
2. Texts become interwoven in more complex ways by means of hyperlinks.
3. Texts can easily be revised, updated and added to.
4. Texts can become collaborative with replies, links and posted comments.
5. Reading and writing paths are often non-linear.
6. Texts become more densely multi-modal (as multimedia allows for a rich range of modes to be used).

FURTHER READING FURTHER READING FURTHER READING FURTHER READING

Perhaps the best source of information about the new literacies made available by new technology, especially the internet, is the website run by the New Literacies Research Team at the University of Connecticut: **www.newliteracies.uconn.edu/** This team is led by Don Leu, who is the world leader currently in thinking about the ways in which new technologies affect literacy. Many of his articles can be read at his personal website: **www.sp.uconn.edu/~djleu/**

DfE (2013) *Teachers' Standards*. London: DfE. **(www.gov.uk/government/uploads/system/uploads/ attachment_data/file/208682/Teachers__Standards_2013.pdf)**

Self-assessment questions

These self-assessment questions are included so you can check how well you have assimilated the knowledge and understanding presented in this book. The answers to these questions are in the following section.

Chapter 2 – Spoken English and Standard English

1. What is Standard English?

2. What three variations affect spoken English?

3. Explain the two main elements of regional variation.

4. What is 'language register'?

5. How can children be helped to recognise and practise the use of Standard English and other dialects?

Chapter 3 – The acquisition of language

1. What are the three main theories of language acquisition?

2. The behaviourist view is based on which psychologist's work?

3. What is the three-part sequence underpinning the behaviourist approach?

4. The generative/innatist approach was based on whose theory?

5. What was the main criticism of the behaviourist approach?

6. What is 'motherese'?

7. Briefly describe the social/interactive approach.

8. What is the LAD and which theory does it support?

9. What is the LASS and which theory does it support?

10. Why is it important that children have opportunities to experiment with language/ be wrong sometimes?

Chapter 4 – Representing sound in writing

1. What is phonological awareness?

2. What are the following:

    a) A syllable?
    b) Onset?
    c) Rime?
    d) A phoneme?

3. How many vowel sounds and consonant sounds are there in English?

4. What is the IPA?

5. What is phonics teaching?

6. Name three common consonant digraphs.

7. What is the visual strategy for learning spellings that was suggested by Margaret Peters?

8. Why is it important to teach fluent letter formation early in the teaching of handwriting?

Chapter 5 – Words, vocabulary and morphology

1. Name five languages that have influenced English following invasion and settlement of the British Isles.

2. What was the main reason for the standardisation of written English between 1400 and 1800?

3. What do the following prefixes mean? Give an example of their use.

   a) Ad-
   b) Ambi-
   c) Ante-
   d) Ant(i)-

4. What is etymology?

5. Name three of the six processes that have caused new words to enter English.

6. What is morphology and why is it important for children to study it?

7. What is a morpheme?

8. What are the two types of affix?

9. Give an example of an inflexional suffix for each of the following:

   a) A noun
   b) An adjective
   c) The past participle of a regular verb
   d) The present participle of a regular verb

Chapter 6 – The grammar of the sentence in Standard English

1. What are three benefits of teaching children about grammar?

2. What is a sentence?

3. Which of the following are sentence fragments and which are run-on sentences?

   a) Many of the women running in the fun-run last week.
   b) In Yorkshire, the cheese made in Wensleydale.
   c) The window catch is broken, it needs mending.
   d) Working far too late for his own good.
   e) The snow is falling, put on your boots.
   f) They shouldn't need help, it is easy to find.

4. List four different possible functions of a sentence.

5. Define these parts of a sentence:

   a) A subject
   b) A predicate
   c) An object

6. What is the difference between a transitive and an intransitive verb?

7. What is a clause?

8. How is a phrase different from a clause?

9. Name four types of phrase.

Chapter 7 – The components of sentences

1. What are the eight main word classes or 'parts of speech' that are components of a sentence?
2. Name the four types of common noun.

3. Which type of noun should be indicated by the use of initial capital letters?

4. Complete the following table of personal pronouns:

	Subject of a sentence	**Object of a sentence**
First person singular		
Second person singular		
Third person singular		
First person plural		
Second person plural		
Third person plural		

5. Which kind of determiner are the following words:

   a) the
   b) a
   c) an
   d) every
   e) several
   f) twenty
   g) third

6. Use the general rules for formation of comparative and superlative adjectives to complete the table:

Adjective	**Comparative form**	**Superlative form**
broad		
sleepy		
intelligent		

7. Which form of regular verbs are the following?

   a) to start
   b) washed

    c) laughing
    d) wink(s)

8. Which form of this irregular verb are the following?

    a) swum
    b) swimming
    c) swim(s)
    d) to swim
    e) swam

9. What are the three types of conjunction?

10. Are the following words adverbs or prepositions?

    a) slow
    b) quickly
    c) through
    d) tomorrow
    e) sudden
    f) where
    g) across
    h) young
    i) beside

Chapter 8 – Punctuation

1. Which of the following definitions is more accurate?

    a) Punctuation is used to show where speakers should take a breath.
    b) Punctuation is used to make clear the grammatical structure of a sentence and to clarify its meaning.

2. Match up the following functions of punctuation with the correct punctuation mark:

3. full stop, comma, colon, semicolon, question mark, exclamation mark, apostrophe, hyphen, dash, brackets, capital letter, inverted commas/speech or quotation marks

    a) Indicates omissions by marking the places where letters are missed out
    b) Links statements that are closely related
    c) Used at the end of a sentence that asks a direct question
    d) Mark off additional information in a stronger way than commas or dashes
    e) Used to create a new noun from two other words
    f) Used to indicate a proper noun
    g) Indicates a hesitation or dramatic pause
    h) Marks off phrases beginning with participles
    i) Used to introduce a list
    j) Indicates direct speech
    k) Used to indicate certain abbreviations
    l) Signifies a sentence where a special note of urgency is required

Chapter 9 – Cohesion: grammar at the level of the text

1. Cohesive references can be made to other parts of the text in two ways. Define these.

2. Name three types of reference tie.

3. What is substitution?

4. What is ellipsis?

5. Explain the four types of conjunction.

6. What is lexical cohesion?

Chapter 10 – The qualities of stories

1. Explain the rationale for the following reasons why stories are so important for children:

   a) To satisfy their curiosity
   b) To help them make sense of the world
   c) To experience the world vicariously
   d) To put them in touch with a common culture
   e) To improve their literacy
   f) To extend their knowledge and experience of language forms
   g) To give them pleasure

2. List three different genres of children's stories.

3. Put the main stages of story structure into the right order:

   - The inciting moment
   - The ending
   - The opening
   - The development
   - The denouement

4. List the alternative names for:

   a) The story opening
   b) The inciting moment
   c) The denouement
   d) The ending

5. What are the suggested criteria for evaluating and making judgements about stories?

Chapter 11 – The qualities of poetry

1. Which poetic devices are used in John Agard's poem *Poetry Jump Up?*

2. In Masefield's classic poem *Cargoes:*

   a) How is the structure organised?
   b) How does Masefield use assonance?
   c) What other devices does Masefield use?

3. From the definitions given, decide which poetry forms are listed:

   a) A poem where the size and shape of the letters, the fonts used, their boldness and their effects support its meaning
   b) Two consecutive lines linked by rhythm and rhyme

c) A poem where the appearance on the page reflects its theme

d) A poem that tells a story, sometimes in ballad form

e) A Japanese verse with 17 syllables distributed over three lines

f) A poem that is written to be acted out

Chapter 12 – The qualities of drama

1. In examining why drama is important, w\hat are the four main functions of drama in primary classrooms?

2. Describe how the following drama activities can make a contribution to children's language and range of experience.

   a) Puppets

   b) Hot seating

   c) Improvisation

   d) Simulation

   e) Tableaux/thought tracking

3. In the layout of play scripts, what are the key elements that must be made clear?

4. What is iambic pentameter?

5. Which are the main elements that should be considered when analysing play scripts?

Chapter 13 – Looking at information books

1. Why should stories not be overused as a major experience in the primary years?

2. What are the criteria that can be used to look critically at information books?

3. Match the correct definitions to the following genres/text types and give an example of each:

   a) Records feelings/events as they occur

   b) Puts forward an argument in favour of a particular point of view

   c) Retells in narrative form a sequence of events

   d) Guides the carrying out of a set of actions

   e) Describes/explains particular phenomena

   f) Presents arguments and information from differing viewpoints before reaching a conclusion based on the evidence

   g) Presents information in an ordered, easily retrievable way

Chapter 14 – Electronic texts

1. Give three examples of everyday situations in which you may need to read an electronic text.

2. Give three examples of everyday situations in which you may need to write an electronic text.

3. What are the three main characteristics that make electronic texts different from traditional print-media texts?

4. What implications do these differences have for the teaching of literacy?

Answers to self-assessment questions

Chapter 2 – Spoken English and Standard English

1. Standard English is largely a matter of using certain grammar, vocabulary and, when written, spelling. It can be spoken in most English accents and does not have a correct pronunciation.

2. Historical, regional and individual variations affect spoken English.

3. In regional variation:

   a) Dialect is the grammar and vocabulary of language spoken in a particular region.
   b) Accent is the way in which words are pronounced.

4. 'Language register' is the way in which speakers/writers use different words and grammatical formations depending on the situation in which they are communicating.

5. Children can be helped to recognise and practise the use of Standard English and other dialects through speaking and listening tasks about texts in pairs, groups, whole-class activities and drama sessions.

Chapter 3 – The acquisition of language

1. The three main theories of language acquisition are the behaviourist account, the generative/innatist approach and the social/interactive approach.

2. The behaviourist view is based on the work of B.F. Skinner.

3. The three-part sequence underpinning the behaviourist approach is the stimulus-response-reward sequence.

4. The generative/innatist approach was based on Noam Chomsky's theory.

5. The main criticism of the behaviourist approach was that children could produce novel utterances that they had never heard adults say.

6. 'Motherese' is a term used to describe the non-standard ways in which adults talk to children.

7. The social/interactive approach suggests that human beings are programmed to communicate and that children communicate with their carers from birth. They learn language through using it in interaction with others to achieve particular ends.

8. The LAD is the Language Acquisition Device and it supports the generative/innatist theory.

9. The LASS is the Language Acquisition Support System and it is part of the social/interactive approach.

10. It is important that children have opportunities to experiment with language/be wrong sometimes because these are critical elements in the learning of language in the context of real dialogue.

Chapter 4 – Representing sound in writing

1. Phonological awareness is the explicit awareness of units of sound and how they work in speech.

2. a) A syllable is a group of sounds that act as a unit of rhythm in speech and that is usually made up of a combination of consonants and vowels.
   b) Onset is the consonant(s) at the beginning of a syllable.
   c) Rime is the remaining part of a syllable, including a vowel or vowel-like sound and possibly one or more consonants.
   d) A phoneme is the smallest unit of sound in a word.

3. There are approximately 20 vowel sounds and 24 consonant sounds in most accents of English.

4. The IPA is the International Phonetic Alphabet that is used to write sounds precisely, including in some dictionaries.

5. Phonics teaching is teaching children sound-symbol correspondence, i.e. to match sounds with letters and letter combinations and to blend and segment these to create words.

6. Three common consonant digraphs are 'ch', 'th' and 'sh'.

7. The visual strategy for learning spellings that was suggested by Margaret Peters is 'Look, Cover, Write, Check'.

8. It is important to teach fluent letter formation early in the teaching of handwriting because poor letter formation inhibits the correct joining of letters and bad habits in letter formation are hard to change.

Chapter 5 – Words, vocabulary and morphology

1. Five languages that have influenced English following invasion and settlement of the British Isles are Anglo-Saxon, Old Norse (Viking), French, Latin and Greek.

2. The main reason for the standardisation of written English between 1400 and 1800 was the invention of the printing press – the ability to print literature meant that printers had to make decisions about language, including spelling, word choice and expression.

3. What do the following prefixes mean? Give an example of their use.

   a) Ad-   towards, against, at – adhere, admire
   b) Ambi-   both, around – ambidextrous, ambiguous
   c) Ante-   before – antenatal, anteroom
   d) Ant(i)-   against, opposite – antibiotic, antidote

4. Etymology is the study of the origins of words.

5. Three of the six processes that have caused new words to enter English are (any three from) back formation, folk etymology, function-shift, acronyms, blending and clipping.

6. Morphology is the study of the structure of words and it is important for children to study it because they need to be able to break down and assemble words in order to be able to understand the grammar of sentences.

7. A morpheme is the smallest unit of meaning in a word. Free morphemes can stand alone, e.g. 'cat'. Bound morphemes cannot exist alone but are attached to other words, e.g. -s, -ed and -ing.

8. The two types of affix are prefixes, which go before the root/stem of a word, and suffixes, which go after it.

9. Give an example of an inflexional suffix for each of the following:

   a) A noun: -s (either to mark a plural or the possessive)
   b) An adjective: -er or -est
   c) The past participle of a regular verb: -d or -ed
   d) The present participle of a regular verb: -ing

Chapter 6 – The grammar of the sentence in Standard English

1. Three benefits of teaching children about grammar are that having grammatical knowledge can help to put them more in control of their use of language; it can help them in their attempts to communicate and it makes them more effective language users.

2. A sentence is a group of words containing a subject and a predicate that should express a thought that can stand by itself. The simplest definition often used with young children is that 'A sentence begins with a capital letter and ends with a full stop'.

3. Which of the following are sentence fragments and which are run-on sentences?

   a) Many of the women running in the fun-run last week. (Fragment)
   b) In Yorkshire, the cheese made in Wensleydale. (Fragment)
   c) The window catch is broken, it needs mending. (Run-on sentence)
   d) Working far too late for his own good. (Fragment)
   e) The snow is falling, put on your boots. (Run-on sentence)
   f) They shouldn't need help, it is easy to find. (Run-on sentence)

4. Four different possible functions of a sentence are a statement, a question, a command and an exclamation.

5. Define these parts of a sentence:

   a) A subject – what or whom the sentence is about
   b) A predicate – tells us something about the subject and always includes the verb
   c) An object – may be needed to complete a verb's meaning and can be direct or indirect

6. The difference between a transitive and an intransitive verb is that a transitive verb takes an object but an intransitive verb does not.

7. A clause is a group of related words containing a subject and a verb. They can be independent (i.e. they could stand by themselves as discrete sentences) or dependent (i.e. they cannot make sense by themselves).

8. A phrase is different from a clause because it is a group of related words but does not contain a subject and a verb.

9. Four types of phrase are noun phrase, prepositional phrase, adjectival phrase and adverbial phrase.

Chapter 7 – The components of sentences

1. The eight main word classes or 'parts of speech' that are components of a sentence are nouns, pronouns, determiners, adjectives, verbs, adverbs, conjunctions and prepositions.
2. The four types of common noun are concrete, abstract, countable and uncountable.
3. Proper nouns should be indicated by the use of initial capital letters.
4.

	Subject of a sentence	Object of a sentence
First person singular	I	me
Second person singular	you	you
Third person singular	he/she/it	him/her/it
First person plural	we	us
Second person plural	you	you
Third person plural	they	them

5. Which kind of determiner are the following words:

   a) the – definite article
   b) a – indefinite article
   c) an – indefinite article
   d) every – determiner expressing quantity
   e) several – determiner expressing quantity
   f) twenty – cardinal numeral expressing quantity
   g) third – ordinal numeral expressing quantity

6. Use the general rules for formation of comparative and superlative adjectives to complete the table:

Adjective	Comparative form	Superlative form
Broad	broader	broadest
Sleepy	sleepier	sleepiest
Intelligent	more intelligent	most intelligent

7. Which form of regular verbs are the following?

   a) to start — infinitive (to + verb stem)
   b) washed — simple past or past participle
   c) laughing — present participle
   d) wink(s) — simple present

8. Which form of this irregular verb are the following?

   a) swum — past participle
   b) swimming — present participle
   c) swim(s) — simple present
   d) to swim — infinitive (to + verb stem)
   e) swam — simple past

9. The three types of conjunction are co-ordinating, correlative and subordinating.

10. Are the following words adjectives, adverbs or prepositions?

   a) slow   adjective
   b) quickly   adverb
   c) through   preposition
   d) tomorrow adverb
   e) sudden   adjective
   f) where   adverb
   g) across   preposition
   h) young   adjective
   i) beside   preposition

Chapter 8 – Punctuation

1. Punctuation is used to make clear the grammatical structure of a sentence and to clarify its meaning.

2.

   a) Indicates omissions by marking the places where letters are missed out – apostrophe

   b) Links statements that are closely related – semicolon

   c) Used at the end of a sentence that asks a direct question – question mark

   d) Mark off additional information in a stronger way than commas or dashes – brackets

   e) Used to create a new noun from two other words – hyphen

   f) Used to indicate a proper noun – capital letter

   g) Indicates a hesitation or dramatic pause – dash

   h) Marks off phrases beginning with participles – comma

   i) Used to introduce a list – colon

   j) Indicates direct speech – inverted commas/speech or quotation marks

   k) Used to indicate certain abbreviations – full stop

   l) Signifies a sentence where a special note of urgency is required – exclamation mark

Chapter 9 – Cohesion: grammar at the level of the text

1. The two ways in which cohesive references can be made to other parts of the text are:

   • Anaphorical references – these refer readers back to something already mentioned.
   • Cataphorical references – these point the reader forwards and are often used for dramatic effect/to heighten suspense.

2. The three types of reference tie are personal, demonstrative and comparative.

3. Substitution is where a word, phrase or clause is substituted in a following sentence for one with a similar grammatical function rather than repeating the original.

4. Ellipsis is where words are omitted rather than having an inelegant repetition – the reader supplies these to make sense of the sentence.

5. The four types of conjunction are:

   • Additive conjunctions – these add on a clause/sentence as if it were additional infor-mation or an afterthought.
   • Adversative conjunctions – these draw a contrast between the clause/sentence that they introduce/are contained in and the preceding clause/sentence.

- Causal conjunctions – these make a link of cause or consequence between two clauses or sentences.
- Temporal conjunctions – these make a time link, usually of a sequential nature.

6. Lexical cohesion is where two words in a text are semantically related in terms of their meaning, either by reiteration or collocation.

Chapter 10 – The qualities of stories

1. Explain the rationale for the following reasons why stories are so important for children:

   a) To satisfy their curiosity – this builds on children's desire to know what happens next by stimulating their interest.

   b) To help them make sense of the world – everyone, including children, tries to impose order in their lives by telling stories about them.

   c) To experience the world vicariously – stories can provide opportunities to learn from the experiences of others.

   d) To put them in touch with a common culture – children learn much about their own cultural heritage and that of the wider world by reading stories.

   e) To improve their literacy – stories give children opportunities to learn about language at word, sentence and text levels and enable them to develop an understanding of phonics and grammar.

   f) To extend their knowledge and experience of language forms – reading a wide range of stories helps children to learn about the structures and conventions of written language.

   g) To give them pleasure – children need to read for their own enjoyment and not just to develop their language skills.

2. The different genres of children's stories include (any three from): folk and fairy tales; myths and legends; adventure stories; detective stories; school-based stories; love stories; historical stories; magical tales or any others from the many references to different genres across the chapter.

3. Put the main stages of story structure into the right order:

   - The opening – establishing time, setting and characters.
   - The inciting moment – where the state of equilibrium is threatened or normality is changed.
   - The development – the largest section, including further complications, disruptions or events.
   - The denouement – a turning point or event that signals the upcoming ending.
   - The ending – where complications are resolved and issues redressed.

4. List the alternative names for:

   a) The story opening – orientation, exposition or the state of equilibrium.

   b) The inciting moment – breach, disruption or complicating action.

   c) The denouement – resolution.

   d) The ending – redress, reinstatement, coda or conclusion.

5. The suggested criteria for evaluating and making judgements about stories are:

   - Appropriateness
   - Social/political awareness
   - Plot and themes

- Characters
- Language
- Illustrations
- The properties of the book as an object
- Teacher interest

Chapter 11 – The qualities of poetry

1. The poetic devices used in John Agard's poem *Poetry Jump Up* are metaphor, simile, rhyme at the ends of lines and within lines and personification.
2. In Masefield's classic poem *Cargoes:*

   a) The structure is organised into stanzas with the same rhyming pattern and a very similar rhythmical pattern.

   b) Masefield uses assonance to give the lines a lightness and delicacy of tone through a prevailing set of vowel sounds.

   c) Masefield also uses associations and onomatopoeia.

3. From the definitions given, decide which poetry forms are listed:

   a) A poem where the size and shape of the letters, the fonts used, their boldness and their effects support its meaning – a calligram

   b) Two consecutive lines linked by rhythm and rhyme – a couplet

   c) A poem where the appearance on the page reflects its theme – a shape poem

   d) A poem that tells a story, sometimes in ballad form – a narrative poem

   e) A Japanese verse with 17 syllables distributed over three lines – a haiku

   f) A poem that is written to be acted out – a performance poem

Chapter 12 – The qualities of drama

1. In examining why drama is important, the four main functions of drama in primary classrooms are:

   - Drama as story;
   - Drama as an aid to learning;
   - Drama as a resource for moral education;
   - Drama as an aid to language and literacy development.

2. Describe how the following drama activities can make a contribution to children's language and range of experience:

   a) Puppets – can be used to perform an improvised or scripted story.

   b) Hot seating – can be used to explain characters' motives and behaviour.

   c) Improvisation – can lead to presenting devised dialogue as a drama script.

   d) Simulation – requires more pre-planning and research than an improvisation.

   e) Tableaux/thought tracking – using a frozen moment allows children to explore the thoughts of a particular character and the significance of that moment to their character.

3. The key elements that must be made clear in the layout of play scripts are setting, stage directions, character names and dialogue.

4. Iambic pentameter is a rhythmical pattern with five metrical beats to the line – Shakespeare's plays are largely written in iambic pentameter.

5. The main elements that should be considered when analysing play scripts are: appropriateness for the children's maturity, skills and interests (and the teacher's interest); plot and themes; characters; dialogue; use of language; and the overall attractiveness of the book as an object.

Chapter 13 – Looking at information books

1. Stories should not be overused as a major experience in the primary years because children may become over-reliant on fiction-based strategies and mistakenly try to apply rules of fiction to non-fiction.

2. The criteria that can be used to look critically at information books are:

   - How they use facts;
   - Whether they are accurate/biased;
   - How concise they are;
   - How they present specialised vocabulary;
   - Their use of illustration;
   - How they are organised.

3. Match the correct definitions to the following genres/text types and give an example of each:

   a) Records feelings/events as they occur – a record (diary or log-book)
   b) Puts forward an argument in favour of a particular point of view – a persuasive text (a pamphlet or leaflet supporting a specific point of view)
   c) Retells in narrative form a sequence of events – a recount (biography, autobiography or newspaper report)
   d) Guides the carrying out of a set of actions – instructions (recipe book or instruction leaflet)
   e) Describes/explains particular phenomena – a report (explanations, scientific accounts, descriptions)
   f) Presents arguments and information from differing viewpoints before reaching a conclusion based on the evidence – a discussion (an issue book)
   g) Presents information in an ordered, easily retrievable way – a reference text (encyclopaedias or identification guides)

Chapter 14 – Electronic texts

1. Examples of everyday situations in which you may need to read an electronic text include:

   a) Reading a web page;
   b) Reading a pdf document;
   c) Reading a text message on your mobile phone or the instructions on an ATM screen.

2. Examples of everyday situations in which you may need to write an electronic text include:
   a) Writing an assignment or presentation;
   b) Sending an email, text message, twitter or tweet;
   c) Having an instant messaging conversation.

3. The three main characteristics that make electronic texts different from traditional print-media texts are:

   a) They are interactive;
   b) They have different structures;
   c) They employ special symbols (icons/features).

4. The implications these differences have for the teaching of literacy are that teachers must ensure that children have access to both paper-based and electronic texts in order to develop their reading skills and digital literacy, and that they have opportunities to write in both media for a range of purposes and audiences.

Appendix: Irregular verbs in English

Infinitive	Simple present	Simple past	Past participle	Present participle
to arise	arise(s)	arose	arisen	arising
to bear	bear(s)	bore	borne	bearing
to beat	beat(s)	beat	beaten	beating
to become	become(s)	became	become	becoming
to begin	begin(s)	began	begun	beginning
to bend	bend(s)	bent	bent	bending
to blow	blow(s)	blew	blown	blowing
to break	break(s)	broke	broken	breaking
to catch	catch(es)	caught	caught	catching
to do	do(es)	did	done	doing
to eat	eat(s)	ate	eaten	eating
to fall	fall(s)	fell	fallen	falling
to fly	fly, flies	flew	flown	flying
to give	give(s)	gave	given	giving
to go	go(es)	went	gone	going
to hide	hide(s)	hid	hidden	hiding
to know	know(s)	knew	known	knowing
to rise	rise(s)	rose	risen	rising
to see	see(s)	saw	seen	seeing
to sing	sing(s)	sang	sung	singing
to speak	speak(s)	spoke	spoken	speaking
to steal	steal(s)	stole	stolen	stealing
to stride	stride(s)	strode	stridden	striding
to take	take(s)	took	taken	taking
to wear	wear(s)	wore	worn	wearing
to write	write(s)	wrote	written	writing

Glossary

Accent A regional accent refers to the features of pronunciation that convey information about a person's geographical origin.

Alliteration A phrase in which adjacent or fairly closely connected words in a phrase or sentence begin with the same phoneme. It is often used by writers to help to create moods.

Aside A speech made by a character in a play that dramatic convention pretends cannot be heard by the other characters on the stage. It may be addressed to the audience and therefore create an atmosphere of personal involvement, or it may be addressed to nobody in particular and be intended simply to explain the speaker's thoughts, feelings, reactions or motivation.

Association Words often mean more than they say because they carry with them whole suitcases of attached meaning created by the contexts in which we have often found them in our language experience. A skilful writer chooses words carefully to take full advantage of these associations or – as Keats put it – to *load every rift with ore.*

Assonance The repetition of the same vowel sounds in a section of text. This is sometimes referred to as 'verse music'.

Cohesion This is a term with a variety of meanings. Which one is applicable depends on the circumstances. In all cases, though, its general meaning is that of sustained consistency. Cohesion in a story is the linking and the consistency of time and place and characters. Cohesion in a section of text is the linking of paragraphs both in content and in grammatical interdependence. Cohesion in a paragraph refers to the way that sentences interrelate. A good way of seeing this cohesion is to look at the opening words of each sentence to see how the thought has been joined to the thought before. Cohesion in a sentence is achieved through such grammatical matters as consistency of noun/verb match, noun/pronoun match and verb tense.

Dialect A regional dialect refers to the features of grammar and vocabulary that convey information about a person's geographical origin.

Dialogue Dialogue can take place between any number of people in a story or play and in the dramatic context refers to the words on the page provided by a dramatist for characters to say.

Digraph A written representation of a sound using two letters. Consonant digraphs represent consonant sounds (/ch/ in **ch**eese). Vowel digraphs represent vowel sounds but may use letters we usually call consonants (/ae/ in p**ai**n, st**a**tion, s**ay**).

Fiction Fiction means something that is not true. In our chapter on fiction, the word 'stories' has largely been preferred – though stories are not always fiction. Stories can be told in a number of ways – including through pictures, poetry, drama and prose – or any combinations of these. The stories chapter concentrates mainly on prose versions of stories.

Figurative language Figurative language is sometimes simply defined as 'the use of metaphor or simile to create a particular impression or mood'. In fact, metaphor and simile are only two examples of an enormous range of rhetorical devices or ways of using language in order to create deliberate effects. English is rich in such devices and poets are not averse to using them for particular effects when the need arises. Amongst those most familiar are **antithesis,** the balance of words or lines for effect, **hyperbole** or overstatement, and **litotes,** or understatement.

Fronted adverbial An adverb, or adverbial phrase or clause, which occurs at the beginning of a sentence, before the verb it modifies. It may be immediately followed by a comma.

Genre A collection of linguistic practices and narrative conventions that govern the way particular texts are written for particular purposes.

Grapheme The smallest unit in the writing system of a language – a, e, f – are all graphemes. However, the NLS used the term grapheme to mean the way a sound is written down. So /a/ is represented by different graphemes in these words: d**a**y, n**eigh,** p**ai**d. The sound /ch/ is always represented by two letters – **ch**erry, **ch**eese – so we call this a digraph in phonics teaching. However, it is important to remember that ch can also represent other sounds, as in ma**ch**ine.

Imagery A simile or a metaphor.

Language register The term used by linguists to indicate the different ways in which people speak to different audiences for different purposes, which may include such issues as language feel, tenor and mode.

Literal and inferential comprehension Literal comprehension indicates the understanding of a text at surface level. Inferential comprehension indicates the understanding of a text at a rather deeper level by being able to pick up nuances implied but not actually stated by the text. When a politician promises that their party will not increase direct taxation, a person comprehending literally will be grateful that they will have to pay no more in income tax. Another person, understanding inferentially, will be grateful for that too, but realise that they will probably have to pay more in indirect taxation!

Metaphor A compressed comparison in which the signal words 'like' and 'as' are taken away.

Morphemes The smallest unit of meaning in a word.

Onomatopoeia A word or phrase that echoes the sound of its meaning. A good example is Tennyson's magical *murmuring of innumerable bees.*

Onset The consonant(s) that precede the nucleus of a syllable: <u>S</u>un. Some syllables have no onset: eel.

Personification The NLS had a rather convoluted definition of this figure of speech. It was almost a poem in itself. Personification is 'a form of metaphor in which language relating to human action, motivation and emotion is used to refer to non human agents or objects or abstract concepts'. A rough translation is 'pretending that things that are not human, are'.

Phoneme The smallest contrastive unit of sound in a word.

Phonemic awareness Ability to segment words into phonemes and know that spoken words are made up of phonemes.

Phonetics The study of the way humans make, transmit and receive sounds, including all the possible sounds made by humans.

Phonics A method of teaching children to read by teaching them to recognise and use sound-symbol correspondences. Phonics does include some aspects of the phonology of English but it is not the same as phonetics or phonology.

Phonological awareness Awareness of units of sound in speech.

Phonology The study of sound systems of languages, including only those sound contrasts (phonemes) that make a difference to the meaning within language.

Prosody The patterns of rhythm and sound used in poetry. In linguistics, prosodic analysis of a language is based on its patterns of stress and intonation in different contexts. In systemic grammar, it is a foundation for the analysis of syntax and meaning.

Rhyme A rhyme is heard when two words share the same or very similar sound in their final syllable.

Rime The part of a syllable that contains the syllable nucleus (usually a vowel) and final consonants, if any – b*in.* Some words consist of rime only – *eel.*

Semantics The branch of linguistics concerned with meaning. The two main areas are **logical semantics** (relating to matters such as sense, reference and presupposition) and **lexical semantics** (relating to the analysis of word meanings and the relationships between words).

Simile A straightforward comparison between one object, emotion or experience and another using the signal words 'like' or 'as'.

Soliloquy A dramatist's device of having a character, either alone or with other characters present, speak thoughts aloud. If there are other characters present, the audience must accept that they cannot hear the soliloquy speech because it is all taking place inside the soliloquist's head! The soliloquy is a theatrical device invented by Shakespeare and actually used very little since. The best known example is of course Hamlet's great 'To be or not to be?' soliloquy from Act 3, Scene i of *Hamlet.* Laurence Olivier did this soliloquy in his own film of the play as a voice-over.

Stage directions The sections of a drama script in which the writer explains to the play's director and actors how sections of the play are to be presented. These directions may give instructions for set layout, ways in which lines should be said, particular lighting and sound effects, and so on. Stage directions in a text may be long or short. George Bernard Shaw is noted for the length and detail of his directions. He certainly did not want any misunderstanding of his own view of the way in which his plays should be performed! When working with play scripts, primary children often do not at first understand that stage directions do not form part of the play itself and insist on reading them out!

Stanza A verse of poetry. The two words, stanza and verse, are quite often interchangeable.

Style An author's individual and characteristic way of selecting, organising and presenting language.

Subjunctive A verb mood expressing what is imagined or wished or possible. *I wish he were here*. Compare with the indicative mood which expresses reality. *Yesterday he was here.*

Syllable An element of speech that acts as a unit of rhythm. A 'beat' in the rhythm of speech. A syllable usually contains a vowel.

Syllable nucleus A vowel or vowel-like sound at the heart of a syllable.

Syntax The arrangement of words and phrases to create well-formed sentences in a language.

Trigraph A written representation of a sound using three letters. See also **digraph**.

Voice-over A disembodied voice (generally recorded) that speaks over the action on the stage to fill in narrative details or to explain characters' thoughts, feelings, reactions or motivation. The voice may be the voice of one of the characters in the play or the voice of an omniscient narrator – the playwright's voice in fact.

REFERENCES REFERENCES **REFERENCES** REFERENCES REFERENCES

Adams, M.J. (1994) *Beginning to Read: Thinking and Learning about Print.* Cambridge, MA: MIT.

Agard, J. *Hippo Writes a Poem to His Wife,* in Agard, J. (ed.) (1988) *We Animals Would Like a Word With You.* London: Random House.

Agard, J. *Poetry Jump Up,* in Nichols, G. (ed.) (1990) *Poetry Jump Up.* London: Puffin.

Agard, J. (1996) *We Animals Would Like a Word With You.* London: Random House.

Ahlberg, A. (1989) *Heard it In the Playground.* London: Viking Kestrel.

Anderson, E. (1992) *Reading the Changes.* Buckingham: Open University Press.

Andrew, M. and Orme, D. (1990) *The Second Poetry Kit.* Cheltenham: Nelson Thornes.

Applebee, A.N. (1978) *The Child's Concept of Story.* Chicago, IL: Chicago University.

Aristotle (364–347BC) *Poetics* in *Aristotle's Poetics and Rhetoric and Other Essays in Classical Criticism.* London: Dent.

Balaam, J. and Merrick, B. (1987) *Exploring Poetry 5–8.* Exeter: NATE.

Belloc, H. (1940) *Cautionary Verses.* London: Duckworth.

Benson, G. (ed.) (1990) *This Poem Doesn't Rhyme.* London: Viking Kestrel.

Berry, J. (ed.) (1997) *Classic Poems to Read Aloud.* London: Kingfisher.

Bettelheim, B. (1989) *The Uses of Enchantment.* New York: Random House.

Blake, Q. (ed.) (1996) *The Puffin Book of Nonsense Verse.* London: Puffin.

Boon, D. (1998) *Gio's Pizzas.* London: Macdonald.

Booty, John E. (ed.) (1976) *The Book of Common Prayer 1559: The Elizabethan Prayer Book.* Washington, DC: Folger Books.

Braddock, R., Lloyd-Jones, R. and Schoer, L. (1963) *Research in Written Composition.* Champaign, IL: NCTE.

Brownjohn, S. (1980) *Does It Have to Rhyme!* London: Hodder & Stoughton.

Brownjohn, S. (1989) *The Ability to Name Cats.* London: Hodder & Stoughton.

Brownjohn, S. (1990) *To Rhyme or Not to Rhyme?* London: Hodder & Stoughton.

Brownjohn, S. (1994) *O. Frabjous Day*. London: Ginn.

Brownjohn, S. (1996) *Both Sides of the Catflap.* London: Hodder & Stoughton.

Bruner, J. (1986) *Actual Minds, Possible Worlds.* London: Harvard University Press.

Bryant, P. and Bradley, L. (1985) *Children's Reading Problems.* Oxford: Blackwell.

Bryson, B. (1990) *Mother Tongue: The English Language.* London: Penguin.

Carroll, L. (1865) *Alice's Adventures in Wonderland.* London: Macmillan.

Carter, D. (1998) *Teaching Poetry in the Primary School.* London: David Fulton.

Chalker, S. and Weiner, E. (1998) *The Oxford Dictionary of English Grammar*. Oxford: Oxford University Press.

Chaplin, A. (2000) *Love Me Tender.* Leamington Spa: Scholastic.

Chapman, J. (1987) *Reading From 5–11 Years.* Buckingham: Open University Press.

Chomsky, N. (1959) 'A Review of B.F. Skinner's "Verbal Behavior"'. *Language*, 35(1): 26–58.

Cigman, G. (ed.) (1989) *Lollard Sermons.* Early English Text Society 294. Oxford: Oxford University Press.

Clark, E.V. (2002) *First Language Acquisition*. Cambridge: Cambridge University Press.

Clipson-Boyles, S. (1998) *Drama in Primary English Teaching.* London: David Fulton.

Connolly, Y. (ed.) (1981) *Mango Spice: 44 Caribbean Songs.* London: A. & C. Black.

Cope, W. (ed.) (1993) *The Orchard Book of Funny Poems.* London: Orchard Press.

Cripps, C. and Peters, M. (1990) *Catchwords: Ideas for Teaching Spelling.* London: Harcourt Brace Jovanovich.

Crystal, D. (2nd edn) (2003) *The Cambridge Encyclopaedia of The English Language.* Cambridge: Cambridge University Press.

Curry, J. (ed.) (1981) *The Beaver Book of School Verse.* London: Hamlyn.

Curry J. and Curry, G. (eds) (1983) *The Sausage is a Cunning Bird.* London: Hodder & Stoughton.

Dahl, R. (1982) *Revolting Rhymes.* London: Jonathan Cape.

Daniel, D.B. and Reinking, D. (1987) 'The construct of legibility in electronic reading environments', in Reinking, D. (ed.) *Reading and Computers: Issues for theory and practice.* New York: Teachers College Press.

Davies, A. (1997) 'Tom Sawyer'. *Children's Literature in Education,* 28(1): 3–10.

Davies, A. (1986) 'Hoff the Cat Dealer', in Alcock, J. (ed.) (1987) *Playstage: Six Primary School Plays.* London: Egmont.

DfE (2012) *Statutory Framework for the Early Years Foundation Stage.* Runcorn: DfE (www.education.gov.uk/publications/standard/AllPublications/Page1/DFE-00023-2012)

DfE (2013) *2014 Key Stage 2 Tests.* (http://education.gov.uk/schools/teachingandlearning/assessment/keystage2/b00208296/ks2-2013/ks2-2014)

DfE (2013) *Teachers' Standards.* London: DfE. (www.gov.uk/government/uploads/system/uploads/attachment_data/file/208682/Teachers__Standards_2013.pdf)

DfE (2013) *The National Curriculum in England.* London: DfE. (www.gov.uk/dfe/national-curriculum)

Douthwaite, G. (1994) *Picture a Poem.* London: Hutchinson.

Durkin, K., Rutter, D.R. and Tucker, H. (1982) 'Social international and language acquisition: Motherese help you'. *First Language,* 3(8): 107–20.

Forster, E.M. (1949) *Aspects of the Novel.* London: Edward Arnold.

Foster, J. (ed.) (1983) *A Fifth Poetry Book.* Oxford: Oxford University Press.

Foster, J. (ed.) (1989) *Let's Celebrate.* Oxford: Oxford University Press.

Foster, J. (ed.) (1992) *Word Whirls and Other Shape Poems.* Oxford: Oxford University Press.

Fox, C. (1993) *At the Very Edge of the Forest.* London, Cassell.

Garfield, L. (1981) *Fair's Fair.* London: Hodder & Stoughton.

Goswami, U. and Bryant, P.E. (1990) *Phonological Skills and Learning to Read.* Hove: Psychology Press.

Griffiths, V. (1995) *Adolescent Girls and Their Friends: A Feminine Ethnography.* Aldershot: Avebury.

Halliday, M.A.K. (1985) *Spoken and Written Language.* Oxford: Oxford University Press.

Halliday, M.A.K. and Hasan, R. (1976) *Cohesion in English.* Harlow: Longman.

Halliday, M.A.K. and Hasan, R. (1989) *Language, Context and Text Aspects of Language in a social-semiotic perspective.* Oxford: Oxford University Press.

Halliday, M.A.K. and Matthiessen, C.M. (2004) *An Introduction to Functional Grammar.* London: Hodder Education.

Harrison, M. and Stuart-Clark, C. (eds) (1990) *The Oxford Book of Story Poems.* Oxford: Oxford University Press.

Harrison, M. and Stuart-Clark, C. (eds) (1996) *The Oxford Treasury of Classic Poems.* Oxford: Oxford University Press.

Hillocks, G. (1986) *Research in Written Composition: New Directions for Teaching.* Urbana, IL: ERIC and NCTE.

Hoad, T. (ed.) (1986) *The Concise Oxford Dictionary of Etymology.* Oxford: Oxford University Press.

Holderness, J. and Lalljee, B. (eds) (1998) *An Introduction to Oracy: Frameworks for Talk.* London: Cassell.

Holy Bible (1611) *King James Version: A Word-For-Word Reprint of the First Edition of the Authorized Version.* Nashville, TN: Thomas Nelson Publishers.

Hughes, A. (2011) *Online English Grammar.* (www.edufind.com/english/grammar)

Hughes, G.A. and Trudgill, P. (1987) *English Accents and Dialect: An Introduction to Social and Regional Varieties of English.* London: Edward Arnold.

Hughes, M. (1994) 'The oral language of children', in Wray, D. and Medwell, J. (eds) *Teaching Primary English: the State of the Art.* London: Routledge.

Hughes, T. (1970) 'Myth and education'. *Children's Literature in Education,* 1 (1): 55–70.

Jager Adams, M. (1990) *Beginning To Read: Thinking And Learning About Print.* Cambridge, MA: Institute of Technology.

Jones, S., Myhill, D. and Bailey, T. (2013) 'Grammar for writing? An investigation of the effects of contextualised grammar teaching on students' writing'. *Reading and Writing*, 26 (8): 1241–63

King, G. (2000) *Punctuation*. London: Collins Wordpower.

Klein, G. (1993) *Education Towards Race Equality.* London: Cassell.

Leffel, K. and Suskind, D. (2013) 'Parent-Directed Approaches to Enrich the Early Language Environments of Children Living in Poverty'. *Seminars in Speech and Language*, 34 (4): 267–77 (http://tmw.org/wp/wp-content/uploads/2013/09/SSL-00517.pdf)

Lewis, C.S. (1950) *The Lion, The Witch and The Wardrobe.* London: HarperCollins.

Lewis, D. (1992) 'Reading the Range: a small-scale study of the breadth of classroom reading at KS2'. *Reading,* 26 (3): 12–18.

Lewis, M. and Wray, D. (1995) *Developing Children's Non-Fiction Writing.* Leamington Spa: Scholastic.

Littlefair, A. (1991) *Reading All Types of Writing.* Buckingham: Open University Press.

Liu, C. and Rawl, S. (2012) 'Effects of Text Cohesion on Comprehension and Retention of Colorectal Cancer Screening Information: A Preliminary Study'. *Journal of Health Communication: International Perspectives*, 17: sup. 3, 222–40.

Liuzza, R.M. (ed.) (1994) *The Old English Version of the Gospels.* Early English Text Society 304. Oxford: Oxford University Press.

Lively, P. (1975) *The Ghost of Thomas Kempe.* Oxford: Heinemann Educational.

Lunin, L.R. and Rada, R. (1989) 'Hypertext: Introduction and overview'. *Journal of the American Society for Information Science,* 40, 159–63.

Lust, B.C. and Foley, C. (2004) (eds) *First Language Acquisition: The Essential Readings*. Oxford: Blackwell.

Maclean, M., Bryant, P. and Bradley. L. (1987) 'Rhymes, nursery rhymes, and reading in early childhood'. *Merrill-Palmer Quarterly,* vol. 33, 255–82.

Magee, W. (1991) *Madtail, Miniwhale and Other Shape Poems.* London: Puffin.

Masefield, J. *Cargoes,* in Webb, K. (ed.) (1979) *I Like This Poem.* London: Puffin.

Maybin, J. (1994) 'Children's voices: talk, knowledge and identity', in Graddol, D., Maybin, J. and Stierer, B. (eds) *Researching Language and Literacy in Social Contexts.* Clevedon: Multilingual Matters.

McGough, R. (ed.) (1991) *The Kingfisher Book of Comic Verse.* London: Kingfisher.

McNaughton, C. (2004) *Who's Been Sleeping in My Porridge?* London: Walker Books.

Medwell, J., Strand, S. and Wray, D. (2007) 'The Role of Handwriting in Composing for Y2 Children'. *Journal of Reading, Writing and Literacy,* 2 (1): 18–36.

Medwell, J., Strand, S. and Wray, D. (2009) 'The Links between Handwriting and Composing for Y6 Children'. *Cambridge Journal of Education,* 39 (3).

Medwell, J., Wray, D., Poulson, L. and Fox, R. (1998) *Effective Teachers of Literacy: a Report of a Research Project Commissioned by the Teacher Training Agency.* Exeter: University of Exeter.

Merrick, B. (1991) *Exploring Poetry 8-13.* Exeter: NATE.

Mills, A.D. (ed.) (1998) *The Oxford Dictionary of Place Names.* Oxford: Oxford University Press.

Mitton, T. (1997) *Royal Raps.* London: Orchard Press.

Mole, J. (1990) *Catching a Spider.* London: Blackie.

Newby, M. (1987) *The Structure of English: A Handbook of English Grammar.* Cambridge: Cambridge University Press.

Nichols, G. (ed.) (1988) *Poetry Jump Up.* London: Penguin.

Nicholls, J. (1993) *Wordspells.* London: Faber and Faber.

Nunes. T. and Bryant, P. (2006) *Improving Literacy by Teaching Morphemes*. Abingdon: Routledge.

Opie, P. and Opie, I. (2001) (new edn) *The Lore and Language of Schoolchildren.* New York: NYRB Classics.

Ousbey, J. *Gran, Can You Rap?,* in Foster J. (ed.) (1993) *All in the Family.* Oxford: Oxford University Press.

Patten, B. (1990) *Thawing Frozen Frogs.* London: Viking.

Peters, M. (1985, 1967) *Spelling: Caught Or Taught? A New Look.* London: Routledge and Kegan Paul.

Peters, M. and Smith, B. (1993) *Spelling In Context: Strategies For Teachers And Learners.* NFER-Nelson.

Prelutsky, J. (1992) *Poems of A. Nonny. Mouse.* London: Orchard Press.

QCA (1999) *Early Learning Goals.* London: QCA.

Reinking, D. and Rickman, S.S. (1990) 'The Effects of Computer-mediated Texts on the Vocabulary Learning and Comprehension of Intermediate-grade Readers'. *Journal of Reading Behavior,* 22, 395–11.

Reinking, D. and Schreiner, R. (1985) 'The Effects of Computer-mediated Text on Measures of Reading Comprehension and Reading Behavior'. *Reading Research Quarterly,* 20, 536–52.

Rose, J. (2006) *Independent Review of the Teaching of Reading*. London: DfES.

Rosen, M. (ed.) (1985) *The Kingfisher Book of Children's Poetry.* London: Kingfisher.

Rosen, M. (ed.) (1991) *A World of Poetry.* London: Kingfisher.

Rosen, M. (ed.) (1995) *Rap with Rosen.* Harlow: Longman.

Rosen, M. (1997) *Michael Rosen's Book of Nonsense.* London: Macdonald.

Sanger, K. (1998) *The Language of Fiction.* London: Routledge.

Sassoon, R. (1990) *Handwriting: The Way To Teach It.* Cheltenham: Nelson Thornes.

Sayers, Dorothy L. (1946) *Unpopular Opinions.* London: Victor Gollancz.

Sheppard, Gerald T. (ed.) (1989) *The Geneva Bible: The Annotated New Testament, 1602 Edition.* New York: Pilgrim Press.

Skinner, B.F. (1957) *Verbal Behavior.* Englewood Cliffs, NJ: Prentice Hall.

Somers, D. (1994) *Drama in the Curriculum.* London: Cassell.

Sprat, Thomas (2003) *History of the Royal Society (1667),* Section XX. Whitefish, NT: Kessinger Publishing.

Stanley, L.A. (1992) *Rap: The Lyrics.* London: Penguin.

Styles, M. (ed.) (1998) *After Alice: Exploring Children's Literature.* London: Routledge.

Tournier, J. (1985) *Introduction déscriptive à la lexicogénétique de l'anglais contemporain.* Paris: Champion-Slatkine.

Trott, K., Dobbinson, S. and Griffiths, P. (2004) (eds) *The Child Language Reader*. London: Routledge.

Trudgill, P and Hannah J (5th edn) (2008) *International English: A guide to the varieties of standard English*. Routledge, London

Trudgill, P. (2nd edn) (1999) *The Dialects of England.* Oxford: Blackwell.

Truss, L. (2003) *Eats, Shoots and Leaves.* London: Fourth Estate.

University College London (2011) *The Internet Grammar of English* **www.ucl.ac.uk/internet-grammar/ home.htm**.

Vandyck, W. (2005) *The Punctuation Repair Kit.* London: Hodder.

Waterfield, R. (ed.) (1996) *The Rime of the Ancient Mariner and Other Classic Stories in Verse.* London: Puffin.

Wells, G. (1985) *Language, Learning and Education.* Cheltenham: NFER-Nelson.

West, C. (1995) *Long Tales, Short Tales and Tall Tales.* London: Doubleday Wright.

Winston, J. (2000) *Drama, Literacy and Moral Education 5-11.* Harlow: David Fulton.

Woods, P. and Hammersley, M. (1993) *Gender and Ethnicity in Schools.* London: Routledge.

Woolland, B. (1993) *The Teaching of Drama in the Primary School.* Harlow: Longman.

Wray, D. and Medwell, J. (1997) *English for Primary Teachers: an Audit and Self-Study Guide.* London: Letts.

Wright, K. (1987) *Cat Among the Pigeons.* London: Penguin.

Zephaniah, B. (1995) *Talking Turkeys.* London: Puffin.

Note: glossary entries are indicated by *g* following the page number